P9-AQR-732

# The Sharks of North American Waters

*Number Five: The W. L. Moody, Jr., Natural History Series*

Whale shark (*Rhiniodon typus*). Ed Robinson/Tom Stack & Associates

# THE SHARKS
# OF
# NORTH AMERICAN
# WATERS

*by* José I. Castro

*Drawings by* D. Bryan Stone III

*Texas A&M University Press*
COLLEGE STATION

Library of Congress Cataloging in Publication Data

Castro, José I. (José Ignacio), 1948–
   The sharks of North American waters.

   Bibliography: p.
   Includes index.
   1. Sharks—North America—Identification.
2. Sharks—Identification.   3. Fishes—Identifi-
cation.   4. Fishes—North America—Identification.
I. Title.
QL638.9.C35  1983       597'.31'097       82-16720
ISBN 0-89096-140-9

*Manufactured in the United States of America*
**FIRST EDITION**

# CONTENTS

# LIST OF COLOR PLATES

# PREFACE

THE encounters between man and sharks are presently on the increase, as recreational and commercial fisheries expand and as the exploration of the seas pushes into deeper waters. The question "What kind of shark is it?" is often asked by fishermen and biologists alike. This question is usually difficult to answer because of the large number of species of sharks and the lack of field guides to this group of fishes. Consequently, sharks are often misidentified, and rare or unusual specimens go unrecognized and are discarded, resulting in the loss of valuable data. The large size attained by many sharks prevents storage or preservation of entire sharks; therefore, species identification is best performed in the field while the whole shark is still available. Thus, I have endeavored to write a handy field guide for those who encounter sharks in their work or recreation and desire to identify or learn more about them. I have also attempted to summarize the life history of each species found in the area covered and have provided selected references for those desiring to go beyond the scope of this book.

Although sharks are among the most common large vertebrates, we know relatively little about them because of the difficulties of studying sharks. The primitive status of our underwater capabilities and logistical problems make field observations of these fast-moving and far-ranging fishes an almost impossible task. Observations in captivity are also difficult to make because most species of sharks do not adapt to captivity in present-day oceanaria and die shortly after capture. Consequently, we know pitifully little about the behavior and the sensory biology of most sharks.

Thousands of sharks are caught each year in longline fisheries and by recreational anglers. Regrettably, most of these fishes are wasted; few are properly utilized. It is unfortunate that our ability to see sharks in their environment is severely limited. Unlike the bloody and distorted creatures often seen lying in boats or hanging from a pole, living sharks are beautiful and graceful fishes that rival flying gulls and albatrosses in ease of movement. On seeing these supreme predators in the water one can only regret their wanton slaughter. Perhaps we may someday utilize properly the sharks that we catch; we may even learn to observe and identify sharks without harming them, both in the wild and in captivity, just as we do birds and other land animals. Only then will we unravel the many mysteries that surround these interesting fishes.

José I. Castro
Charleston, May, 1982

# ACKNOWLEDGMENTS

As a writer of a field guide, I have relied heavily on published works, as well as on the many people who answered my queries or provided me with specimens. While I cannot thank those whose immortality lies on library shelves, I would like to thank those whose goodwill and cooperation made this work possible.

D. Bryan Stone III prepared all the illustrations. His accurate and elegant work greatly enhances this book. His dedication and patience carried us through the innumerable changes I made on the original drawings. To him I express my deepest gratitude. The illustrations were prepared from photographs of fresh or preserved specimens whenever possible. In many cases we adapted the illustrations published in the original description of a species, particularly in cases of rare deepwater sharks. The illustrations were prepared under my supervision, and I am responsible for any inaccuracies that may have escaped me.

I am indebted to the following specialists: John G. Casey, Alan Lintala, Harold "Wes" Pratt, and Chuck Stillwell for numerous photographs and information, and for their great hospitality and camaraderie at Montauk; Eugenie Clark for her comments and advice; Robert Cummings, Jr., for data on *Pristiophorus*; J. A. F. Garrick for allowing me to read and borrow freely from his as yet unpublished work on *Carcharhinus*; R. Grant Gilmore for photographs and data on *Isurus paucus*; William Eschemeyer for answering questions on West Coast species; William E. Fahy for unpublished data on *Squatina dumerili*; the late Carl Hubbs for data on *Euprotomicrus bispinatus*; Gordon Hubbell for his generous loan of shark jaws; Gerhard Krefft for data on *Etmopterus gracilispinnis*; John McCosker for photographs and data on *Notorhynchus cepedianus*; Frank J. Schwartz for data on *Scyliorhinus meadi*; Pearl M. Sonoda for invaluable assistance at the California Academy of Sciences; Stewart Springer for answering many questions; Larry G. Talent for data on *Triakis semifasciata* and *Mustelus californicus*; Leighton R. Taylor for the use of his thesis on Heterodontidae; Leray A. de Wit for data on *Squatina* and *Triakis*; Warren Zeiller, Charles A. Buie, and Olivia Peña for their help at the Miami Seaquarium. To these individuals I extend my sincere gratitude, while retaining full responsibility for any errors of fact or omission.

I am very grateful to my friends in Ascension Island, Marion and Bonnie McDowell, Douglass Augustus, Jimmy Young, and Ken Jourdan, for their superb help during my expedition and visits to that island and for sharing with me some very exciting diving. I also thank my other Ascension friends for their assistance in all my shark fishing and tagging endeavors.

I also owe special thanks to the seafood brokers, fishermen, and sportsmen who provided me with much-needed specimens and to friends who helped me with my many tasks: Bill Aldret, Mark Almond, Melinda W. Bannon, Steve Crosby, John and Betty DeVane, Dale Favero and the members of the Charleston Shark Club, Wes Fuller, Frank Gummere, Jim Hair, Jeff Holden, Robert C. Johnson, Jr., Bob Kelly, C. A. Kennedy, Woody McCord, Ivan and Joyce Schultz, Mike Schultz, Sandy Schwarz, Billy Simmons, Hugh "Red" Simmons, George Steele, Rick Stringer, Gorden H. Timmons, Jeff Tracy, Ted Vees, Charles Winburn, Jay Winburn, and Tony Winburn. My friends Edward K. Burch and David Auten, who perished at sea, assisted me in many ways. Felicia C. Coleman and Jennifer E. Ripple assisted me with bibliographic matters. Alston C. Badger, Leslie Dane, Christopher C. Koenig, and Kathleen Meuli encouraged me throughout the project. Kathleen Meuli and Cookie Mishoe typed the manuscript. John McEachran reviewed the manuscript and supplied details in many Gulf of Mexico species. To all these people and to those whose names I have inadvertently omitted, I express my sincere gratitude.

# The Sharks of North American Waters

"What's the use of their having names," the Gnat said, "if they won't answer to them?"

"No use to *them*," said Alice; "but it's useful to the people who name them, I suppose."

—Lewis Carroll, *Through the Looking Glass*

# INTRODUCTION

THE purpose of this book is to provide a handy guide for identification of sharks inhabiting North American waters. It includes all the species reported within 500 nautical miles of the shores of the United States and Canada, from the Arctic Ocean to the twentieth parallel of North latitude, including the Gulf of California, the Gulf of Mexico, and part of the Caribbean Sea. It also includes a few deep-water species from adjacent areas, anticipating their presence in North American waters. It is designed for scientists, fishermen, and anyone else interested in identifying sharks. It provides concise summaries of diagnostic characters, similar species, distribution, biology, reproduction, economic importance, fishing methods, and literature references for each of the species covered.

This book consists of two parts. The first is a general account of sharks: their evolution, anatomy, reproduction, distribution, and economic uses. The second part consists of an illustrated key to the families of sharks, descriptions of each family, species identification keys for each family, species accounts, and illustrations of each species.

The keys found in this book are aids for shark identification; they use easily observable external features such as shape, proportions, color, shape of the teeth, or geographic range for identifying sharks. These keys are not based on taxonomic or phylogenetic relationships; their design follows diagnostic convenience. The keys are of the standard dichotomous type; each key consists of a series of alternatives presented in numbered couplets. Starting with the first couplet, the reader should select the alternative that best fits the specimen being identified and follow it to the next indicated couplet, continuing the process until the family or species is identified.

To identify a shark, first turn to the "Key to the Families." Determine which family it belongs to using the key, and confirm the identification with the figure on the right margin. Then, turn to the species keys for the selected family and determine the species of shark using that key. The identification can then be confirmed by referring to the species account and the figure.

There are 108 species accounts, which summarize our present knowledge of each species. Some accounts are brief because of our limited knowledge about some sharks. All the accounts are written in the same format to facilitate comparisons.

The species accounts begin with the common name in boldface type. The common names used are those designated by the American Fisheries Society in Special Publication No. 12, *A List of Common and Scientific Names of Fishes from the United States and Canada*, by Robins et. al (1980). When a common name has not been designated but a vernacular name exists, the latter is used. Species lacking common or vernacular names are designated by the scientific name only. The scientific name of each shark appears in italics after the common name, followed by the author or authors that named the shark and the year that the name was published. Each scientific name consists of two words in Latin or in latinized

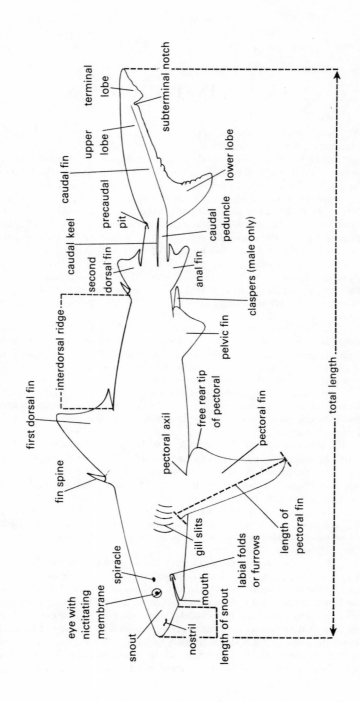

terminal
lobe

subterminal notch

upper
lobe

caudal fin

lower lobe

precaudal
pit

caudal
peduncle

caudal keel

second
dorsal fin

anal fin

interdorsal ridge

claspers (male only)

pelvic fin

first dorsal fin

free rear tip
of pectoral

fin spine

pectoral axil

pectoral fin

length of
pectoral fin

gill slits

spiracle

eye with
nictitating
membrane

mouth

labial folds
or furrows

snout

nostril

length of snout

total length

4   *Sharks of North American Waters*

form. The first word is the genus or generic name; the second word is the species or specific name. Some authors' names are enclosed in parentheses, indicating that the author originally placed the shark in a different genus than the one to which it is presently assigned. The scientific name used is that currently used in the literature. Most sharks have several obsolete scientific names, published after the original description; these names, known as synonyms, are invalid. When a synonym is still in use, although no longer valid, it follows in parentheses.

The description of the shark includes the most important diagnostic characteristics that can be easily observed in the field. The shape and number of teeth are also given, as the teeth are often an important diagnostic characteristic. The number of teeth in each side of the upper jaw is written before the number of teeth in each side of the lower jaw. For example, U 12–1–12, L 15 or 16–2–15 or 16, indicates twelve teeth on the left side of the upper jaw, one tooth in the center of the jaw (symphysis), and twelve teeth on the right side of the upper jaw; fifteen or sixteen teeth on the left side of the lower jaw, two teeth in the center, and fifteen or sixteen on the right side. In cases where the center of the jaw cannot be distinguished readily, the total number of teeth in that jaw is indicated. For example, U 24 to 30, L 28 to 32, indicates twenty-four to thirty teeth in the upper jaw and twenty-eight to thirty-two in the lower jaw. The shape of the dermal denticles is given whenever it is used to discriminate among species. The color given is that of live or freshly caught specimens, since the color of most sharks will fade or dull shortly after death. The length given is total length, measured in a straight line from the tip of the snout to the tip of the tail (see sketch). Length measurements are in centimeters, followed in parentheses by the customary equivalents in feet and tenths of feet or, in the case of sharks less than ten feet long, in inches. Weights are given in kilograms with pound equivalents in parentheses.

Similar species occurring in the same area are listed with their distinguishing characteristics. Usually the most similar species is listed first, and the least similar is listed last.

The range given for a species is its total known range, including the approximate limits of North American distribution and areas where the species may be locally common. A species may be referred to as tropical, temperate, polar, etc., depending on the waters it inhabits. Tropical waters are those where the surface temperature is 20°C (68.5°F) or higher. Temperate waters include a wide zone ranging from 20°C on the side towards the equator to 10°C (50°F) on the polar side. Species living in the warmer part of the temperate zone are called warm-temperate species; those on the polar side are called cold-temperate species. Polar waters are those where the surface temperature is usually below 10°C. The range of a species is a three-dimensional space bound by its tolerance limits to physical or biotic factors. Temperature is one of the most important factors affecting the distribution of sharks; it decreases rapidly with depth, from maxima of 20–25°C at the surface to 2°C at depths greater than 1,100 fathoms. Whereas the temperature of deep waters is uniform and stable regardless of latitude or season, the temperature of surface waters is highly variable, changing with latitude and season. Thus, species inhabiting deep waters live under stable conditions with few barriers to their distribution and are often widely distributed; species inhabiting surface waters are often migratory and move about seasonally seeking favorable conditions. In temperate latitudes the warmest temperatures are found close to shore in summer; in winter coastal waters can cool off rapidly, while offshore waters remain warmer and more stable. It follows that a species adapted to warm waters may be found close to shore in the northern parts of its range during the summer; when the temperature begins to fall in autumn, it may seek warmer off-shore waters or migrate southward. A cool-water-adapted species may be found close to the surface in the northern parts of its range, while in the southern parts it may inhabit much deeper waters where correspondingly cooler temperatures are found.

The general section on biology gives a summary of known habitat including depth and temperature preferences, feeding habits including what species it preys upon, predators, migrations, growth rates, etc.

The section on reproduction gives mode of reproduction, size at sexual maturity for both sexes, mating and birth seasons, length of the gestation period, location of nursery areas, size of the pups at birth, and litter size. When the size of the pups at birth is unknown, the size of the smallest free-swimming specimen known is given.

The section on relation to man lists commercial uses, economic loss from predation or interference with fisheries, uses as laboratory animals, toxicity of the flesh, and sporting qualities. This section also includes whether the species is known to attack man or presents a potential threat to swimmers or divers.

The section on fishing provides the usual fishing methods, preferred baits, depth of capture, and times and areas of best fishing.

Selected references are given for each species. These references have been chosen because they contain important or recent data, life histories, new size or range records, or extensive bibliographies. The references cited can be found in the bibliography in the back of the book.

Each shark covered is illustrated by a profile figure, snout outline, and upper and lower teeth outlines. The dermal denticles are illustrated whenever they are used for diagnostic purposes.

Deep-water species of wide distribution that have not been reported from our area are included in an appendix, anticipating their presence in North America.

# Evolution

Sharks belong to a class of fishes known as Chondrichthyes or cartilaginous fishes, which also includes rays and chimaeras. These fishes are characterized by having entirely cartilaginous skeletons and by lacking true bones. Parts of their skeletons (the skull, spines, and vertebrae) are often strengthened by the deposition of calcium salts, and, when sufficiently calcified, they may resemble bone. However, calcified cartilage remains microscopically distinct from bone. True bony tissues, if present in Chondrichthyes, are confined to the bases of their teeth and dermal denticles.

Cartilage disintegrates shortly after death; thus the skeletons of cartilaginous fishes are seldom preserved as fossils. Only their teeth and calcified parts are hard enough to be fossilized; the softer body parts are preserved only under exceptional conditions. Consequently, the fossil record of the cartilaginous fishes consists mainly of teeth, spines, and vertebrae. Although these are abundant fossils, it is difficult and often impossible to determine the characteristics of the fishes that bore them. Thus, the evolutionary history of the cartilaginous fishes is incomplete, and their relationships to other groups of fishes are still largely unclear.

The Chondrichthyes are divided into two major groups: the Holocephalans or chimaeras and the Elasmobranchs or sharks and rays. The chimaeras are a small group (about 35 species) of fishes that inhabit deep, cool waters. They are characterized by long tapering bodies, gill slits covered by an operculum (gill cover), upper jaw fused to the cranium, smooth naked skin, and teeth modified into a few grinding plates. The Elasmobranchs are the dominant cartilaginous fishes today, numbering about 780 species. They are characterized by cylindrical to flattened bodies, gill slits not covered by an operculum, upper jaw not fused to the cranium, skin covered by dermal denticles or placoid scales, and numerous cutting or crushing teeth.

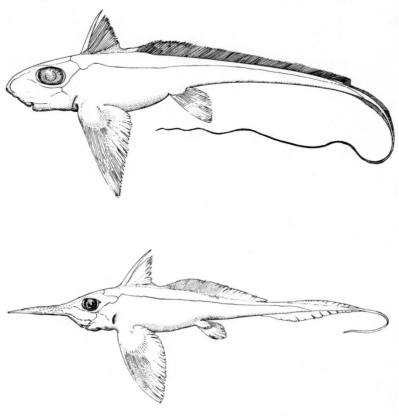

**CHIMAERAS**

The Elasmobranchs have evolved along two general trends: sharks and rays. The sharks have cylindrical to moderately depressed (dorsoventrally flattened) bodies, gill slits on the sides of the head, pectoral fins clearly marked off the head, and well-developed tails used for swimming with a sculling motion. The rays have moderately depressed to greatly depressed very wide bodies, gill slits on the ventral side of the head, pectoral fins fused to the head, and well-developed to whiplike tails. Rays with whiplike tails have well-developed pectoral fins used for locomotion with an up and down movement; those with well-developed tails, such as the sawfishes, propel themselves with the tail just as sharks do.

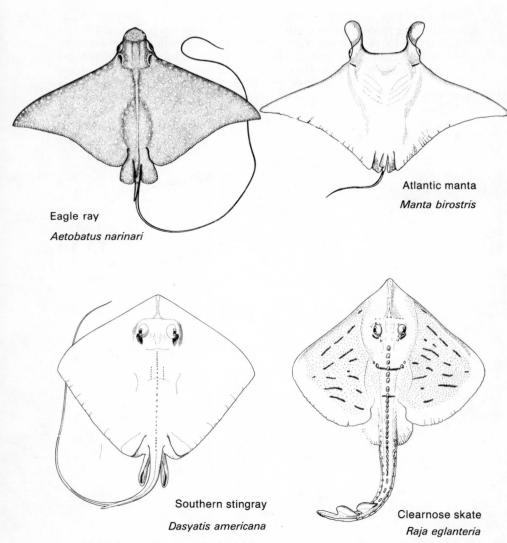

Eagle ray
*Aetobatus narinari*

Atlantic manta
*Manta birostris*

Southern stingray
*Dasyatis americana*

Clearnose skate
*Raja eglanteria*

Sharks first appear as fossils in the rocks of the Devonian period, which started some 400 million years ago and lasted for about 50 million years. The Devonian is also known as the Age of Fishes because it was during that period that fishes flourished, becoming the dominant creatures in the sea. In Devonian times, sharks were not the dominant predators they are today but were small creatures, often preyed upon by the much larger armored fishes that dominated those seas. These Devonian sharks, known as cladodonts, constitute the most primitive level in the evolution of sharks and may be considered to approximate the central stem from which later sharks evolved. They take their name from their multicuspid teeth (cladodont = branched tooth), which are characterized by one large, conical, central cusp with two or more lateral cusps and by disclike, flattened bases. The best known of the cladodont sharks is *Cladoselache*, a fossil shark from the late Devonian period of which there are numerous well-preserved fossils. These fossils are found in black shales along the south shore of Lake Erie, in what geologists call the Cleveland Shales; these shales originated from fine-grained mud and produced exceptionally fine fossils, which preserved not only teeth and vertebrae but also the structure of internal parts such as kidneys and muscles. *Cladoselache* was a rather small fish, 90–120 cm (35–47 in), with a terminal mouth, a definitely "sharklike" body, and a large tail. It had two dorsal, two pectoral, and two pelvic fins, just as modern sharks do, but lacked an anal fin. The fins were broad-based, which probably made them stiff and relatively inflexible in life. A hard, cartilaginous spine protruded through the skin at the base of these fins. The tail had two outwardly equal lobes and large lateral keels. Its large terminal mouth was adapted for seizing and tearing, indicating the role of a pelagic predator. Although it is probable that internal fertilization appeared in the earliest sharks, *Cladoselache* apparently lacked the copulatory claspers associated with internal fertilization in later sharks; this may be a matter of poor preservation or may represent a reproductive specialization.

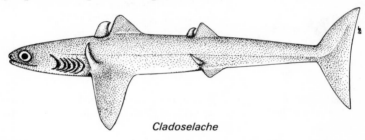

*Cladoselache*

The cladodonts vanished by the end of the Paleozoic era about 225 million years ago but left behind their presumed descendants, the *hybodont* sharks, more progressive fishes that form an intermediate level in shark evolution. The hybodonts appeared during the late Devonian and reached their zenith during the Carboniferous period (345–280 million years ago), when sharks became the dominant creatures in the seas. These sharks had improved maneuverability and loco-

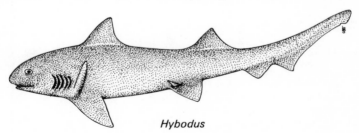

*Hybodus*

motion provided by their narrow-based fins, which were movable and flexible like those of modern sharks. Hybodonts were characterized by two types of teeth: those at the front of the jaws were pointed, cutting teeth, while those at the back were flat, crushing teeth (hybodont = "humpback" tooth). This dentition allowed them to feed on both fishes and the numerous shelled invertebrates that inhabited those seas. Copulatory claspers had developed on the pelvic fins of the males, indicating that they had internal fertilization. An anal fin first appeared in these sharks, located just in front of the caudal fin. Many hybodonts are known only from their teeth, and their fossil record is less complete than that of their predecessors. *Hybodus*, a common shark of the Mesozoic era, is a typical hybodont.

During the Mesozoic the hybodonts provided the stock that evolved into the modern sharks and the related rays. Starting at the end of the Jurassic period, which lasted from 190 to 135 million years ago, new sharks with more progressive feeding and locomotive adaptations began to appear in the fossil record. These new sharks had shortened protrusible jaws placed in a more ventral position, which could produce a gouging bite of considerable force. In addition, they had calcified vertebrae, which provided better attachment for muscles and produced a more stable spinal column, thus improving swimming. These early modern sharks, represented by *Paleospinax*, established the evolutionary pattern for to-

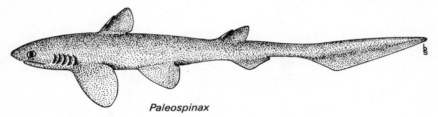

*Paleospinax*

day's sharks and rays. By the end of the Cretaceous period, 135 to 65 million years ago, the hybodonts had become extinct and all the modern groups of sharks had been established.

Since the Cretaceous, the evolution of sharks has proceeded along the two general trends of sharks and rays. The sharks continued as pelagic predators with cylindrical bodies; they number about 350 species today. The rays, which evolved as bottom-dwellers with flattened bodies, number about 430 species today. The separation of these two groups is not complete, as there is a continuum of transitional forms, such as angel sharks, guitarfishes, sawsharks, and sawfishes, which possess characteristics of both sharks and rays.

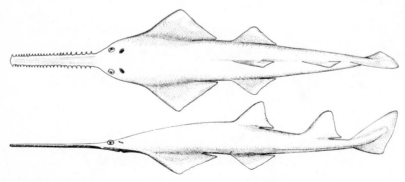

Sawfish
*Pristis pectinatus*

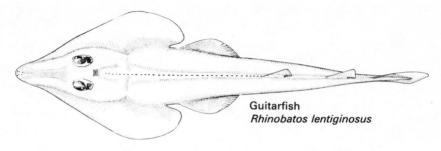

Guitarfish
*Rhinobatos lentiginosus*

## Anatomy

### External Anatomy

THE SKIN: The rough, sandpaperlike texture of shark skin comes from the presence of minute scales embedded in the skin. These scales are known as *dermal denticles* or *placoid scales* and are so minute that they must be observed under a microscope or a powerful lens. A dermal denticle consists of a *basal plate* that anchors it securely to the skin, a constricted *neck*, and a *spine* or *crown*, which protrudes through the skin. The spine is composed of *dentine* covered by a hard layer of *vitrodentine* and has a central *pulp cavity* that opens through the basal plate and contains the blood vessels that nourish the dentine. The shape of the denticles is quite variable and is often used for species identification. However, in a given shark the denticles may vary slightly from one part of the body to another and also may vary with age. The dermal denticles illustrated here for identification purposes are from adult sharks, from an area just below the first dorsal fin.

THE AMPULLAE OF LORENZINI: The *ampullae of Lorenzini* are small vesicles that form a complex and extensive subcutaneous sensory system around the shark head. Each *ampulla* consists of a bundle of sensory cells innervated by several nerve fibers in a long jelly-filled *canal or tubule* that opens to the outside by a small *pore*. The surface of the shark head is covered by these small pores, which are visible to the naked eye. (By pressing on the snout of a freshly killed shark, one can cause the clear jelly that fills the canals to exude through the pores.) The ampullae of Lorenzini detect weak electric fields at short ranges, enabling sharks to find prey buried in the sand (such as stingrays), even in the absence of visual or olfactory clues. It is possible that they may respond to mechanical stimuli as well.

THE NOSTRILS: The *nostrils* or *external nares* are the openings of the olfactory organs and are situated on the ventral surface of the snout. The olfactory

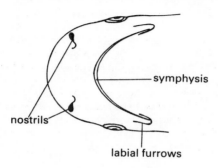

organs are blind sacs and usually do not communicate with the mouth; thus they take no part in breathing, and their function is solely olfactory. The nostrils may be partially covered by a *nasal flap*. *Nasal barbels* are slender sensory projections located near the nostrils or mouth of fishes.

THE EYE: The design of the shark eye follows that of the basic vertebrate eye, except that it is laterally compressed. In addition to the basic structures, the shark eye possesses a *tapetum lucidum*, a mirrorlike reflecting layer located behind the retina. The tapetum consists of a layer of parallel, platelike cells filled with silver guanine crystals. These crystals reflect light that has already passed through the retina, restimulating the retina a second time as the light passes out, thus making it more efficient under low-light conditions. The tapetum of sharks is perhaps the most efficient in the animal kingdom (twice as effective as the cat's), approaching 90 percent reflection at certain wavelengths.

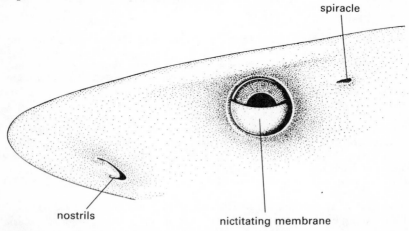

spiracle

nostrils

nictitating membrane

Some sharks also possess a *nictitating membrane* or *nictitans*, an additional eyelid that protects the eye from mechanical injury. It consists of an opaque, dense, denticle-covered membrane, which is extended over the eye at the time of biting or when the shark passes close to objects.

THE SPIRACLE: The spiracle is a rudimentary or vestigial first gill slit that provides oxygenated blood directly to the eye and brain through a separate blood vessel. Generally it is very reduced or absent in active, fast-moving sharks.

THE GILL SLITS: *Five to seven pairs of gill slits* or external gill openings are located on the sides of the head. During breathing, water enters through the mouth, passes into the pharynx and through the gills, and exits through the gill slits. The respiratory exchange of oxygen and carbon dioxide takes place on the surface of the *gill filaments*.

THE MOUTH: In sharks the mouth is subterminal or, rarely, terminal. A terminal mouth, typical of the frill shark and the whale shark, is located at the anterior end of the shark, and the snout does not protrude in front of it. A subterminal mouth is located in a ventral position, and the snout protrudes in front of it. This ventral position allows the snout to become an area of sensory perception (with nostrils and ampullae of Lorenzini), which samples the water just ahead of the mouth. A ventral mouth also provides pre-oral planing surfaces (as in the hammerhead sharks), which may increase maneuverability in feeding; a ventral mouth

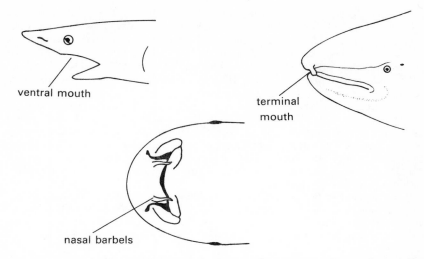

ventral mouth

terminal mouth

nasal barbels

also accompanies shortened jaws, which provide a greater biting force. The mouth may have *labial folds* or *furrows* around its corners.

THE TEETH: In sharks the teeth are derived from the dermal denticles or placoid scales, and thus they are structurally similar. In essence the teeth are modified and enlarged dermal denticles that have evolved for cutting, seizing, or crushing prey. Each tooth consists of a *root* that firmly implants the tooth in the connective tissue of the jaw and a *crown* that protrudes from the jaw. That part of the crown that adjoins the root is termed the *base*, and the pointed projections of the crown are termed the *cusps* or *cusplets*, depending on their size relative to one another. In some sharks (such as the sand tiger shark) smaller *lateral* or *basal denticles* may arise from the base of the crown. The shape of the teeth is highly variable and well adapted to the shark's diet. Teeth may be triangular and plate-like and have serrated edges, clearly designed for cutting; others may be long, pointed, and designed for grasping prey; yet others may have low, blunt crowns designed for crushing invertebrates. Different species may have only one type of tooth, or they may have cutting teeth in the upper jaw and grasping in the lower jaw, depending on their diet.

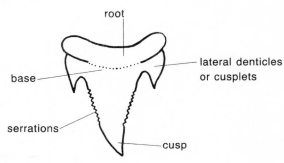

root

base

lateral denticles or cusplets

serrations

cusp

The teeth are arranged in rows along the border of each jaw. Other rows of replacement teeth lie behind along the gums and move forward as the front teeth wear out. Because of the considerable biting force exerted by sharks, their teeth are often broken or damaged while feeding. However, lost or damaged teeth are replaced after a few days. The shape and number of teeth are two of the best diagnostic characteristics for species identification. The teeth illustrated in this guide are from upper and lower jaws near the center.

THE LATERAL LINE: The lateral line is a series of fluid-filled canals that lie just beneath the skin of the head and along the sides of the body. The lateral line along with the internal ear and perhaps the ampullae of Lorenzini comprise a complex system of receptors that transforms underwater sound or mechanical disturbance into nerve impulses that allow sharks to orient to sound or particle motion. The exact mechanism of how these organs are stimulated and how the information is integrated is unclear.

THE FINS: The fins are steering, stabilizing, or propulsive surfaces. Sharks may have one or two fins along the middorsal line, and these are termed *first dorsal fin* and *second dorsal fin*. These fins act as antiroll stabilizers and may or may not have *spines* at their origin. The spines are defensive and may be associated

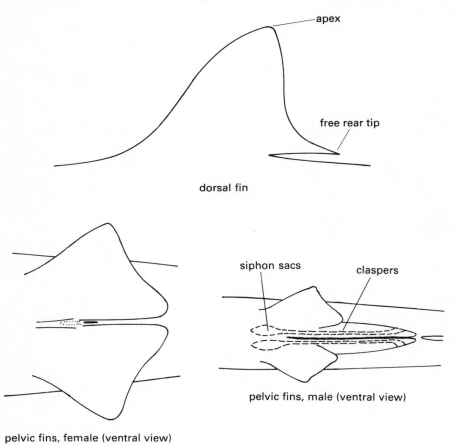

apex

free rear tip

dorsal fin

siphon sacs      claspers

pelvic fins, male (ventral view)

pelvic fins, female (ventral view)

with skin glands that produce irritating substances. A pair of large *pectoral fins* originate behind the head and extend outward like the wings of an airplane; these fins are used for steering. A pair of *pelvic fins* are found in the posterior part of the trunk around the *cloaca*; these fins also act as stabilizers. In male sharks the pelvic fins are specialized into stout, tubelike copulatory organs called *claspers*. A single *anal fin* is located ventrally between the pelvic fins and the caudal fin. The anal fin is absent in some families. The tail region consists of the *caudal peduncle* and the *caudal fin*. The caudal peduncle may bear small notches known as *precaudal pits* just ahead of the caudal fin, and it may be horizontally flattened into *lateral keels*, which may help to strengthen the tail. The caudal fin comprises most of the tail region and is the major source of propulsion. This fin is moved with a sculling motion, generating the forward thrust that pushes the shark through the water.

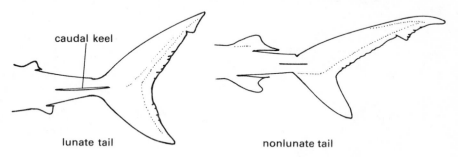

caudal keel

lunate tail

nonlunate tail

The caudal fin consists of an *upper lobe* and a *lower lobe*. The upper lobe may have a *subterminal notch* and a clearly defined *terminal lobe*; it may be *lunate* and have equally large upper and lower lobes; or it may be *non-lunate* and have a larger upper lobe with a reduced or absent lower lobe. (The term lunate is used instead of the more familiar term homocercal because the latter implies similar upper and lower caudal lobes resulting from similar underlying skeletal support; this is not the case in sharks with lunate tails.) Lunate tails are associated with well-developed keels on the caudal peduncle and are found in mackerel and basking sharks. A longitudinal skin ridge, the *interdorsal ridge*, may be present on the dorsal midline between the two dorsal fins.

with interdorsal ridge

without interdorsal ridge

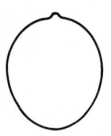

cross section of body between dorsal fins

## Internal Anatomy

THE LIVER: If one opens the belly of a shark by making an incision from the level of the pectoral fins to the origin of the pelvic fins, the first organ encountered is the liver. It is a large, soft, oily organ, which occupies most of the body cavity and may comprise as much as 25 percent of the body weight; it consists of two large, pointed lobes, which range from light greenish gray to dark brown in color. In sharks the liver serves two functions: first it provides for energy storage, as all the fatty reserves are concentrated in this organ; second, it acts as a hydrostatic organ by storing lighter-than-water oils, which decrease the density of the shark's body, providing buoyancy and counteracting the natural sinking tendency of sharks.

DIGESTIVE TRACT: If the liver is pushed aside, the esophagus and the stomach are revealed. These two organs are contiguous, without a clear external line of demarcation; the esophagus is characterized by numerous internal fingerlike projections or *papillae*, while the stomach bears longitudinal folds known as *rugae*.

The anterior part of the J-shaped stomach is saclike and voluminous and is known as the *cardiac stomach*; it is in this organ that one can often identify the remains of the shark's last meal. The posterior part of the stomach, known as the pyloric stomach, is much narrower and bends anteriorly; it terminates on a constriction known as the *pylorus*. After the pylorus, the digestive tract continues as a short duodenum, which leads to a much larger *spiral valve*. The spiral valve is an internally twisted or coiled organ that serves to increase the absorptive surface of the intestine. Usually the spiral valve resembles a carpenter's auger enclosed in a tube, but it may also be rolled up on itself in scroll fashion. The posterior end of the spiral valve leads to the *rectum* and the *anus*. The anus opens into the *cloaca*, a chamber where the digestive, urinary, and genital tracts open to the outside.

THE PANCREAS: The *pancreas* is a digestive gland consisting of two connected lobes, usually pinkish in color; a *ventral lobe* lies ventral to the duodenum, while a *dorsal lobe* lies dorsal to it. Pancreatic secretions enter the duodenum through a duct in the ventral lobe.

THE SPLEEN: The spleen is the dark organ lying against the stomach; it is triangular or elongated in shape. It is not a digestive gland but part of the lymphatic system and has no connection with the digestive tract.

THE RECTAL GLAND: The *rectal gland* or digitiform gland is a small, fingerlike organ that opens by a duct into the rectum. It acts as a salt gland, removing relatively large quantities of excess sodium chloride (salt) from the blood; it secretes a colorless solution of sodium chloride at about twice the concentration found in the plasma and higher than that of seawater.

THE MALE UROGENITAL TRACT: Removal of the digestive tract exposes the male gonads or *testes* and the *kidneys*. In mature males a pair of large, elongated or cylindrical testes can be seen at the anterior end of the body cavity dorsal to the liver; both testes are equally developed, and they are whitish or yellowish in color. In immature sharks the testes are an inconspicuous mass of whitish tissue at the anterior end of the body cavity. In many species the testes are embedded on the anterior end of a long *epigonal organ* whose function is believed to be hemopoietic (blood-cell forming). Sperm are produced in each testis and conveyed through minute ductules (ductus efferens) into a highly convoluted *epidydimis* which can be seen along the vertebral column on either side of the dorsal aorta. Posteriorly the epidydimis passes into the ductus deferens (or vas deferens), which is a sperm-storage or spermatophore-forming organ. In many sharks sperm are aggregated and packed in rounded or ovoid small masses known as spermato-

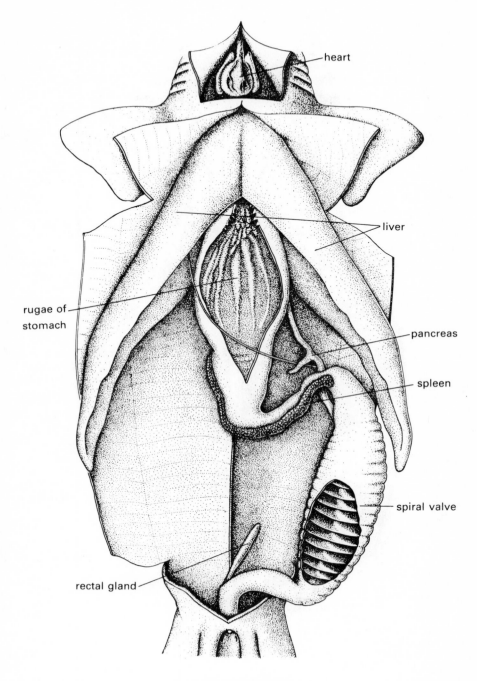

heart

liver

rugae of
stomach

pancreas

spleen

spiral valve

rectal gland

DIGESTIVE SYSTEM

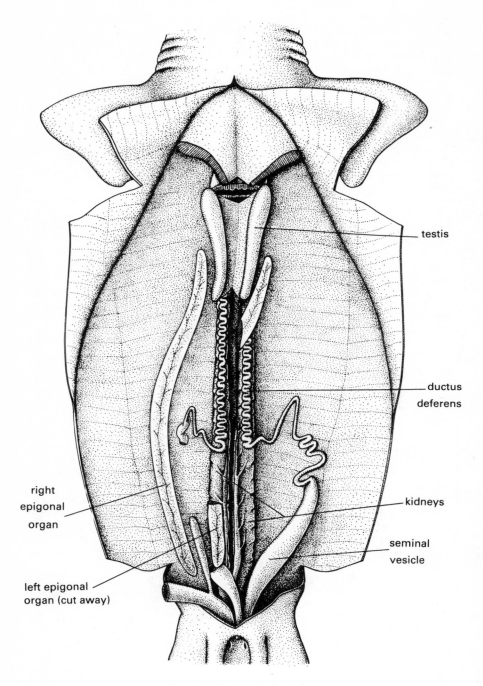

testis

ductus deferens

right epigonal organ

kidneys

seminal vesicle

left epigonal organ (cut away)

MALE UROGENITAL SYSTEM

phores, each containing a very large number of sperm. It is believed that the function of the spermatophore is to protect the sperm and to prevent loss of sperm by leakage into the water during copulation. In immature males the ductus deferens is a straight tube on the ventral surface of the kidneys; in sexually mature males the anterior part of the ductus deferens is highly coiled, while the posterior part is a straight tube that enlarges to form the *seminal vesicles*. The posterior end of the seminal vesicles forms an outpocketing on its ventral side, the *sperm sac*. The size of the sperm sac is highly variable depending on species. The two sperm sacs unite posteriorly to form the *urogenital sinus*, a cavity enclosed by a conical projection, the *urogenital papilla*, which protrudes into the cloaca. In male sharks the median edge of the pelvic fins forms tubelike copulatory organs known as *claspers*. During mating the claspers are turned forward and presumably one is inserted into the female. Sperm or spermatophores are forcibly ejected with the aid of contractile saclike organs known as *siphon sacs*. These organs lie just beneath the skin of the ventral side of the body and extend anteriorly almost to the level of the pectoral fins, where they end blindly. Their function seems to be to force sperm from the cloaca through the claspers and out into the female by means of a sea water current produced upon contraction. It is believed that the siphon sacs produce a secretion involved in copulation, perhaps as a lubricant.

The kidneys are the dark red organs seen on either side of the vertebral column. They are actually located outside the body cavity and separated from it by a membrane (peritoneum). The kidneys are drained into the cloaca by the ureters.

THE FEMALE UROGENITAL TRACT: Removal of the digestive tract will expose the female urogenital tract. A pair of *ovaries* may be seen at the anterior end of the body cavity dorsal to the liver. The appearance of the ovaries varies with the sexual condition of the specimen. In immature females they are small and smooth; in mature females they are large and of granulated appearance, often bearing large eggs on the surface. In some sharks both ovaries are functional; in others only one ovary is developed, usually the right one, and it is embedded in the anterior end of a long *epigonal organ*. When eggs are released from the ovary, they pass through the *ostium* into the *oviducts*, which are long tubes that run the length of the body cavity. A *shell gland* can be seen as an enlargement of the anterior part of each oviduct; it secretes a membrane that encloses the eggs as they pass through the oviduct. The shell gland may also act as the site of sperm storage and fertilization. The posterior part of each oviduct is enlarged to form the *uterus*, where the embryonic shark develops. The two uteri unite posteriorly to form a chamber, the *vagina*, which opens into the cloaca by a large aperture.

The kidneys are the long, dark red organs seen on either side of the vertebral column. In the female the anterior part of the kidney is very reduced, and urine is produced only in the posterior part. The kidneys are drained by paired *ureters*, which unite posteriorly to form the *urinary sinus*. The urinary sinus is enclosed by a conical projection, the *urogenital papilla*, which opens by a pore into the cloaca.

THE HEART: The heart can be exposed by making an incision from the mouth to the pectoral girdle; it lies in a cavity known as the pericardial cavity. In sharks the heart is an S-shaped tube that receives blood from the body at its posterior end and pumps it out to the gills through the anterior end. It consists of four chambers, from posterior to anterior, the sinus venosus, atrium, ventricle, and conus arteriosus. Venous blood returning to the heart first enters the sinus venosus, a thin-walled triangular sac posterior to the ventricle. The thick, muscular ventricle pumps blood into the conus arteriosus; from the conus arteriosus five afferent branchial arteries carry the blood to the gills. The oxygen–carbon dioxide

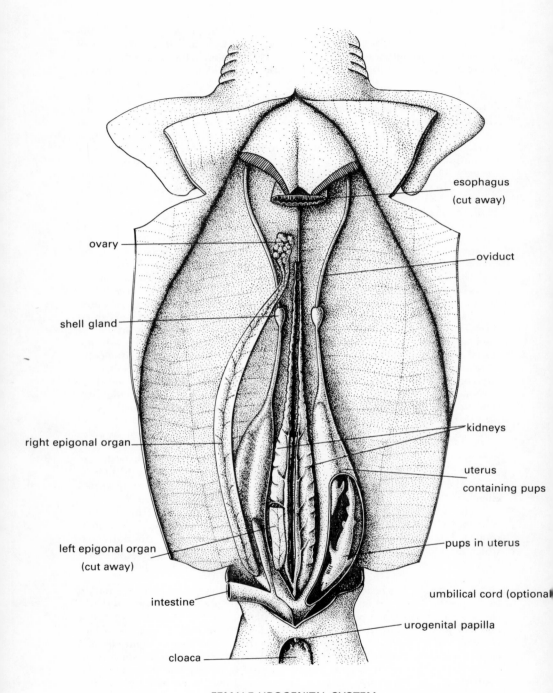

esophagus
(cut away)

ovary

oviduct

shell gland

right epigonal organ

kidneys

uterus
containing pups

left epigonal organ
(cut away)

pups in uterus

intestine

umbilical cord (optional)

urogenital papilla

cloaca

FEMALE UROGENITAL SYSTEM

exchange takes place in the gill filaments. The efferent branchial arteries take blood from the gills to the dorsal aorta and thence to different parts of the body.

THE SKELETON: The cartilaginous skeleton of sharks is divided into axial and appendicular portions. The axial skeleton consists of the skull and the vertebral column. The skull consists of a chondrocranium, which houses the brain and sense organs, and a splanchnocranium, which composes the jaws and gill arches. The skull lacks the sutures and joints that separate the bones of the skull of other vertebrates; it is often strengthened by the deposition of salts and may become quite hard. The appendicular skeleton consists of the *pectoral* and *pelvic girdles* and the median fin cartilages; these girdles do not articulate with the vertebral column. The median fin cartilages provide support for the fins; they consist of cartilaginous supports known as *pterygiophores*, which bear parallel, elastoid rays known as *ceratotrichia*.

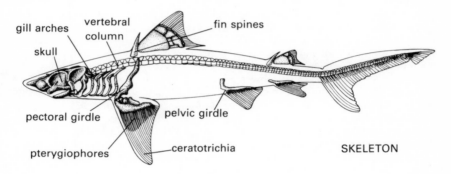

gill arches    vertebral    fin spines
               column

skull

pectoral girdle         pelvic girdle

pterygiophores       ceratotrichia         SKELETON

## Reproduction

The primitive mode of reproduction in fishes is the production of very large numbers of eggs and sperm, which are shed into the water, where fertilization occurs. This process is known as oviparity and is typical of most bony fishes. The embryos of oviparous fishes are provided with only a small amount of yolk and consequently hatch in an undeveloped or larval condition and require weeks or months to complete development. Both eggs and young are highly vulnerable to predators and environmental factors for prolonged periods and suffer heavy mortality.

The evolutionary success of sharks is partly due to their reproductive adaptations that depart from oviparity. The most significant of these are *internal fertilization* and the production of *small numbers of large young*, which hatch or are born as active, fully developed miniature sharks or "pups." The embryos spend their developmental stages within their mother's body and so receive protection during their most vulnerable stages. The pups are born at a relatively large size, reducing the number of potential predators and competitors while increasing the number of potential prey, thus enhancing their chances of survival.

All sharks have internal fertilization. The male shark inseminates the female with the use of its claspers; during mating the claspers are turned forward and one is inserted into the female. Sperm are then forcibly ejected with the aid of the contractile, saclike siphons. Mating in sharks has seldom been observed or reported. Detailed descriptions are available only for a few of the small species that can be kept in captivity. In some small sharks the male wraps its body around the female, which remains stretched out and immobile. In other sharks, such as the horn shark, the male holds the female by grasping one of her pectoral fins with his mouth and then maneuvers his tail around the female so he can insert a clasper. Very little is known about the mating activities of large sharks. The lemon shark is probably the only large shark whose mating behavior has been reported. A pair of lemon sharks observed while mating were swimming side by side, heads slightly apart and bodies close together, swimming in almost perfect synchrony. Other large pelagic sharks are believed to mate in this way. In many species the females bear tooth marks in their fins and head regions, which are believed to be evidence of courtship or mating activity, but these activities remain to be observed.

The number of young produced each season is small, usually ranging from two to twenty, although large females of some species can carry litters of a hundred or more pups. The production of large young requires that great amounts of nutrients be available to the developing embryo to nurture it to large size. Sharks have evolved diverse means of nourishing their embryos, such as the production of eggs with very large yolks, the ingestion of egg yolks by the embryos, and the direct transfer of nutrients from mother to embryo through a yolk sac placenta. Traditionally these adaptations have been grouped into three modes of reproduction: oviparity, ovoviviparity, and viviparity.

Oviparity in sharks is the most primitive condition, and it is a modified oviparity, different from that of the bony fishes. Oviparous sharks lay large eggs that contain sufficient yolk to nourish the embryo through development and allow it to emerge as a fully developed miniature shark. These eggs are enclosed in leathery cases that are deposited on the bottom without further contact with the parent. The egg cases are usually rectangular or conical; rectangular egg cases have long tendrils at every corner for attachment to bottom plants or rocks; conical egg cases have a spiral flange around them, which probably serves for burying in soft bottoms. The egg cases are produced when the egg passes through the

 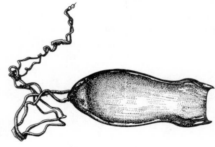

egg cases of oviparous sharks

shell gland; when freshly laid they are soft and pale, but they harden and darken within a few hours. The only protection for the embryo is its tough leathery case composed of protein fibers. The development of these eggs is temperature-dependent and usually lasts a few months. The pups of oviparous sharks are relatively small because their growth is limited by the amount of nutrients stored in the egg. The embryos of the oviparous whale shark, the largest living fish, measure only 36 cm (14 in), a size exceeded by the embryos of many ovoviviparous or viviparous sharks. Oviparity is found in only four families of sharks: the bullhead sharks, the nurse sharks, the catsharks, and the whale shark.

Ovoviviparity, also known as aplacental viviparity, is the most common mode of reproduction in sharks. The rich, yolky eggs of ovoviviparous sharks hatch in the uterus before the embryos are fully developed. The embryos then continue to grow in the uterus without forming a placental connection with the mother and are born after their development has been completed. The embryos are nourished by yolk stored in a *yolk sac* that is attached to the embryo by a *yolk stalk*; both of these structures are fully absorbed prior to birth. It is likely that in some ovoviviparous sharks, such as the tiger shark, the lining of the uterus secretes nutritive fluids that are absorbed by the embryos, providing nourishment after the nutrients stored in the egg have been consumed. In other ovoviviparous sharks,

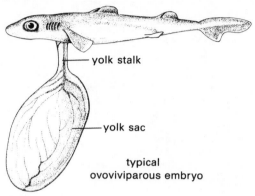

yolk stalk

yolk sac

typical
ovoviviparous embryo

such as the sand tiger, the yolk sac and the yolk stalk are absorbed very early in their development; thereafter the embryos nourish themselves by swallowing unfertilized eggs and smaller embryos in the uterus, in a form of embryonic cannibalism called oviphagy. These embryos consume very large amounts of yolk acquiring greatly distended throats and enormous *yolk stomachs*. In these sharks

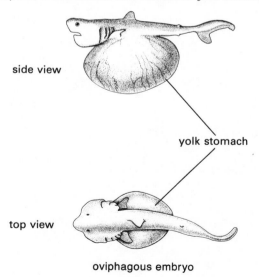

side view

yolk stomach

top view

oviphagous embryo

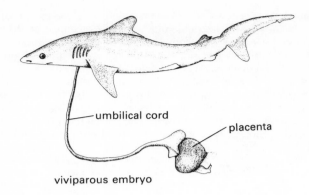

umbilical cord

placenta

viviparous embryo

usually only one embryo survives in each uterus, having eaten its smaller siblings. The cow sharks, the frill shark, sand tiger sharks, goblin sharks, mackerel sharks, basking sharks, thresher sharks, false catsharks, saw sharks, angel sharks, squaloid sharks, ribbontail catsharks, some nurse sharks, some smooth dogfishes, and some catsharks are ovoviviparous.

Viviparity, or placental viviparity, is the most advanced mode of reproduction. The embryos of viviparous sharks are initially dependent on stored yolk but are later nourished by the mother through a placental connection. In viviparous sharks the yolk stalk grows long, having a very reduced yolk sac at its end; where the yolk sac comes in contact with the mother's uterus, it becomes modified into a *yolk sac placenta*. Here the tissues of embryo and mother come in intimate contact, and nutrients are passed on to the embryo. In other viviparous sharks the uterine lining produces a nutritive fluid (often called uterine milk), which bathes the embryos in the uterus. These embryos have highly branched yolk stalks, which are believed to absorb this fluid. Viviparity is confined to some smooth dogfishes, the requiem sharks, and the hammerhead sharks.

## Migrations

Most sharks undertake periodic migrations determined by the availability of food, their reproductive cycles, or environmental factors. Some of these migrations are daily movements covering short distances, while others are seasonal movements covering great distances or even transatlantic movements of unknown extent and duration.

Many species migrate in pursuit of their prey. Some sharks follow their prey along daily vertical migrations, spending the day at great depths and ascending to the upper layers at night. Others spend the day in offshore areas and approach the shore at night in search of food. Yet others appear to follow their prey along annual migration routes that may cover thousands of miles.

The migrations of many species are related to their reproductive cycles. Some sharks travel to specific areas for mating, often gathering into very large schools composed of individuals of uniform size or sex. The females of many species migrate to specific nursery areas to shed their eggs or give birth to pups. Frequently the nursery areas are in highly productive coastal or estuarine waters, where the abundant small fishes and crustaceans provide ample food for the growing pups.

Environmental factors such as temperature, oxygen solubility, light, and oceanic currents affect the migrations of sharks. However, the specific effects upon sharks of environmental factors or their interactions are complex and poorly understood. The effects of temperature are of prime importance because temperature affects not only water density and oxygen solubility but also the metabolic rate of sharks. Sharks are cold-blooded or poikilothermic animals, and with a few exceptions their body temperature conforms to that of the surrounding water. Each species lives within a relatively narrow temperature range determined by its own metabolic or regulatory adaptations. Seasonal temperature changes induce many species to migrate in order to remain within their temperature preferences or tolerance limits. Sharks such as the spiny dogfish follow yearly migration routes closely attuned to the water temperature. Generally their migrations are directed northward and inshore in summer and southward and offshore in winter.

All these migrations are poorly understood because of the difficulties of studying or tracking free-ranging sharks. Most of our knowledge of shark migrations has been derived from tagging studies. Tagging consists of attaching numbered metal or plastic markers to sharks, recording the date and location (and ideally the size and weight). If the shark is recaptured at a later date, it is possible to discern the general direction of its travels, and when the shark has been carefully measured at the times of tagging and recovery, it is possible to obtain data on growth and longevity.

Shark tagging programs first appeared in the 1930s, but they did not become productive until the mid-sixties, when effective, long-wearing tags were developed. Recently some shark tagging programs have become popular, engaging large numbers of scientists and amateurs who tag a few thousand sharks each year. Recoveries are very low, usually 1 to 5 percent of tagged sharks, because there are no large-scale commercial fisheries for sharks and because tags are often shed (due to mechanical failure, erosion, or rejection by body tissues). At present, the recovery of a tagged shark that has been at liberty more than ten years after tagging is a rare event, and in many cases valuable information is lost because the shark is not measured or reported.

# Fishing

Shark fishing gear must be tailored to the species being sought as well as to the local conditions. The gear used for recreational or non-commercial purposes is usually limited to handlines and rod and reel. Handlines are by far the most efficient method for catching single sharks. Handlines consist simply of a stout cord, a float, a short wire leader, and a hook. The line is usually secured to the boat; the float acts as a shock absorber and serves to wear out the fish. When fishing for large sharks from dinghies or small boats, one should be prepared to sever the line if there is danger of the boat being swamped or if it becomes obvious that one "needs a bigger boat."

When fishing with rod and reel from a boat, a 6/0 reel and 50-lb line will handle all but the largest sharks. The leaders used should be long, about twice the length of the expected shark, to prevent the line from abrading and parting upon contact with the shark's tail. Pier or beach fishing for large sharks requires more specialized tackle; reels 10/0 to 16/0 are used, as one must have enough line to tire out the fish. It is often necessary to take the bait far out to sea in a boat to keep it away from the surf zone. Small sharks can be caught on light or ultralight tackle, providing fun and food for the table.

Longlines are the most popular method for catching large sharks on a commercial scale. Longlines are multiple hook systems that can attain considerable lengths—up to twenty-five miles. Longlines can be made to float on the surface or they can be anchored to the bottom. Floating longlines were initially developed by the Japanese for catching tuna, and more recently they have been modified for swordfish and sharks. A longline consists of a very long horizontal main line, usually ¼-inch nylon rope, with numerous vertical lines or gangions attached to it. The gangions consist of ³⁄₁₆-inch nylon lines of varying lengths and bear one or more hooks on short wire leaders. Evenly spaced floats keep the line from sinking. Radar reflectors or marking flags are placed at the ends. The lines on a floating longline need not be very stout, as the entire line will act as a drag and move under the pull of a fish, often with several fish pulling against each other.

Anchored longlines are used in coastal waters, where navigation or traffic precludes the use of floating longlines. Because the line is anchored, it must be heavy enough to hold the largest expected sharks, as the line will be held in a fixed position and could become quite taut. Thus, anchored longlines are made of heavier material than floating longlines. These lines are usually set parallel to the current so that the chumming effect of the bait will be concentrated. The anchored longline has declined in popularity and is seldom used today.

Gill nets are long, wall-like nets that entangle fish that attempt to swim through them. Gill nets are seasonally very effective in shallow water for catching small to medium sharks that are active just beyond the surf zone. They are less expensive to operate than longlines since they do not require bait; trapped fish act as bait or attractant for other fish, which are in turn entangled in the net. The size of the mesh used for sharks is four-inch stretched mesh or longer, depending on local conditions. Although gill nets can be very effective, they also have several drawbacks. Gill nets are difficult to manage in rough weather and often catch many unwanted species, such as rays, in very large numbers. Gill nets kill sharks by stopping their forward movement and preventing water from circulating through their gills, quickly suffocating them. However, a large shark caught on a light gill net can turn it into a tangled mess before dying.

Trawls are towed nets that strain the water through the mesh, leaving the fish in a bag. The main types of towed nets are the otter trawl and the midwater or pelagic trawls. The otter trawl derives its name from the "otter-boards" or "doors" attached to the ends of the towed net; these otter-boards resemble massive wooden doors liberally strengthened by iron bands, and they act as kites spreading the net horizontally. The otter trawl is used for catching animals that live on the bottom, and it is very popular in coastal fisheries. Sharks are usually an accidental catch in many otter-trawl operations such as shrimping. Otter trawls can also be used in deep waters for research work.

Midwater or pelagic trawls use additional doors to keep the net spread vertically as well as horizontally. They are used for catching fish that live in the water column, off the bottom. These trawls have little commercial use in North America; they are primarily research tools.

Harpoons are spears modified for fishing. They consist of a barbed spear or "lily iron" attached to floats or a boat. Harpoons are used for the largest sharks, such as the basking shark or the whale shark. The harpoon is thrust at a fish on the surface, and its barbs anchor it firmly in the flesh. The fish tires out quickly from pulling the boat or floats. In the past the European basking shark fisheries used harpoons to catch their prey; the harpoon is presently used in India for the pursuit of whale sharks.

The hooks used for shark fishing vary with the type of fishing and with the size of shark being pursued. The most popular ones are stout hooks with long shanks, 1½ to 2 inches across the curve of the hooks. Most sharks have large mouths and can swallow relatively large hooks.

Generally live or fresh bait is used for sharks. Live bait is best as it produces auditory and electric stimuli lacking in dead bait. Bait used for sharks should be very fresh; contrary to popular belief, most sharks do not scavenge for rotten flesh. Freshly thawed bait that was frozen while fresh is also suitable. Stingrays make excellent bait for numerous sharks; oily fishes such as bonito or small tunas are also very effective.

## Utilization

Sharks can yield more marketable products than any other single group of fishes: their flesh is used for food; their liver yields oils and vitamins; they can be rendered into fish meal or fertilizer; their skin can be processed into leather or shagreen; they are used for biomedical research and for dissection in biology or anatomy courses; they offer great sport to the fisherman; and their teeth often become jewelry or even offensive weapons.

The principal use of sharks is food. In many countries shark fisheries have existed for hundreds of years; by contrast, in North America sharks have been traditionally considered inedible or unappetizing. The main reason for this reputation is ammonia formation in the flesh and the consequent foul smell (urea found in their blood quickly breaks down after death, releasing ammonia). Furthermore, the idea that they are man-eaters probably makes them even more unappetizing. However, when properly handled and prepared, the boneless, white shark steaks constitute excellent table fare and shark fin soup must be considered a delicacy.

The flesh of most sharks is edible; only that of the Greenland shark has been proven poisonous. Other species reputed to be mildly poisonous are the sharpnose sevengill shark and the sixgill shark, although the case against these two is far from clear. Shark flesh is highly perishable, and extreme precautions must be taken to preserve it immediately after a shark is caught. Sharks should be bled immediately after capture, preferably by hanging them and cutting off the tail. After bleeding, carcasses should be cleaned meticulously, butchered immediately, and frozen quickly. Soaking fillets in salt water prior to use will eliminate unpleasant odors; the fillets can then be treated as those of any other gamefish.

Sharks are also used in the production of fish meal, a valuable protein supplement used for feeding livestock. Fish meal is obtained by first boiling scraps or whole carcasses in water to get rid of the oil. The cooked scrap is then pressed to further remove the oil; it is then dried over a fire, and the dried product is ground into a coarse powder.

Many sharks have been pursued for their liver oils. In the past basking sharks were pursued for their huge livers, which yielded many barrels of lamp oil. More recently shark liver oils were used for extracting vitamin A. In 1937 it was discovered that the liver of the spiny dogfish contained about ten times the amount of vitamin A found in cod liver oil, a traditional source. Vitamin A was usually imported from Europe, and in early World War II supplies were interrupted. An intensive fishery for sharks developed overnight along the Pacific coast of the United States, with the soupfin shark and the spiny dogfish as the main quarries. This fishery reached its climax in 1939, when over 9 million tons were landed. By 1942 the price of high-quality shark liver had risen to thirteen dollars per pound, luring hundreds of people into the business of shark fishing. Because of overfishing and the catching of females and young in the nursery areas, the fishery had been depleted by 1946. The synthesis of vitamin A in 1950 marked the end of this fishery. Shark liver oils have also been used as a paint and cosmetic base, as lubricants, for tanning, and in numerous pharmaceuticals. Nowadays there is little demand for shark liver oils.

Shark skin has been used for its abrasive properties, as well as processed into leather. In the past the dried-up skins of sharks, known as shagreen, were used as fine sandpaper. At one time shagreen was also used to cover the hilts of Japanese and German swords, since its rough surface provided a firm grip even when the hilt was bloodied. Once the rough dermal denticles are removed, shark skin can be processed into leather. The first large-scale uses of shark leather started around 1920, when chemical processes were developed for the removal of the skin denticles; the removal of the denticles is commercially known as de-armoring and consists of soaking the skins in acid, usually hydrochloric. For details of this process see Tressler and Lemon (1951) and Rogers (1922).

Sharks evolved very early in the history of the vertebrates. Consequently, they are often used as examples of primitive fishes; thousands of spiny dogfish are dissected every year by biology and anatomy students; nurse sharks and spiny dogfish are popular laboratory animals in biomedical research as models of the primitive immune system; smooth dogfish are used in electromagnetic experiments.

The many species of large sharks that inhabit coastal waters offer a challenge to the sportsman without the greater expense of pursuing offshore gamefishes. Although surpassed by the billfishes in fighting qualities, sharks are very popular with sportsmen because they are large, plentiful, and easier to hook.

Sharks' teeth have found numerous uses. In many primitive societies they were used for spear points or for making saws. Nowadays they are popular jewelry items.

In spite of all the products obtainable from sharks, economic realities have prevented the development of large, commercial shark fisheries. First, sharks are difficult to handle given their large size and potential for inflicting injury. Second, they must be butchered immediately to prevent spoilage, an arduous task for tired fishermen at sea. Third, shark populations cannot support prolonged, intensive fisheries because of their low reproductive potential; sharks bear few young, which grow and mature slowly, and thus they must be managed very conservatively. They are reproductively similar to marine mammals such as seals and should be managed according to similar principles. Nevertheless, more and more people are discovering shark as an inexpensive but tasty dish, and at present consumption of shark is rapidly increasing.

## Shark Attacks

There is a great deal of misinformation on shark attacks and the danger they pose to man. First, it should be understood that sharks and man evolved many, many millions of years apart. The feeding patterns that have made sharks successful predators were evolved millions of years ago, long before the appearance of man. Sharks eat fish and other marine animals; man is not included in any shark's diet and can only be considered an accidental prey.

Nevertheless, some sharks are known to attack man. Most "shark attacks" involve people handling hooked or snared sharks; some involve spearfishermen handling wounded fish, and only a few result from the deliberate feeding or fighting activities of sharks.

Sharks are predators with extraordinarily acute senses that allow them to detect and track down wounded or dying fishes. As predators, sharks must balance the energy spent in chasing and capturing prey against the energy to be obtained from eating it. Consequently, sharks usually select weak, sick, injured, or dying prey because it is far easier to catch than healthy prey. A speared fish in the water is the source of the olfactory, auditory, electric, and visual stimuli that attract sharks. Sharks quickly track these stimuli to their source and may attempt to take a fish from a diver or may even mistake the diver for the fish, with disastrous results.

The attractive stimuli are not limited to those produced by wounded fish. In many cases swimmers or divers themselves produce the attractive stimulus. To a white shark, a diver clad in a black wetsuit, splashing on the surface or releasing air bubbles, may present an image that is very similar to that of a seal, its natural prey. Adding the olfactory and auditory stimuli from a wounded fish may initiate the feeding behavior. Even when divers are attacked by white sharks, in the great majority of cases, the shark does not pursue the attack beyond the initial bite. Perhaps there is a missing component in the feeding process or perhaps the neoprene rubber wetsuit or human flesh does not taste like seal blubber.

Some shark attacks are clear cases of intentional feeding. On many occasions, the victims of air and sea disasters, often wounded and in a panic, have been set upon and devoured by frenzied sharks. Other cases may be the result of a territoriality drive in sharks, which mistake the diver for a competitor or an attacker. These attacks are characterized by slashing wounds with little loss of tissue. These wounds are produced by the raking motion of the upper jaw only; apparently there is no intention to feed associated with these attacks. A stereotyped agonistic behavior usually precedes these attacks. Sharks displaying aggression shake their heads repeatedly and swim erratically with a hunched-up back, pectoral fins pointing down, and nose pointing up.

# KEY TO THE FAMILIES

1.  Snout prolonged into a flat sawlike blade with teeth and barbels on sides . . . . . . . . . .

    PRISTIOPHORIDAE
    Sawsharks
    Page 70

    Snout without flat, sawlike blade . . . . . . . . . . . . . . . . . . 2

2.  Eyes on top of head, body flattened and skatelike . . . . . . .

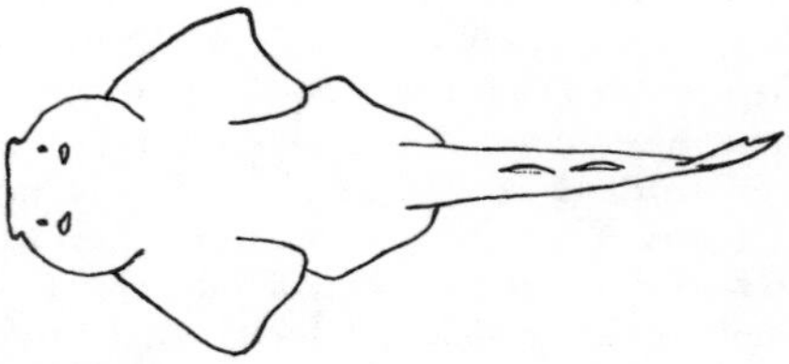

    SQUATINIDAE
    Angel sharks
    Page 71

    Eyes on the sides of the head, body cylindrical, not flattened
    . . . . . . . . . . . . . . . . . . . . . . . 3

3.  Gill slits 6 or 7, only one dorsal fin . . . . . . . . . . . . . . . . . . . . 4
    Gill slits 5, two dorsal fins . 5

4.  First gill slit pair joined under throat, mouth almost terminal
    . . . . . . . . . . . . . . . . . . . . . . .

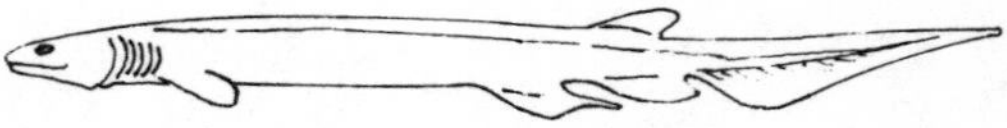

    CHLAMYDOSELACHIDAE
    Frill shark
    Page 35

    First gill slit pair not joined under throat, snout projecting ahead of mouth . . . . . . . . . .

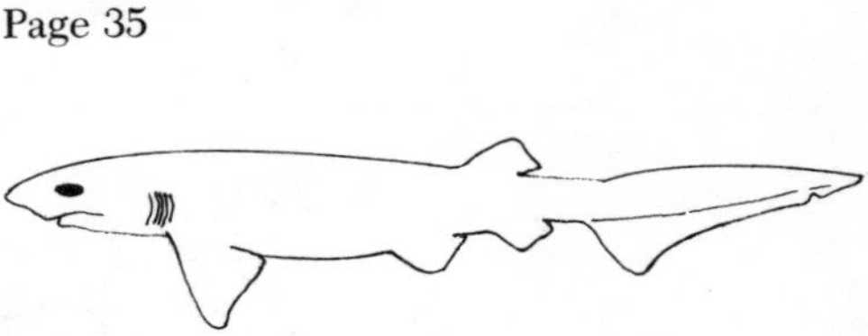

    HEXANCHIDAE
    Cowsharks
    Page 36

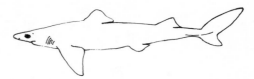

5.  Anal fin absent . . . . . . . . . . .     SQUALIDAE
                                              Dogfish sharks
                                              Page 40

    Anal fin present . . . . . . . . . .  6

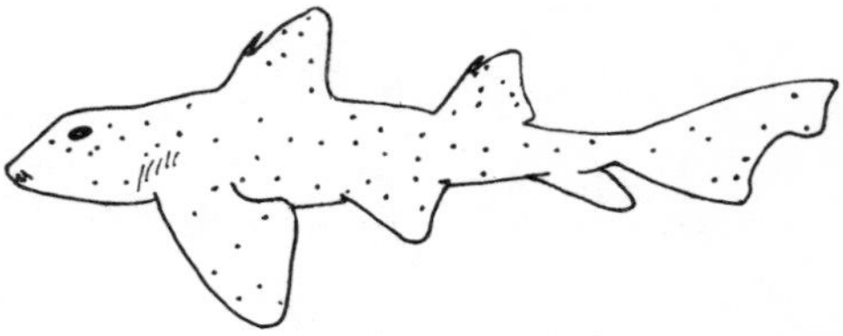

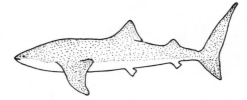

6.  Dorsal fins with a spine . . .     HETERODONTIDAE
                                       Bullhead sharks
                                       Page 73

    Dorsal fins without a spine.   7
7.  Mouth terminal . . . . . . . . . .   8
    Mouth  ventral,  not  termi-
    nal; snout projecting ahead of
    mouth . . . . . . . . . . . . . . . . .   9

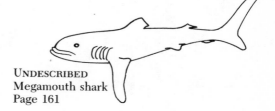

8.  Body  covered  with  white
    spots, nostrils with short bar-
    bels . . . . . . . . . . . . . . . . . . .       RHINIODONTIDAE
                                                     Whale shark
                                                     Page 78

    Body not covered with white
    spots (Other characters to be
    determined,  presently  un-
    described species) . . . . . . . .     UNDESCRIBED
                                           Megamouth shark
                                           Page 161

9.  Nasal barbels present . . . . .   **GINGLYMOSTOMATIDAE**
    Nurse shark
    Page 76

    Nasal barbels absent . . . . . . 10

10. Caudal fin as long or almost as
    long as body . . . . . . . . . . . .   **ALOPIIDAE**
    Thresher sharks
    Page 82

    Caudal fin shorter than body
    . . . . . . . . . . . . . . . . . . . . . . 11

11. Head flattened, shovel or
    hammer shaped, eyes at end
    of lobes . . . . . . . . . . . . . . .   **SPHYRNIDAE**
    Hammerhead sharks
    Page 151

    Head normal, not hammer or
    shovel shaped, not flattened
    . . . . . . . . . . . . . . . . . . . . . . 12

12. Tail with pronounced lateral
    keels . . . . . . . . . . . . . . . . . . 13
    Tail without pronounced lat-
    eral keels . . . . . . . . . . . . . . 14

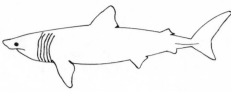

13. Gill slits very long, often with gill rakers, teeth minute and numerous . . . . . . . . . . . . . .

CETORHINIDAE
Basking sharks
Page 86

Gill slits normal, teeth large and few in number . . . . . . .

LAMNIDAE
Mackerel sharks
Page 88

14. Fifth gill slit anterior to base of pectoral fin . . . . . . . . . . . . . . 15
Fifth gill slit over or posterior to base of pectoral fin . . . . . 16

15. Snout prolonged into a flat, flexible blade . . . . . . . . . . .

SCAPANORHYNCHIDAE
Goblin shark
Page 160

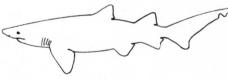

Snout normal, lacking flat blade . . . . . . . . . . . . . . . . . .

ODONTASPIDIDAE
Sand tiger sharks
Page 79

16.  First dorsal fin much longer (six to seven times) than high . . . . . . . . . . . . . . . . . . . . .

**PSEUDOTRIAKIDAE**
False catsharks
Page 113

First dorsal fin not longer than high . . . . . . . . . . . . . . . . . . . . 17

17.  First dorsal fin over or behind origin of pelvic fins . . . . . . .

**SCYLIORHINIDAE**
Catsharks
Page 95

First dorsal fin anterior to origin of pelvic fins. . . . . . . . . . 18

18.  Precaudal pit present . . . . .

**CARCHARHINIDAE**
Requiem sharks
Page 123

Precaudal pit absent . . . . . . 19

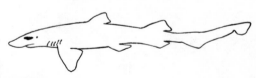

19.  Dorsal fins equal in size, teeth pointed, with lateral denticles . . . . . . . . . . . . . . . . . . . . .

**PROSCYLLIDAE**
Ribbontail catsharks
Page 112

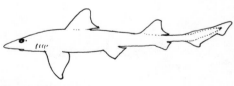

First dorsal fin higher than second dorsal fin, teeth usually blunt and pavementlike

**TRIAKIDAE**
Smoothhound sharks
Page 114

# FAMILY AND SPECIES DESCRIPTIONS

## Family Chlamydoselachidae—Frill shark

The Chlamydoselachidae are a family whose only living representative is the frill shark, the most primitive living shark.

### Frill shark
*Chlamydoselachus anguineus* Garman 1884

DESCRIPTION: The frill shark is an eellike shark with a *terminal mouth* with long jaws, six large gill slits with large gill covers, and a single dorsal fin set very far back, posterior to the pelvic fins. The lower jaw reaches almost to the tip of the snout, and *the first pair of gill covers is continuous across the throat* giving this shark a frilled appearance. The terminal mouth, an incompletely segmented vertebral column, and poorly calcified vertebrae are believed to be primitive characters. The teeth have *three large, fanglike cusps* with two smaller cusps between them. The teeth form interlocking rows, have inwardly directed points, and are alike in both jaws. Their number is variable, averaging U 13–13, L 13–1–13. The color is brown, darker at the edge of the fins. Some specimens have lighter undersides. Average size is 130–150 cm (51–59 in), adult females being slightly larger. The largest recorded specimen was a female 196 cm (77 in) long.

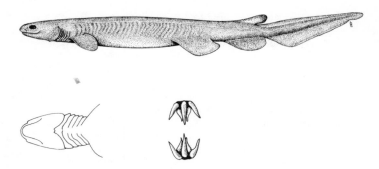

SIMILAR SPECIES: The sixgill shark and the bigeye sixgill shark also have six gills, but their gill covers are not continuous across the throat, and their lower jaws only reach under the eye.

RANGE: The frill shark probably has worldwide distribution in deep waters. Specimens have been reported from Japanese waters, the northeastern Atlantic from Madeira to Arctic Norway, South Africa, and California.

BIOLOGY: This is a deep water species usually reported from 300–500 fathoms. It has distensible jaws with inwardly directed teeth, which indicate that it may feed upon prey of a diameter approximating its own. Analyses of stomach contents have not revealed its usual prey because all captured specimens had empty, or nearly empty, stomachs. It is likely that after a large meal a gorged fish may lie quiescent until its meal has been digested, indifferent to prey and baited hooks. This shark has a fold of tissue in the mouth believed to act as a breathing valve. This structure would allow it to breathe while motionless or resting on the bottom.

REPRODUCTION: Development is ovoviviparous. Females may contain up to 12 fertilized eggs measuring about 12 cm (4.7 in) in diameter, enormous in proportion to the size of the fish. Full-term embryos have never been reported, but birth probably occurs when the embryos reach 50–60 cm (19–24 in). The smallest known free-swimming specimen measured 61 cm (24 in).

RELATION TO MAN: It is a scarcely caught fish, and only about seventy-five specimens have been recorded. Although some specimens have been obtained in Japanese fish markets, the frill shark is too difficult to capture to be of much economic importance.

FISHING: Most specimens have been accidental catches. In the past, Japanese fishermen used squid as bait in waters 300–500 fathoms deep. One California specimen was caught in a gill net set at the surface over deep water.

REFERENCES: Gudger 1940; Gudger and Smith 1933; Noble 1948; B. G. Smith 1937; J. L. B. Smith 1967; Wheeler 1962.

# Family Hexanchidae—Cowsharks

The family Hexanchidae includes the sixgill and sevengill sharks, a small group of deep-water fishes. The family is easily recognized by the presence of six or seven gill slits, subterminal mouths, and a single dorsal fin set posterior to the pelvic fins. The only other sharks with six gill slits are the frill shark and one of the sawsharks, and they are both easily identified; all other sharks have five gill slits. The teeth of cowsharks are dissimilar in the upper and lower jaws; the upper teeth are fanglike, and the lower teeth are sawlike and rectangular. Their development is ovoviviparous. Four species are presently recognized.

1.  Six pairs of gill slits . . . . . . . . . . . . . . . . . . . . . . . . . . . . . . . . . . . . . . . . . . . . . . . 2
    Seven pairs of gill slits . . . . . . . . . . . . . . . . . . . . . . . . . . . . . . . . . . . . . . . . . . . 3
2.  Five large, broad, sawlike teeth on each side of the lower jaw (maximum size about 180 cm [70 in]) . . . . *Hexanchus vitulus* (p. 38)
    Six large, broad, sawlike teeth on each side of the lower jaw . . . . *Hexanchus griseus* (p. 37).
3.  Snout broadly rounded, dorsal surface with numerous dark spots (inhabiting Pacific waters) . . . . *Notorynchus cepedianus* (p. 38)
    Snout narrowly tapering, dorsal surface uniformly dark without spots . . . . *Heptranchias perlo* (p. 40)

Blue shark (*Prionace glauca*). Howard Hall

Leopard shark ((*Triakis semifasciata*). Tom McHugh, Nat'l. Audubon Soc. Coll.,
    Photo Researchers

Bull shark (*Carcharhinus leucas*). Tom Stack/Tom Stack & Associates

Sand tiger shark (*Odontaspis taurus*). Russ Kinne, Nat'l. Audubon Soc. Coll.,
Photo Researchers

Scalloped hammerhead (*Sphyrna lewini*). Howard Hall

Horn shark (*Heterodontus francisci*). Howard Hall

Lemon shark (*Negaprion brevirostris*). Tom McHugh, Nat'l. Audubon Soc. Coll.,
Photo Researchers

Swell shark (*Cephaloscyllium ventriosum*). Howard Hall

# Sixgill shark
*Hexanchus griseus* (Bonnaterre) 1788

DESCRIPTION: The sixgill shark can be recognized by its single dorsal fin, *six gill slits*, and *six large, broad, sawlike teeth on each side of the lower jaw*. Teeth number U 9 or 10–9 or 10, L 6–1–6, disregarding the minute, budlike teeth on the corners of the jaws. The teeth on the lower jaw are much broader and more sawlike than the upper teeth and have one small central tooth. Color is dark gray or brown with lighter or whitish undersides. A 400-cm (13-ft) specimen weighed 240 kg (528 lb), and one 467 cm (15 ft) long weighed 500 kg (1,300 lb). Largest on record was a female 482 cm (15.8 ft) long. Reports of a specimen 807 cm (26.5 ft) long are now known to be erroneous.

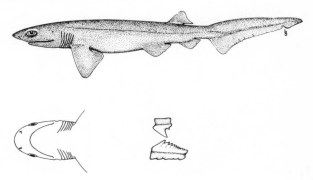

SIMILAR SPECIES: The bigeye sixgill shark has five teeth on each side of the lower jaw. The frill shark has a terminal mouth and fanglike teeth.

RANGE: The sixgill shark has worldwide distribution in deep temperate and tropical waters. In North American waters it has been reported from British Columbia to California and from North Carolina to Florida and the Gulf of Mexico. Immatures have been reported from Puget Sound and San Francisco Bay. It appears to be common in deep waters along the northern coast of Cuba.

BIOLOGY: This is a common, bottom-dwelling, deep-water species, usually reported from depths of 100–600 fathoms. It is active by night, often visiting surface waters. It feeds on crustaceans and a wide variety of fishes, including hake, grouper, swordfish, and small marlins.

REPRODUCTION: Development is ovoviviparous. Females are believed to reach maturity at about 450 cm (14.9 ft). Size of the males at maturity is not known because of previous confusion with the bigeye sixgill shark. The litters are large, up to 108 pups having been reported. The pups measure 60–70 cm (24–28 in) at birth. Free-swimming young of 60–75 cm (24–30 in) have been reported

RELATION TO MAN: It is too scarcely taken in North American waters to be of economic importance, possibly because of the lack of a deep-water fishery. In Cuba it has been used for oil and fish meal. The flesh is said to have a purgative effect.

FISHING: Most specimens are caught at night on the bottom in 100–300 fathoms. During the day this fish is seldom caught in less than 200 fathoms.

REFERENCES: Bass, D'Aubrey, and Kistnasamy 1975*d*; Bigelow and Schroeder 1948; Hart 1973; Kato, Springer, and Wagner 1967; Miller and Greenfield 1965.

## Bigeye sixgill shark
*Hexanchus vitulus* Springer and Waller 1969

DESCRIPTION: The bigeye sixgill shark is recognized by its single dorsal fin, *six gill slits*, and *five large, broad, sawlike teeth* on *each side of the lower jaw.* The upper teeth are long and pointed; the lower teeth are broad and sawlike, with one small central tooth. Teeth number U 9–9, L 5–1–5, disregarding the minute, budlike teeth on the sides of the mouth. Color is gray above with lighter undersides. Average specimens measure 158–175 cm (62–69 in) and weigh around 20 kg (44 lb). Maximum size is 180 cm (71 in).

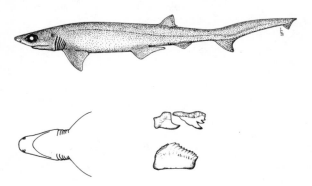

SIMILAR SPECIES: The sixgill shark has six large, broad teeth on each side of the lower jaw. The frill shark has a terminal mouth and fanglike teeth.

RANGE: The bigeye sixgill shark probably has worldwide distribution in deep water. Specimens have been reported from the Bahamas, Florida, the Philippines, and the Indian Ocean.

BIOLOGY: Very little is known about this species, which was first described in 1969. It is known to be a deep-water shark, and most specimens have been captured at depths of 220 fathoms. A small tuna was reportedly found in the stomach of a bigeye sixgill shark, suggesting that it may visit surface waters.

REPRODUCTION: Development is ovoviviparous. The pups measure about 40 cm (16 in) at birth. Thirteen pups were reported from a 163-cm (64-in) female.

RELATION TO MAN: None.

FISHING: Most specimens have been caught on the bottom at depths of 120–220 fathoms.

REFERENCES: Bass, D'Aubrey, and Kistnasamy 1975d; Forster et al. 1970; Springer and Waller 1969.

## Sevengill shark
*Notorynchus cepedianus* Peron 1807 (= *Notorynchus maculatus*)

DESCRIPTION: The sevengill shark is recognized by its *seven gill slits, a flattened head with a broadly rounded snout*, a single dorsal fin and numerous *dark spots on the dorsal surface*. The upper teeth are long and pointed; lower teeth are broad and sawlike. Teeth number U 7–1–7, L 6–1–6, counting the large teeth only. Color is sandy gray to reddish brown with dark spots above and whitish below. A partial albino has been reported. Most specimens caught are immatures

70–125 cm (28–49 in) and weigh 2–9 kg (5–20 lb). An adult male 197 cm (78 in) weighed 35 kg (77 lb). Largest on record was a female 264 cm (104 in) that weighed 107 kg (235 lb).

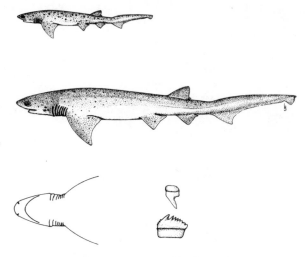

SIMILAR SPECIES: The sharpnose sevengill shark also has seven gill slits, but it has a pointed snout and lacks the spots on the dorsal surface.

RANGE: The sevengill shark is found throughout the Pacific and Indian oceans. In the eastern Pacific it has been recorded from British Columbia to the Straits of Magellan. Young and immatures are very common in San Francisco, Tomales, and Monterey bays.

BIOLOGY: This is a common shark and a frequent denizen of marine aquaria; however, very little is known about its biology. It has been reported to feed on chimaeras, small sharks, and mackerel. Although pups and immatures are often captured in bays, the adults are seldom taken. It is likely that the females enter bays to give birth to their pups and are inhibited from feeding while in the nursery areas.

REPRODUCTION: Development is apparently ovoviviparous. The smallest mature male known measured 197 cm (78 in). Females with large embryos have not been reported. The smallest free-swimming specimen recorded measured 53 cm (21 in). Litters are probably large, since a female carrying eighty-three large eggs has been reported.

RELATION TO MAN: Small amounts of flesh are found in California markets, where it is considered one of the most palatable sharks. It is often exhibited in marine aquaria, where it lives for several months but requires force-feeding. Human remains were found in the stomach of one specimen, and a provoked attack on a diver occurred in a California aquarium.

FISHING: Young and immatures are easily caught in the nursery areas during late summer and fall. Best fishing is reported from depths of 3–6 fathoms. A sevengill shark is an aggressive fish, and one just pulled out of the water will attempt to bite at anything.

REFERENCES: Hart 1973; Herald 1968; Kato, Springer, and Wagner 1967; Pequeño 1979.

## Sharpnose sevengill or perlon shark
*Heptranchias perlo* (Bonnaterre) 1788

DESCRIPTION: The sharpnose sevengill shark is recognized by its *seven gill slits*, a narrow tapering snout, and a single dorsal fin. The upper teeth are fang-like, with the side teeth having small lateral denticles; the lower teeth are broad and sawlike, except for the small symmetrical central tooth. Teeth number U 9 to 11–9 to 11, L 5–1–5. Color is brownish gray with paler undersides. The tips of the dorsal and caudal fins are black. Average size is 100 cm (39 in), but adult females may reach 137 cm (54 in).

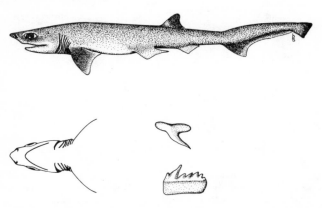

SIMILAR SPECIES: The sevengill shark also has seven gill slits, but its snout is broad and round, and it has spots on its dorsal surface.

RANGE: It probably has worldwide distribution in deep tropical and warm-temperature waters. Specimens have been reported from the Mediterranean, Australia, New Zealand, Japan, South Africa, and northern Cuba. A small specimen was caught in deep water off South Carolina.

BIOLOGY: This is a deep-water species of the edges of the continental shelf, where it appears to be most abundant in depths of 100–250 fathoms. It feeds on squid and small fishes. Very little is known about its habits.

REPRODUCTION: Development is ovoviviparous. Maturity is reached at 85–90 cm (33–35 in). Litters consist of nine to twenty pups, which measure about 25 cm (10 in) at birth.

RELATION TO MAN: In North American waters it is too scarce to be of economic importance. It is considered a nuisance off the Spanish coast because it is blamed for consuming large numbers of hake. The flesh is said to be mildly poisonous.

FISHING: Usually it is caught on longlines in 100–250 fathoms, occasionally in shallower waters. When caught, it behaves aggressively and attempts to bite.

REFERENCES: Bass, D'Aubrey, and Kistnasamy 1975*d*; Bigelow and Schroeder 1948; Garrick and Paul 1971.

## Family Squalidae—Dogfish Sharks

The Squalidae are a large family of sharks, also known as squaloids, characterized by a "sharklike" body, lateral eyes, prominent spiracles, two dorsal fins with or without spines, and no anal fin (only the angel sharks and the sawsharks also lack the anal fin). The squaloids are primarily small sharks of cool or deep waters (only a few reach large size) and they include the only polar sharks known. The group is apparently displaced from shallow tropical and warm-temperate waters by more advanced and larger sharks. Development is ovoviviparous.

This is a diverse group of sharks often considered to be composed of several families depending on the absence or presence of dorsal-fin spines, body tubercles, and teeth shape. The interrelationships of the squaloid sharks are poorly understood because of the lack of an adequate fossil record; consequently numerous classification schemes have been proposed. Here I follow Nelson (1976) and retain all the sharks with "sharklike" bodies, lateral eyes, and no anal fin in the family Squalidae. Presently about seventy-five species are recognized, and their number increases yearly as surveys of deep waters continue; at least twenty-six species are found in our area.

1. Dorsal fins each with a spine . . . . . . . . . . . . . . . . . . . . . . . . . . . . . . . . . . 2
   Second dorsal fin without a spine . . . . . . . . . . . . . . . . . . . . . . . . . . . . . . 18
2. Upper teeth with one cusp only . . . . . . . . . . . . . . . . . . . . . . . . . . . . . . . . 3
   Upper teeth with three to seven cusps . . . . . . . . . . . . . . . . . . . . . . . . . . 10
3. Snout length greater than distance from center of mouth to pectoral
   fin origin, denticles on sides of body pitch-fork-shaped on stalks
   standing nearly erect . . . . *Deania profundorum* (p. 60)
   Snout length less than distance from center of mouth to pectoral fin
   origin, denticles on sides of body low or scalelike . . . . . . . . . . . . . . . 4
4. Upper and lower teeth similar . . . . . . . . . . . . . . . . . . . . . . . . . . . . . . . . . 5
   Upper and lower teeth dissimilar, lowers much broader than uppers . . 8
5. Second dorsal fin smaller than first . . . . . . . . . . . . . . . . . . . . . . . . . . . . 6
   Second dorsal fin as large as first; first dorsal fin origin posterior to
   free rear tips of pectoral fins . . . . *Squalus asper* (p. 57)
6. Small white spots scattered over dorsal side; origin of first dorsal fin
   well behind free rear tips of pectoral fins . . . . *Squalus acanthias*
   (p. 55)
   Color uniform, lacking white spots; origin of first dorsal fin over free
   rear tips of pectoral fins . . . . . . . . . . . . . . . . . . . . . . . . . . . . . . . . . . . . 7
7. Pectoral fins with deeply concave rear margins and pointed free rear
   tips; dermal denticles on sides of body narrow and with a single
   point . . . . *Squalus cubensis* (p. 59)
   Pectoral fins with moderately concave rear margins and rounded
   free rear tips; dermal denticles on sides of body broad, with three
   points . . . . *Squalus blainvillei* (p. 58)
8. Dorsal fins with very small, inconspicuous spines; free rear tips of
   pectoral fins rounded . . . . *Centroscymnus coelolepis* (p. 61)
   Dorsal fins with conspicuous spines, free rear tips of pectoral fins
   pointed . . . . . . . . . . . . . . . . . . . . . . . . . . . . . . . . . . . . . . . . . . . . . . . . . 9
9. Denticles on sides of body with longitudinal ridges ending on thorn-
   like point . . . . *Centrophorus uyato* (p. 54)
   Denticles on sides of body with ridges on anterior margin only, lacking point on posterior margin . . . . *Centrophorus granulosus*
   (p. 53)
10. Upper and lower teeth similar, teeth in both jaws with three to five
    cusps . . . . . . . . . . . . . . . . . . . . . . . . . . . . . . . . . . . . . . . . . . . . . . . . . . 11
    Upper and lower teeth dissimilar, lower teeth with one cusp only . . . . 12

11. Rear margins of pectoral fins, when laid back, not reaching a perpendicular at point of emergence from skin of first dorsal fin spine by a distance of at least 25 percent as long as eye; inhabiting North Atlantic waters .... *Centroscyllium fabricii* (p. 45)

Rear margins of pectoral fins, when laid back, reaching almost to a perpendicular at point of emergence from skin of first dorsal fin spine; inhabiting eastern Pacific waters .... *Centroscyllium nigrum* (p. 46)

12. Upper margin of caudal fin nearly as long as from tip of snout to rear edges of pectoral fins; pectoral fins with a fringe of naked, hornlike rays (ceratotrichia) .... *Etmopterus schultzi* (p. 51)

Upper margin of caudal fin shorter than distance from tip of snout to rear margins of pectoral fins, pectoral fins lacking a fringe of naked, hornlike rays.................................................. 13

13. Interspace between dorsal fins much shorter than distance from tip of snout to first gill slit opening ............................... 14

Interspace between dorsal fins as long as, or longer than, distance from tip of snout to first gill slit opening........................ 15

14. Rear margins of the pectoral fins reaching the level of first dorsal fin origin .... *Etmopterus bullisi* (p. 46)

Rear margin of pectoral fins not reaching the level of the origin of the first dorsal fin origin .... *Etmopterus gracilispinis* (p. 47)

15. Dermal denticles on sides of body with low, flat crowns and four-pointed bases .... *Etmopterus pusillus* (p. 50)

Dermal denticles on sides of body thornlike or bristlelike, with sharp points................................................. 16

16. A noticeable pale, yellowish spot on top of the head................ 17

Lacking a pale, yellowish spot on top of the head .... *Etmopterus princeps* (p. 49)

17. Head in front of spiracle about as long as distance from spiracle to pectoral fin axil; skin on underside of snout rough with denticles .... *Etmopterus hillianus* (p. 48)

Head in front of spiracle about as long as distance from spiracle to pectoral fin origin, skin on underside of snout naked, lacking denticles .... *Etmopterus virens* (p. 52)

18. First dorsal fin with a spine, second dorsal fin base twice as long as first dorsal fin base .... *Squaliolus laticaudus* (p. 69)

First dorsal fin without a spine.................................... 19

19. First dorsal fin originating well ahead of pelvic fins................. 20

First dorsal fin originating over or behind origin of pelvic fins ....... 25

20. Second dorsal fin base more than twice as long as first dorsal fin base, rear tip of first dorsal fin slightly over origin of pelvic fins .... *Euprotomicrus bispinatus* (p. 65)

Second dorsal fin base about as long as first dorsal fin base .......... 21

21. Rear tip of first dorsal fin over or behind the pelvic fins ............. 22

Rear tip of first dorsal fin well ahead of pelvic fins.................. 23

22. Second dorsal fin lower than first .... *Isistius brasiliensis* (p. 67)

Second dorsal fin higher than first .... *Isistius plutodus* (p. 68)

23. Lower teeth with triangular, erect cusps, and serrated edges .... *Dalatias licha* (p. 64)

Lower teeth with oblique, smooth-edged cusps ................... 24

24. First dorsal fin origin almost as near to snout tip as to tip of caudal

fin; inhabiting Pacific waters . . . . *Somniosus pacificus* (p. 63)
First dorsal fin origin nearer to snout tip than to tip of caudal fin;
inhabiting Atlantic waters . . . . *Somniosus microcephalus* (p. 62)
25. Large dermal denticles (up to 15 mm in diameter if single but to 35
mm if compound), irregularly distributed, with scalloped bases
and finely ridged spines . . . . *Echinorhinus brucus* (p. 43)
Large dermal denticles (up to 4 mm in diameter), uniformly distributed over the body, with stellate bases and strongly ridged
spines . . . . *Echinorhinus cookei* (p. 44)

## Bramble shark
### *Echinorhinus brucus* (Bonnaterre) 1788

DESCRIPTION: The bramble shark has the *first dorsal fin located over or behind the origin of the pelvic fins*. The teeth have several smooth-edged cusps,
with the largest cusp curved toward the corners of the mouth; they number U 10
to 13–10 to 13, L 11 to 13–11 to 13, and are similar in both jaws. The body is
*covered by large spinelike dermal denticles*. These denticles are *sparse and irregularly distributed*; they measure up to 1.5 cm (.6 in) in diameter at the base and
larger when two or more are joined together; their bases have a scalloped edge,
and the spines are finely ridged. In adults, the underside of the snout is covered
with large denticles. Color varies from dark gray or brown to black above, with
metallic hues and often with darker or brownish blotches; the undersides are
paler or whitish. A specimen 216 cm (85 in) weighed 78 kg (173 lb). The bramble
shark grows to about 245 cm (96 in).

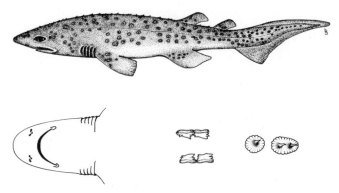

SIMILAR SPECIES: The more common prickly shark has smaller, uniformly
distributed dermal denticles, less than 0.4 cm (0.16 in) in diameter and never
joined together; the base of its denticles is stellate and the spines are heavily
ridged.

RANGE: It is probably cosmopolitan in deep temperate and tropical waters. It
is often reported from the eastern Atlantic and the western Indian oceans, but it is
very rare in the western Atlantic. Only three specimens have been reported from
the North American east coast in the last hundred years; reports of specimens
from the west coast are doubtful because of confusion with the prickly shark.

BIOLOGY: Very little is known about its habits. It appears to be more abundant in depths of 200–500 fathoms; occasionally it is found in shallow water.

REPRODUCTION: Development is ovoviviparous. The pups probably reach about 40 cm (16 in) at birth. A litter of twenty-four pups has been reported.

RELATION TO MAN: None.

FISHING: It is usually caught in depths greater than 100 fathoms. Catches should be preserved and reported, given their rarity.

REFERENCES: Bigelow and Schroeder 1948; Collyer 1953; Garrick 1960*a*; Garrick and Moreland 1968; Hubbs and Clark 1945; Musick and McEachran 1969; Silas and Selvaraj 1972.

## Prickly shark
*Echinorhinus cookei* Pietschmann 1928

DESCRIPTION: The prickly shark has a *first dorsal fin located over or behind the origin of the pelvic fins*. The teeth have several smooth-edged cusps, with the longest cusp curved toward the corners of the mouth; they number U 10 to 12–10 to 12, L 11 to 14–11 to 14, and are similar in both jaws. The juveniles have single-cusped teeth. The body is *covered by very large dermal denticles*. These denticles measure up to 0.4 cm (0.16 in) in diameter at the base; they are *uniformly distributed* over the body, and they have stellate bases and strongly ridged spines. In adults the underside of the snout has very small dermal denticles and is almost smooth. Color is grayish brown above and below; the underside of the snout and around the mouth are white, and the fins are black-tipped. A 295-cm (116-in) specimen was reported to weigh 222 kg (490 lb). The species is reputed to reach 400 cm (13.1 ft).

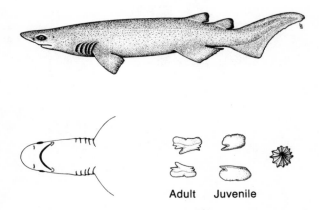

Adult    Juvenile

SIMILAR SPECIES: The bramble shark has larger, irregularly distributed denticles with rounded bases, scalloped edges, and finely ridged spines.

RANGE: The prickly shark inhabits tropical and temperate waters of the Pacific Ocean. Our only records are from southern California, where it is rare.

BIOLOGY: Almost nothing is known of its habits. It appears to be a deep-water species that frequently visits surface waters.

REPRODUCTION: Development is ovoviviparous. The young are probably born at about 40 cm (16 in).

RELATION TO MAN: None.

FISHING: Most specimens recorded were accidental trawl catches in 40–50 fathoms. A few specimens have been caught on rod and reel on the bottom in about 20 fathoms.

REFERENCES: Bass, D'Aubrey, and Kistnasamy 1976; Garrick 1960*a*; Silas and Selvaraj 1972.

## Black dogfish
### *Centroscyllium fabricii* (Reinhardt) 1825

DESCRIPTION: The black dogfish is characterized by two dorsal fins with prominent spines, and a *second dorsal fin originating over the pelvic fins*. The teeth have three (sometimes four or five) sharp, smooth-edged cusps, the central cusp being the largest. Teeth number U 34–34, L 34–34, and are *similar in both jaws*. The dermal denticles are minute, thornlike, and with ridged, stellate bases. Juveniles are ink black below and slightly lighter or chocolate brown above, with the dorsal and pectoral fins margined and the pelvics tipped with white, and with white fin spines. Half-grown and *adult specimens are black throughout*, with white fin spines. It is likely that this is a luminescent shark, although it has not actually been reported to emit light. Average size is 60–75 cm (24–30 in); maximum size is about 84 cm (33 in).

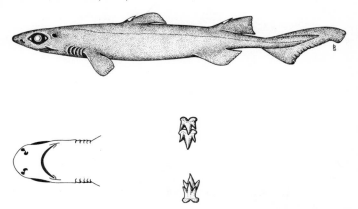

SIMILAR SPECIES: Other Atlantic coast dogfishes lack the tricuspid teeth in the lower jaw.

RANGE: The black dogfish inhabits the subpolar waters of the North Atlantic from the Davis Strait to the Shetlands. In North American waters it ranges from the Davis Strait to the Virginia coast. It is common from the Davis Strait to Nova Scotia.

BIOLOGY: This is a deep-water species that may approach the surface only in arctic latitudes and during the coldest and darkest months. Specimens have been captured at the surface through the ice in winter, down to 730 fathoms. Most captures occur in depths of 300–500 fathoms and temperatures of 3.5–4.5°C (38–40°F). It is known to feed on squid, pelagic crustaceans, and jellyfish.

REPRODUCTION: Development is ovoviviparous. Its reproductive processes have not been described.

RELATION TO MAN: None.

FISHING: It is caught on longlines or in deep-water trawls at depths greater than 200 fathoms.

REFERENCES: Bigelow and Schroeder 1948, 1954, 1957; Leim and Scott 1966; Templeman 1963.

## Pacific black dogfish
### Centroscyllium nigrum Garman 1899

DESCRIPTION: This small shark has two dorsal fins of equal size, each with a long spine. The teeth have three (occasionally four or five) sharp, smooth-edged cusps, the median cusp being the largest, and are *similar in both jaws*. The dermal denticles are thornlike, erect, with stellate bases, and set far apart. Color is deep black above and below, with white dorsal spines and a *narrow white edging* on the dorsal, pectoral, and pelvic fins. Average size is about 30 cm (12 in); it grows to at least 40 cm (16 in).

SIMILAR SPECIES: Other Pacific coast dogfishes lack the tricuspid teeth in the lower jaw.

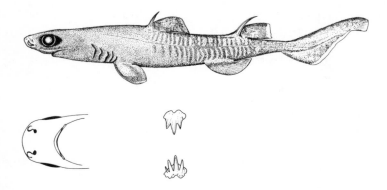

RANGE: The Pacific black dogfish inhabits the eastern Pacific from California to Central America; it has also been reported from the Hawaiian area. It is a rare catch in our area.

BIOLOGY: This is a deep-water species; most specimens are caught in 400–625 fathoms. It has been reported to feed on shrimp, but nothing else is known of its habits.

REPRODUCTION: Development is probably ovoviviparous. It reaches maturity at about 40 cm (16 in). Nothing else is known of its reproductive processes.

RELATION TO MAN: None.

FISHING: It is caught in deep-water trawls.

REFERENCES: Beebe and Tee-Van 1941; Bigelow and Schroeder 1957; Garman 1899, 1913; Gilbert 1905; Hubbs, Follett, and Dempster 1979.

### Etmopterus bullisi Bigelow and Schroeder 1957

DESCRIPTION: This small shark is characterized by a slender body, two dorsal fins, each with a spine, a *first dorsal fin originating over* the rear tips of the pectoral fins, and an interspace between the *dorsal fins that is shorter* than the distance from the tip of the snout to the first gill slit. The upper teeth have three smooth-edged cusps, the central cusp being much larger; the lower teeth have a single cusp with a nearly horizontal cutting edge and a notch on its outer margin. Teeth number U 18 to 20, L 27 to 31. The dermal denticles are thornlike and erect; those on the back and sides are *arranged in regular longitudinal rows*. Color is dark brown above with a pale yellowish spot on top of the head, slightly darker or blackish below, and with distinct flank markings. These markings are evident only upon close observation, as the sides are almost as dark as the ventral side. The fins are light-colored. There is a pale band along the dorsal midline with a series of black dots along its center; presumably these dots are luminescent organs. Most specimens captured have been juveniles 18–24 cm (7–9 in). The size of the adults is not yet known.

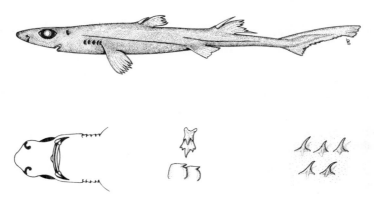

SIMILAR SPECIES: The broadband dogfish has bristlelike dermal denticles. In other similar sharks the interspace between the dorsal fins is longer than the distance from the tip of the snout to the first gill slit.

RANGE: This shark inhabits the western Atlantic from North Carolina to the Caribbean Sea. It is common throughout its range.

BIOLOGY: This is a deep-water species usually found in 200–350 fathoms. It feeds on small crustaceans and squid. It is capable of swallowing whole relatively large squid, probably by distending its jaws.

REPRODUCTION: Development is presumably ovoviviparous. Nothing else is known of its reproductive processes.

RELATION TO MAN: None.

FISHING: It is caught in deep-water trawls.

REFERENCES: Bigelow and Schroeder 1957; Schwartz and Burgess 1975.


## Broadband dogfish
### *Etmopterus gracilispinis* Krefft 1968

DESCRIPTION: This small shark has two dorsal fins, each with a spine, an *interdorsal space shorter* than the distance from the tip of the snout to the first gill slit, and *pectoral fins ending far short* of the dorsal fin origin. The upper teeth have five cusps, with the median being the largest. The lower teeth have one outwardly pointing cusp. Teeth number about U 27, L 28. The dermal denticles are high and bristlelike. The underside of the snout is rough with denticles. Color is dark brown above and black below, with black winglike markings on the flanks.

This dogfish has a pale yellowish spot on top of the head. It is known to reach 33 cm (13 in).

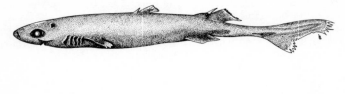

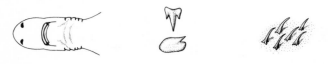

SIMILAR SPECIES: *E. bullisi* has pectoral fins that reach the level of the first dorsal fin origin. Other small squaloids have an interdorsal space longer than the distance from the tip of the snout to the first gill slit.

RANGE: The broadband dogfish has been reported from the western North Atlantic (Virginia and Florida) and from both sides of the South Atlantic. It is probably widely distributed in the Atlantic.

BIOLOGY: This is a deep-water species that has been caught at depths of 225–333 fathoms. It is believed to ascend in the water column at night, as many other species do. Nothing else is known of its habits.

REPRODUCTION: Development is probably ovoviviparous. A newborn specimen 13 cm (5 in) has been reported. A 26-cm (10-in) male was reported as immature.

RELATION TO MAN: None.

FISHING: It is caught in deep-water trawls.

REFERENCES: Krefft 1968*a*; Schwartz and Burgess 1975.


## *Etmopterus hillianus* (Poey) 1861

DESCRIPTION: This small shark is characterized by two dorsal fins, each with a spine, a distance from the spiracle to the tip of the snout that is *almost as long as* the distance from the spiracle to the pectoral fin axil, and an interspace between the pelvic fins and the caudal fin that is as long as the distance from the tips of the pectoral fins to the origin of the pelvic fins. The upper teeth usually have five cusps (rarely three or seven), with the central cusp being much larger. The lower teeth have one cusp with a nearly horizontal cutting edge and a notch on its outer margin. Teeth number about U 12–12, L 18–18. The dermal denticles are bristlelike, with long tapering points and stellate bases concealed in the skin. The underside of the snout is rough with dermal denticles. Color is chocolate brown above, with a pale yellowish spot on top of the head; the undersides are black with black patches extending upward behind the pelvic fins. Small, black dots are scattered over the top of the head and continue rearward into a single row along the midline; two to four rows of narrow black dashes extend along the sides. These black dots and dashes are presumably luminescent. Average size is about 25 cm (10 in). It grows to at least 32 cm (13 in).

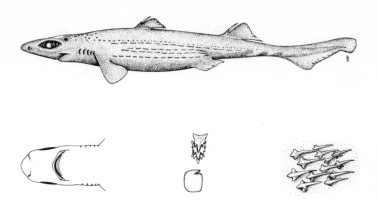

SIMILAR SPECIES: *E. virens* lacks dermal denticles on the underside of the snout. *E. bullisi* and *E. gracilispinis* have an interdorsal space much shorter than the distance from the tip of the snout to the first gill slit. *E. pusillus* has a longer interdorsal space, almost as long as the distance from the tip of the snout to the pectoral fin axil. In *E. princeps* and *E. schultzi* interspace between the pelvic fins and the caudal fin is much shorter than the distance from the rear tips of the pectoral to the origin of the pelvic fins.

RANGE: This small shark is found from the West Indian region and southern Florida to the offings of Chesapeake Bay. It has been reported as common around Cuban waters.

BIOLOGY: It appears to be confined to deep water; it has been reported from depths of 208 to 392 fathoms. Nothing else is known of its habits.

REPRODUCTION: Development is ovoviviparous. Males mature at about 25 cm (10 in); females mature at about 30 cm (12 in). Litters consist of up to five pups, which measure about 9 cm (4 in) at birth.

RELATION TO MAN: None.

FISHING: It is caught in deep-water trawls.

REFERENCES: Bigelow and Schroeder 1948, 1957; Schwartz and Burgess 1975.

## *Etmopterus princeps* Collett 1904

DESCRIPTION: This small shark has a slender body and two dorsal fins, each with a spine. The upper teeth have five smooth-edged cusps, with the central cusp being much larger and the outermost cusps being much smaller. Small specimens may have teeth with only three cusps. The lower teeth have a single, strongly oblique cusp with a notch on its outer margin. Teeth number about U 29 to 32, L 40 to 50, their number varying with age. The dermal denticles are *low, thornlike*, nearly erect, with the point turned rearward, with prominent ridges and squarish bases. Color is *uniform blackish brown or black*, occasionally with darker undersides. It *lacks a pale yellowish spot on top of the head*. It does not appear to be luminescent. Average size is about 55 cm (22 in). It grows to about 75 cm (30 in).

SIMILAR SPECIES: *E. hillianus* and *E. virens* have conspicuous body markings. *E. pusillus* has a yellowish spot on top of the head and low, four-pointed dermal denticles. *E. schultzi* has frilled pectoral fins, a yellowish spot on top of the head, and much more slender dermal denticles. *E. bullisi* has a more anterior second dorsal fin and a yellowish spot on top of the head, and its dermal denticles

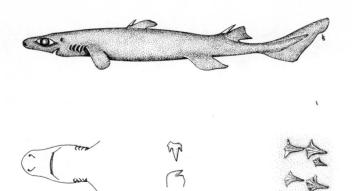

are arranged in rows. *E. gracilispinis* has distinct winglike flank markings, and the interspace between its dorsal fins is less than the distance from the snout to the first gill slit.

RANGE: This shark is known from both sides of the North Atlantic. In the east it has been reported from the Faroes and Hebrides and off the Strait of Gibraltar. In North America it occurs off southern Nova Scotia to southern New England. It is common throughout its range.

BIOLOGY: This shark is confined to deep waters; it has been reported from depths of 310 to 1,134 fathoms. Its habits and diet have not been reported.

REPRODUCTION: Development is presumably ovoviviparous. A 55-cm (22-in) male was reported as mature.

RELATION TO MAN: None.

FISHING: It is caught only in deep-water trawls.

REFERENCES: Bigelow, Schroeder, and Springer 1953; Leim and Scott 1966.

## *Etmopterus pusillus* (Lowe) 1839

DESCRIPTION: This small shark has two dorsal fins, each with a spine, and an interdorsal space longer than the distance from the tip of the snout to the first gill slit. The upper teeth have three to five (usually three) triangular, smooth-edged cusps, the median cusp being much larger; the lower teeth have one strongly oblique, smooth-edged cusp with a deep notch on its outer margin. Teeth number U 22 to 26, L 17 to 19–1–17 to 19. The dermal denticles have *low, flat crowns* and *four-pointed bases,* and they are randomly distributed. Color is uniform black above and below, except for a pale yellowish spot on top of the head and the rear edges of dorsal fins, which are whitish and nearly translucent. Average size is about 45 cm (18 in). The largest specimen on record measured 47 cm (19 in).

SIMILAR SPECIES: The other squaloid sharks in the area lack the flat, four-pointed denticles.

RANGE: It has been reported from both sides of the North and South Atlantic, Japan, and the east coast of Africa. It is probably cosmopolitan in deep water.

BIOLOGY: It is a deep-water species, specimens having been caught in about 250 fathoms. It is known to feed on squid, other small sharks, and small bony fishes.

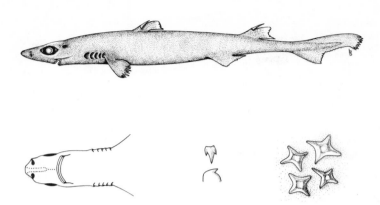

REPRODUCTION: Males up to 39 cm (15 in) and females up to 47 cm (19 in) have been reported as immature. Its reproductive processes have not been described.

RELATION TO MAN: None.

FISHING: It is caught in deep-water trawls.

REFERENCES: Bass, D'Aubrey, and Kistnasamy 1976; Bigelow, Schroeder, and Springer 1955; Krefft 1968a.

## *Etmopterus schultzi* Bigelow, Schroeder, and Springer 1953

DESCRIPTION: This small shark is characterized by two dorsal fins, each with a spine; *pectoral fins with a broad fringe of naked, hornlike rays* (ceratotrichia); and an upper lobe of the caudal fin *about as long as* the distance from the tip of the snout to the rear edges of the pectoral fins. The upper teeth have five to eight (usually seven) pointed, smooth-edged cusps, with the median cusp being the much larger. The lower teeth have one cusp with a nearly horizontal cutting edge

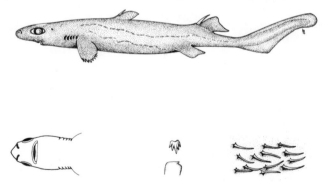

and a notch on its outer margin. Teeth number U 32 to 38, L 32. The dermal denticles are *minute, bristlelike,* and *strongly curved backwards* and have four-pointed bases. Color is dark sooty gray above, with a pale yellowish spot on top of the head, and black below. There are two irregular lines of short, narrow, black markings along each side, and a single line along the dorsal midline. These black markings are difficult to discern and could possibly be luminescent, but no light emission has been reported. Average size is about 27 cm (11 in); it probably reaches 30 cm (12 in).

SIMILAR SPECIES: The other squaloid sharks in the area lack the pectoral fins with conspicuous ceratotrichia.

RANGE: This shark has been reported from the northern Gulf of Mexico, where it appears to be common.

BIOLOGY: This is a deep-water species; most captures have been reported from 210–400 fathoms. It is known to feed on squid.

REPRODUCTION: No data available.

RELATION TO MAN: None.

FISHING: It is caught in deep-water trawls.

REFERENCES: Bigelow, Schroeder, and Springer 1953; Compagno 1978.

## Green dogfish
*Etmopterus virens* Bigelow, Schroeder, and Springer 1953

DESCRIPTION: This small shark is characterized by two dorsal fins, each with a spine, and a distance from the spiracle to the tip of the snout about as long as the distance from the spiracle to the pectoral fin origin. The upper teeth have five cusps, occasionally four, with the median cusp being much larger than the others; the lower teeth have one cusp with a nearly horizontal cutting edge and a notch on its outer margin. Teeth number about U 29 to 34, L 24 to 32. The dermal denticles are conical and thornlike and have squarish bases concealed in the skin. The skin on the lower surface of the snout, up to the mouth, *lacks dermal denticles.* Color is dark sooty brown or black above and below, with two narrow, pale bluish gray *longitudinal stripes along the sides*; the stripes merge together on the rear portion of the trunk, forming a conspicuous pattern of *darker and paler flank markings*. There is a pale yellowish spot on top of the head. The belly of a freshly caught specimen shines with a *bright green iridescence*, hence the name; this iridescence is lost upon preservation. Average size is 20–25 cm (8–10 in). It probably reaches 30 cm (12 in).

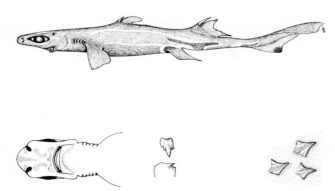

SIMILAR SPECIES: *E. hillianus* has longer, bristlelike dermal denticles; the lower surface of its snout is rough with denticles; it has different markings on the sides and the rear portion of the trunk; and fresh specimens lack any trace of iridescence. *E. bullisi, E. princeps, E. pusillus,* and *E. schultzi* have uniform color and lack the markings on the rear portion of the trunk. *E. gracilispinis* has bristlelike dermal denticles on the underside of the snout.

RANGE: The green dogfish is known only from the northern Gulf of Mexico, where it appears to be common.

BIOLOGY: This is a small shark that appears to live in dense schools confined to moderately deep waters, 190–260 fathoms. It feeds primarily on squid or octopus. The cephalopod beaks and eyes commonly found in the stomach contents of the green dogfish are so large that the shark's jaws must have been greatly stretched at the time of swallowing. It has been suggested that dense schools of these sharks attack prey much larger than themselves, biting off chunks of their prey with their sharp lower teeth.

REPRODUCTION: Development is ovoviviparous. Maturity is reached at about 19 cm (7 in). The gestation period is believed to last about one year. Litters consist of one to three pups, which measure about 9 cm (4 in) at birth.

RELATION TO MAN: None.

FISHING: It is caught in deep-water trawls.

REFERENCES: Bigelow and Schroeder 1957; Bigelow, Schroeder, and Springer 1953; Eisert 1969; S. Springer 1967.

## Gulper
### *Centrophorus granulosus* (Bloch and Schneider) 1801

DESCRIPTION: The gulper is characterized by two dorsal fins with spines, a second dorsal fin smaller and lower than the first, and *pectoral fins with long and pointed free rear tips*. The upper teeth are triangular, pointed, smooth-edged, *symmetrical all along the central part of the jaw*, and slightly oblique at the corners. The lower teeth have strongly oblique cusps with microscopically fine serrations, a notch on their outer margins, and overlapping bases. Teeth number U 33 to 40, L 14 or 15–1–14 or 15. The dermal denticles are low and squarish; their anterior edges have five to seven ridges that converge rearward. Color is light brown to cinnamon brown above, lighter below. Average size is about 150 cm (59 in) and 27 kg (60 lb). It is said to reach 182 cm (72 in).

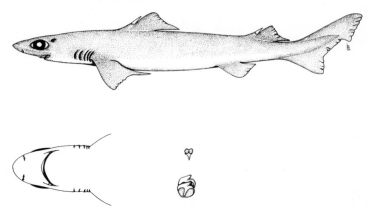

SIMILAR SPECIES: The pectoral fins with long, pointed free rear tips distinguish it from most other squaloid sharks. *Centrophorus uyato* has pectoral fins with shorter free rear tips, upper teeth with more oblique cusps, and elongated dermal denticles.

RANGE: The gulper has been found in the eastern Atlantic from Portugal to North Africa, the Mediterranean, and the western Atlantic from the Carolinas to the Gulf of Mexico. There is also a doubtful record from Japan. It is obviously widely distributed in the Atlantic, but it is a rare catch in our area.

BIOLOGY: This is a deep-water species; specimens have been trawled from about 200 fathoms. Nothing else is known of its habits.

REPRODUCTION: Development is ovoviviparous. The pups measure about 35 cm (14 in) at birth. Litters consist of four to six pups.

RELATION TO MAN: None.

FISHING: It is usually caught in deep-water trawls.

REFERENCES: Bigelow and Schroeder 1957; Bigelow, Schroeder, and Springer 1955; Fowler 1941.

## *Centrophorus uyato* (Rafinesque) 1810

DESCRIPTION: This small shark has a slender body, two dorsal fins, each with a spine, a second dorsal fin slightly smaller than the first, and pectoral fins with *long and pointed free rear tips*. The upper teeth have narrow, *triangular, smooth-edged cusps* and squarish bases; the cusps become increasingly oblique toward the corners of the mouth. The lower teeth are larger than the upper and have *oblique, smooth-edged cusps notched on their outer margins*. Teeth number U 18 or 19–1–18 or 19, L 16–0 or 1–16. The dermal denticles are ovoid, narrowing rearward to a point, with one strong central ridge flanked by two weaker lateral ridges. Color is grayish brown above, paler or whitish on the sides and below. The gill region is bluish, and the *lining of the mouth is very dark grayish blue*. It is reported to reach 98 cm (39 in).

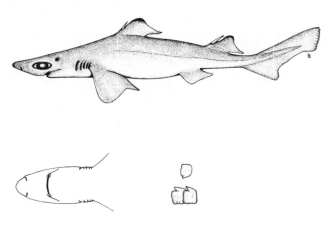

SIMILAR SPECIES: The gulper, generally much larger, has pectoral fins with much longer, pointed free rear tips and dermal denticles not narrowing rearward to form a point but with five to seven ridges diverging rearward.

RANGE: It has been reported from the eastern Atlantic from Gibraltar to off Angola, the Mediterranean, and the Gulf of Mexico.

BIOLOGY: This shark inhabits continental slopes, usually at depths of 100–500 fathoms (although it has been reported at depths of 27–765 fathoms). Its diet and habits have not been reported.

REPRODUCTION: No data available.

RELATION TO MAN: None.

FISHING: It is caught in deep-water trawls.

REFERENCES: Bigelow, Schroeder, and Springer 1953; Hureau and Monod 1973; Tortonese 1956.

## Spiny dogfish
### *Squalus acanthias* Linnaeus 1758

DESCRIPTION: The spiny dogfish is characterized by two dorsal fins, each with a spine, a first dorsal fin usually originating posterior to (occasionally over) the free rear tips of the pectoral fins, a second dorsal fin considerably *smaller* than the first, pectoral fins with curved rear margins and rounded free rear tips, and a *narrow anterior nasal flap*. The teeth have strongly oblique, smooth-edged cusps with a strong notch on their outer margin, forming a continuous cutting edge. Teeth number U 14–14, L 11 or 12–11 or 12, and are similar in both jaws. The dermal denticles are three-pointed with a strong central ridge and broad, wing-like extensions on either side of the central ridge. Color is slate gray or brownish gray above, *usually with small white spots scattered over the body*, and pale gray, grayish white, or pure white below. An albino from Norwegian waters has been reported. Average size is 75–105 cm (30 to 40 in) and 3.1–4.5 kg (7–10 lb). Maximum size is about 130 cm (51 in) and 9.1 kg (20 lb).

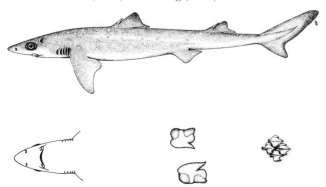

SIMILAR SPECIES: The roughskin spiny dogfish has a second dorsal fin almost as large as the first; it has very large dermal denticles (over 1 mm) and lacks the white spots on the body. The Cuban dogfish and Blainville's dogfish have the origin of the first dorsal fin over the midpoint of the inner margin of the pectoral fin, and they lack the white spots on the body. The Pacific Ocean population of the spiny dogfish is considered to be a different subspecies, *S. acanthias suckleyi*.

RANGE: The spiny dogfish inhabits the temperate and subarctic latitudes of the North Atlantic and North Pacific oceans. It has also been reported from the Mediterranean and Black seas. Along the east coast of North America it ranges from Greenland (only as a rare stray) to northern Florida (winter only). On the west coast it ranges from the Bering Sea to Baja California. It is locally common during migration from Newfoundland to North Carolina and from northern British Columbia to northern California.

BIOLOGY: The spiny dogfish is the most abundant as well as the most economically important shark off the North American coasts; hence, it is the best known. It is a highly gregarious fish that forms very large, highly localized schools, usually composed of hundreds or thousands of sharks of uniform size or sex. These schools exhibit north-south coastal movements and onshore-offshore movements that are not completely understood. These migrations are controlled by temperature, as the spiny dogfish prefers waters at 6–11°C (43–52°F). It is found from the surface to depths of 400 fathoms or more.

The spiny dogfish is found from Georges Bank to the New Jersey coast in March or April, after the temperature has risen above 6°C (43°F). As the waters south of Cape Cod begin to warm up above 15°C (59°F), schools of the spiny dogfish move north, appearing off Newfoundland and the Labrador coast in June or July. As the northern waters begin to cool with the onset of autumn, the schools move south and into deeper water, reaching waters off the Carolinas in November or December. The schools usually remain off the Carolinas or in deep water until early spring, when they begin their northward migration once again.

The spiny dogfish is an opportunistic feeder, which preys on numerous small fishes and invertebrates, taking whatever is locally abundant. Its reported prey includes capelin, cod, haddock, hake, herring, menhaden, ratfish, krill, squid, octopus, and many others. The name dogfish was adopted because the schools of this shark, called "packs" by fishermen, are often seen relentlessly pursuing schools of smaller fish.

This is a slow-growing, long-lived fish that attains a maximum age of twenty-five to thirty years. Studies based on spine growth indicate a growth rate of about 3.5 cm (1.4 in) a year, while tagging studies suggest a slower rate of 1.5 cm (0.6 in) a year. Its few enemies are the larger sharks such as the blue shark, the porbeagle shark, and the tiger shark and, of course, man.

REPRODUCTION: Development is ovoviviparous. Males reach maturity at 80–100 cm (31–39 in) and an estimated age of eleven years; females mature at 100–124 cm (39–49 in) and an estimated age of eighteen to twenty-one years. In the North Atlantic mating takes place during the winter months. While the fertilized eggs are in the oviduct, a thin, horny, transparent shell is secreted around them. This shell usually encompasses several eggs and is known as a "candle." It dissolves when the embryos are about nine months old. Gestation lasts approximately twenty-two to twenty-four months. The nursery areas are unknown but are believed to be in deep water in the wintering grounds as females with pups ready for birth are seen occasionally off the Carolinas in January. Litters range from two to eleven pups, with seven being the average. The pups measure 20–30 cm (8–12 in) at birth.

RELATION TO MAN: In the past the spiny dogfish was fished for its liver oil which was used for tanning, lubrication, and illumination. During World War II it was the subject of an intensive fishery; its liver oil was used for vitamin A extraction. That fishery died out after vitamin A was synthesized. Presently the species is used for reduction into oil and fish meal (used mainly in dog and cat food), and it is a popular laboratory animal. Thousands of spiny dogfish are dissected by students every year at colleges and universities. Although its flesh is quite palatable, only small quantities of spiny dogfish flesh are found in American markets.

In North America the spiny dogfish is considered the bane of commercial fishermen because of the great damage it causes to the net fisheries. Large numbers of spiny dogfish often become entangled in nets, and their removal is a tedious process that results in great loss of fishing time and excessive wear and tear of nets. When catches are large enough (catches of 2,000–4,500 kg of spiny dogfish are not unusual), nets may be lost or ruptured. The hook-and-line fisheries for groundfish such as cod and haddock are also devastated by the sudden appearance of large schools of spiny dogfish. Once these large schools appear, fishing for other species practically comes to a halt, as the spiny dogfish either drive other fishes away or beat them to the bait. Loss of fishing stock through predation is also attributed to it. By contrast, in European waters it is sought after as a valuable food fish. In England it is marketed as grayfish or flake and is widely used for the popular dish of fish and chips.

Numerous elaborate schemes for the elimination of spiny dogfish have been devised and implemented in areas affected by its presence. These schemes, which have ranged from bounties to the blasting of schools, have usually failed because they were short-sighted or naive. The best control method is utilization for human food.

FISHING: It is easily caught both on hook and line or in trawl nets throughout its range when it is locally common. It offers little challenge to the angler. It should be handled with care because the dorsal spines are said to be slightly venomous.

REFERENCES: Aasen 1964; Alverson and Stansby 1963; Bearden 1965a; Bigelow and Schroeder 1948, 1957; Ford 1921; Frøiland 1975; Garrick 1960c; Halstead 1970; Hess 1964; Hisaw and Albert 1947; Holden and Meadows 1962; Holland 1957; A. C. Jensen 1966, 1969; Templeman 1963, 1968.

## Roughskin spiny dogfish
*Squalus asper* Merrett 1973

DESCRIPTION: The roughskin spiny dogfish is characterized by two dorsal fins, each with a spine, a first dorsal fin originating *posterior* to the free rear tips of the pectoral fins, a second dorsal fin *almost as large* as the first, very broad pectoral fins with rounded free rear tips, and a *very broad anterior nasal flap*. The

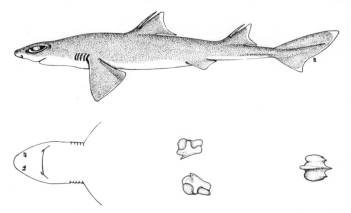

teeth have strongly oblique, smooth-edged cusps with a strong notch on their outer margins, forming a nearly continuous cutting edge. Teeth number U 12 to

14–12 to 14, L 11 or 12–11 or 12, and are similar in both jaws. The dermal denticles are *very large*, usually 0.08–0.09 percent of the total length (about three times larger than those of comparable-size specimens of similar species), or more than 1.1 mm in grown specimens. The dermal denticles of juveniles are leaf-shaped with a strong central ridge; those of the adults have a strong central ridge terminating in a point and flanked on either side by winglike extensions and weaker ridges. Color is brown to brownish gray above, paler or whitish below. Average size is about 90 cm (35 in). It grows to at least 118 cm (46 in).

SIMILAR SPECIES: The spiny dogfish has smaller dermal denticles, a second dorsal fin smaller than the first, and, usually, white spots scattered over the body. Blainville's dogfish and the Cuban dogfish have a more anterior first dorsal fin, which originates over the pectoral fin, and smaller dermal denticles (about 0.3 mm in adult specimens).

RANGE: The roughskin spiny dogfish has been reported from the western Indian Ocean and the Gulf of Mexico. Recently it has been caught in deep water off South Carolina. It is undoubtedly widely distributed in deep water.

BIOLOGY: This is a poorly known species, which was not described until 1973. Most specimens have been isolated captures in 120–330 fathoms. Its diet includes squid and small fishes. Nothing else is known of its habits.

REPRODUCTION: Development is ovoviviparous. The size at maturity has not been determined, but specimens 85 cm (33 in) long were reported as mature. Litters of twenty-one and twenty-two pups have been reported.

RELATION TO MAN: None.

FISHING: It has been caught with both hook and line and trawling gear in deep waters.

REFERENCES: Bass, D'Aubrey, and Kistnasamy 1976; Compagno 1978; Garrick 1960c; Merrett 1973.

## Blainville's dogfish
*Squalus blainvillei* (Risso) 1826

DESCRIPTION: Blainville's dogfish is characterized by two dorsal fins, each with a spine, a first dorsal fin originating over the *midpoint* of the inner margin of the pectoral fin, a second dorsal fin smaller than the first, and pectoral fins with

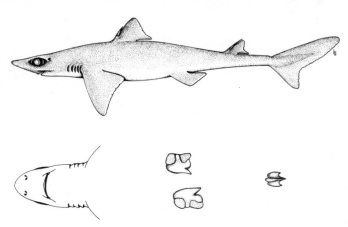

slightly curved rear margins and *rounded free rear tips*. The teeth have strongly oblique, smooth-edged cusps with a strong notch on their outer sides, forming a nearly continuous cutting edge. Teeth number U 13–1–13, L 11–1–11, and are similar in both jaws. The dermal denticles are *broad* and *three-pointed* and have a strong central ridge. Color is gray-brown above, white below. The posterior edges of the fins are white-edged in juveniles but barely so in adults. Average size is about 75 cm (30 in); maximum size is at least 100 cm (39 in).

SIMILAR SPECIES: The Cuban dogfish has pectoral fins with curved posterior margins and pointed free rear tips, and its dermal denticles have a single narrow point. The spiny dogfish and the roughskin spiny dogfish have the origin of the first dorsal fin posterior to the free rear tip of the pectoral fins.

RANGE: Blainville's dogfish is cosmopolitan in deep tropical and temperate waters. It has been caught in the Gulf of Mexico.

BIOLOGY: This is a deep-water species usually reported from depths of 180–400 fathoms, usually on the bottom. Its diet includes crustaceans, squid, and small fishes. Its habits are poorly known.

REPRODUCTION: Development is ovoviviparous. Maturity is reached at 60–70 cm (24–28 in). The gestation period is about two years. The litters consist of four to nine pups, usually six. The pups measure 22–26 cm (9–10 in) at birth.

RELATION TO MAN: None.

FISHING: It is usually caught in midwater or bottom trawls.

REFERENCES: Bass, D'Aubrey, and Kistnasamy 1976; Bigelow and Schroeder 1948; Chen, Taniuchi, and Nose 1979; Garrick 1960c, 1961; Merrett 1973.

## Cuban dogfish
*Squalus cubensis* Howell-Rivero 1936

DESCRIPTION: The Cuban dogfish is characterized by two dorsal fins, each with a spine, a first dorsal fin originating over the midpoint of the inner margin of the pectoral fin, a second dorsal fin smaller than the first, and pectoral fins with *curved posterior margins* and *pointed free rear tips*. The teeth have strongly

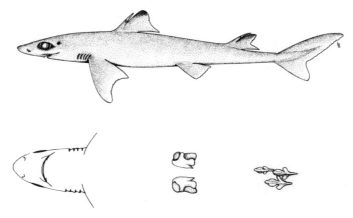

oblique, smooth-edged cusps with a strong notch on their outer margins forming a nearly continuous cutting edge. Teeth number U 13–13, L 13–13, and are similar in both jaws. The dermal denticles are *lanceolate*, with a strong central ridge that divides anteriorly into two to three ridges and with a broad winglike extension on either side of the central ridge. Color is dark gray above and pale gray below. The upper lobes of both dorsal fins are black; the other fins are white-edged. Average size is 75 cm (30 in). It is said to reach 110 cm (43 in).

SIMILAR SPECIES: Blainville's dogfish has pectoral fins with rounded free rear tips, and its dermal denticles are three-pointed. The spiny dogfish and the rough-skin spiny dogfish have the first dorsal fin originating over or posterior to the free rear tips of the pectoral fin.

RANGE: The Cuban dogfish inhabits the waters of the Atlantic coast of North America from North Carolina to Florida and the Gulf of Mexico, the Caribbean, and the western Atlantic south to Brazil.

BIOLOGY: This is a little-known, bottom-dwelling species, which forms dense schools in 65–200 fathoms. Its habits and diet have not been reported.

REPRODUCTION: Development is ovoviviparous. Litters of about ten embryos have been recorded.

RELATION TO MAN: It is used for the preparation of oil.

FISHING: It is caught in bottom trawls at depths greater than 30 fathoms.

REFERENCES: Bigelow and Schroeder 1948, 1957; Compagno 1978; Garrick 1960c.


## *Deania profundorum* Smith and Radcliffe 1912

DESCRIPTION: This small shark is characterized by a *broad, flat, very long snout*, its length greater than the distance from the center of the mouth to the origin of the pectoral fins; two dorsal fins each with a spine, the second one being larger than the first; and a noticeable, *low keel or flap of skin between the pelvic fins and the caudal fin*. The teeth vary markedly with size and sex. In small specimens the teeth of both jaws have oblique cusps. Adult males have teeth with erect, slender, smooth-edged cusps and squarish bases on both jaws; adult females have lower teeth with oblique cusps. Teeth number U 26 to 31, L 26 to 30. The dermal denticles are three-pointed, *pitchfork-shaped, on a tall stalk* that stands nearly erect on the skin. Color is dark gray above, slightly lighter below. Average size is about 50 cm (20 in); maximum size is about 76 cm (30 in).

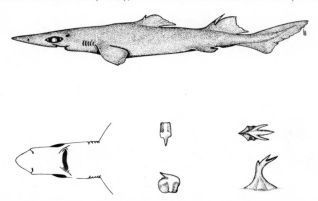

SIMILAR SPECIES: Other squaloid sharks in the area have shorter snouts and lack the low keel between the pelvic fins and the caudal fin.

RANGE: It has been reported from the Philippine Sea, off the southeast and southwest coasts of Africa, and off North Carolina. It is probably widely distributed in deep waters.

BIOLOGY: This is a poorly known deep-water species, which has been reported from 160–976 fathoms. It is known to feed on crustaceans, squid, and lantern fishes.

REPRODUCTION: Development is probably ovoviviparous. Males mature at about 70 cm (28 in). The embryos have not been described.

RELATION TO MAN: None.

FISHING: It is caught in deep-water trawls.

REFERENCES: Bass, D'Aubrey, and Kistnasamy 1976; Cadenat 1960; Compagno 1978; Garrick 1960b; Smith and Radcliffe 1912; S. Springer 1959.

## Portuguese shark
*Centroscymnus coelolepis* Bocage and Capello 1864

DESCRIPTION: The Portuguese shark is characterized by a moderately stout body, *two dorsal fins with very small, inconspicuous spines at their origins,* and a second dorsal fin slightly larger than the first. The upper teeth are long, pointed, and smooth-edged. The lower teeth have short, broad, strongly oblique cusps and large, overlapping bases. Teeth number about U 58, L 40. The dermal denticles of the young and juveniles have three points and are widely spaced; those of the adults are very large, scalelike, and closely overlapping. The juveniles are dark blue, the half-grown are black, and the adults are chocolate brown, above and below. Average size is 90–107 cm (35–42 in); maximum size is about 120 cm (47 in).

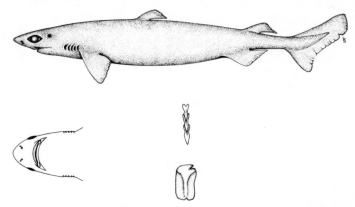

SIMILAR SPECIES: The Greenland shark has spineless dorsal fins, and its denticles are thorny. The kitefin shark has spineless dorsal fins and triangular, pointed teeth with serrated edges.

RANGE: The Portuguese shark inhabits both sides of the North Atlantic, from the Grand Banks to Delaware Bay in the west, and from Iceland and the Faroes south to the Azores and Cape Verde Islands. It has also been reported from the western Mediterranean and Japanese waters. It appears to be scarce in North American waters, but this is probably misleading because of the lack of a deep-water fishery.

BIOLOGY: This shark inhabits very deep waters; it has been taken from 185 to 1,487 fathoms, with most captures at depths greater than 500 fathoms, and in temperatures of 5–6°C (41–43°F). It is said to be sluggish and to feed on small fishes.

REPRODUCTION: Development is ovoviviparous. Litters of thirteen to fifteen pups have been reported. The pups measure 27–30 cm (11–12 in) at birth.

RELATION TO MAN: In the past it was the object of a deep-water fishery off Portugal, hence the name. It is of no commercial importance in North American waters.

FISHING: In the past most specimens were caught on halibut lines at depths greater than 180 fathoms.

REFERENCES: Bigelow and Schroeder 1948, 1954, 1957; Leim and Scott 1966; Templeman 1963.

## Greenland shark
*Somniosus microcephalus* Bloch and Schneider 1801

DESCRIPTION: The Greenland shark is a stout shark, *usually very large*, with *two spineless dorsal fins of nearly equal size*, the *first one originating about midway on the trunk*. The upper teeth have long, pointed, smooth-edged cusps; the *lower teeth have strongly oblique, smooth-edged cusps* and large, overlapping bases. Teeth number U 48 to 52, L 50 to 52. The dermal denticles are conical and curved rearward, with fluted sides and squarish bases. Color is brown, black, purplish gray, or slaty gray above and below; the back and sides may have a violet tinge, or they may have scattered dark bands or white spots. Two chalk-white specimens (albinos?) were reported early in this century. Average size is 340 cm (11.1 ft) and 285 kg (627 lb). The largest specimen on record measured 640 cm (21.0 ft) and weighed 1,022 kg (2,250 lb).

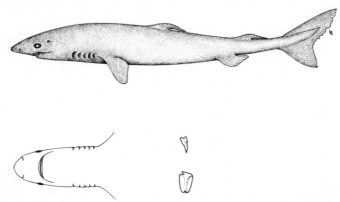

SIMILAR SPECIES: The prickly shark and the bramble shark have the first dorsal fin originating over or posterior to the origin of the pelvic fins. The kitefin shark has lower teeth with triangular cusps and serrated edges. The Portuguese shark resembles a small Greenland shark, but it has dorsal fins with small, inconspicuous spines and overlapping, scalelike dermal denticles, instead of the thornlike denticles of the Greenland shark. The Greenland shark is replaced in the Pacific Ocean by the Pacific sleeper shark, which has a more posterior first dorsal fin, broader upper teeth, and a shorter distance between the rear tip of the second dorsal fin and the origin of the caudal fin.

RANGE: The Greenland shark inhabits the North Atlantic Ocean from polar latitudes to the North Sea in the east and the Gulf of Saint Lawrence in the west, occasionally straying southward. In North American waters it is found from Baffin Bay to the Gulf of Saint Lawrence, being common throughout that range. It occasionally strays into the Gulf of Maine and rarely south to Cape Hatteras in deep waters.

BIOLOGY: This is the only shark regularly found in the polar waters of the Atlantic Ocean, where the temperatures are 2–7°C (35–45°F). It is a deep-water species that comes to the surface only during the cooler months. In summertime most specimens seem to live in 100–400 fathoms, but some have been caught as deep as 600 fathoms. During winter the Greenland shark approaches the surface, often coming to the edge of the ice. It feeds on capelin, char, halibut, herring, lumpfish, salmon, numerous other fishes, and seals. Fast-moving fishes are often found with their tails bitten off in the stomach of this proverbially sluggish shark; invariably, the tails are missing from the stomach contents, indicating that the fish were swallowed head first. An interesting explanation has been offered to account for the ability of such a sluggish shark to catch fast-moving fishes. In Greenland waters most of these sharks have a parasitic copepod firmly attached to the cornea of each eye. These copepods range from 3 to 70 mm (0.1 to 2.7 in) in size and are whitish yellow in color. It is speculated that these copepods may be luminescent and may act as a lure, attracting prey to the shark. This possible case of mutualism requires confirmation. This species often gathers in large numbers around sealing or whaling operations, feeding on offal or carrion. Tagging studies have shown the Greenland shark to be a very slow-growing fish; medium-size specimens seem to grow 1 cm (0.4 in) or less per year. One tagged specimen grew from 262 cm to 270 cm in sixteen years; another grew from 285 cm to 300 cm in fourteen years, a third grew from 271 cm to 272 cm in two years.

REPRODUCTION: Development is ovoviviparous. Very little is known about the reproductive processes of this shark, which was presumed to be oviparous until a few years ago because the embryos had never been reported. The pups measure about 38 cm (15 in) at birth; ten pups have been reported in one litter.

RELATION TO MAN: It has been fished for its liver oil along the coasts of Norway, Iceland, and Greenland from olden times. In Greenland it is also used for dog food. It often enters fjords in autumn and plays havoc with fishing nets. The flesh is poisonous when fresh, and it must be dried or boiled several times before consumption.

FISHING: In Greenland, large hooks baited with fresh or salted seal blubber are used on longlines in 140–300 fathoms, most sharks being caught in 160–220 fathoms. In winter fisheries it is often lured to the surface by a light. Once on the surface it is extremely sluggish and offers little resistance.

REFERENCES: Beck and Mansfield 1969; Berland 1961; Bigelow and Schroeder 1948, 1957; Bjerkan and Koefoed 1957; Dunbar and Hildebrand 1952; Hansen 1963; A. S. Jensen 1914; Leim and Scott 1966; Lineaweaver and Backus 1970; McAllister 1968.

## Pacific sleeper shark
*Somniosus pacificus* Bigelow and Schroeder 1944

DESCRIPTION: The Pacific sleeper shark is a stout shark, usually large, with *two spineless dorsal fins of nearly equal size*, the *first one originating midway on the trunk*. The upper teeth have long, pointed, smooth-edged cusps and overlapping bases; the *lower teeth have strongly oblique, smooth-edged cusps* and large overlapping bases. Teeth number about U 26–1–26, L 26–1–26. The dermal denticles are conical, curved rearward, and with fluted sides. Color is blackish brown to slate gray above, slightly lighter below, often with darker streaklike mottling on the back. Average size is about 365 cm (12.0 ft) and 320–365 kg (700–800 lb). The largest specimen on record measured 396 cm (13.0 ft), but it is said, without supporting evidence, to grow to 760 cm (25.0 ft).

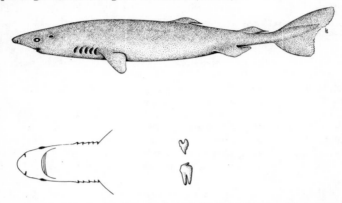

SIMILAR SPECIES: The prickly shark and the bramble shark have the first dorsal fin originating over or posterior to the pelvic fins. The kitefin shark has lower teeth with triangular cusps and serrated edges. The Portuguese shark has small, inconspicuous dorsal fin spines and scalelike dermal denticles. The Pacific sleeper shark is replaced in the Atlantic Ocean by the Greenland shark, which has a more anterior first dorsal fin, narrower upper teeth, and a larger space between the rear tip of the second dorsal fin and the origin of the caudal fin.

RANGE: The Pacific sleeper shark inhabits the North Pacific Ocean from polar latitudes to Japan in the west and California in the east. In North American waters it ranges from the Bering Sea to Puget Sound, occasionally straying to central California.

BIOLOGY: This is a shark of polar and subpolar latitudes, a deep-water species that occasionally comes to the surface. It is a voracious eater, consuming large quantities of halibut, soles, salmon, and many other fishes. Its diet also includes octopus, squid, crabs, seals, and carrion.

REPRODUCTION: Development is presumably ovoviviparous. Females with up to 300 eggs have been recorded. Nothing else is known about its reproductive processes.

RELATION TO MAN: It may take hooked salmon or halibut from longlines, but it has little economic impact.

FISHING: It is occasionally caught on longlines or in trawling gear.

REFERENCES: Bright 1959; Garman 1913; Gotshall and Jow 1965; Hart 1973; Phillips 1953.

## Kitefin shark
*Dalatias licha* (Bonnaterre) 1788

DESCRIPTION: This small shark has *two spineless dorsal fins, the first one originating forward on the trunk.* The upper teeth have long, narrow, smooth-edged, pointed cusps; the *lower teeth have triangular, erect cusps with serrated edges* and overlapping bases. Teeth number U 9–1–9, L 9–1–9. The denticles are squarish, with three weak ridges united rearward in a point of variable length. Color is dark gray or brown above and below, with the fin margins being whitish or pale. Average size is about 120 cm (47 in) and 8 kg (18 lb). The largest specimen on record measured 182 cm (72 in).

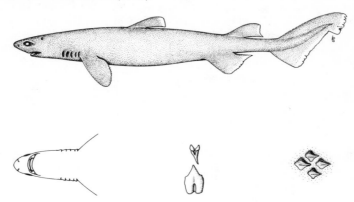

SIMILAR SPECIES: The triangular, pointed lower teeth with serrated edges distinguish it from other squaloid sharks in the area.

RANGE: The kitefin shark has been reported from the North Atlantic, the eastern Atlantic from the Shetlands to tropical west Africa, the Mediterranean, the western Pacific, and the southwestern Indian Ocean; it has not been reported from the eastern Pacific, the South Atlantic, or the northwestern Indian Ocean. Although it is common in deep water in the eastern Atlantic and along the east coast of southern Africa, it is very rare off North American coasts. The only specimens from our area come from Georges Bank and the Gulf of Mexico.

BIOLOGY: This is a deep-water shark usually found at depths of 140–330 fathoms. One of the few North American specimens was caught in about 50 fathoms, indicating that it is not confined exclusively to deep water. It feeds on numerous bony fishes, rays, crabs, and squid.

REPRODUCTION: Development is ovoviviparous. Males probably reach maturity at about 95 cm (37 in), females at about 120 cm (47 in). Litters range from ten to sixteen pups, which measure about 30 cm (12 in) at birth.

RELATION TO MAN: In olden days the skin was used for sandpaper (shagreen). It has no economic importance nowadays.

FISHING: It is usually taken in deep-water trawls or on longlines.

REFERENCES: Bass, D'Aubrey, and Kistnasamy 1976; Bigelow and Schroeder 1948, 1957; Bigelow, Schroeder, and Springer 1955; De Groot and Nijssen 1976; Fowler 1941; Garrick 1960*b*.

## Pigmy shark
*Euprotomicrus bispinatus* Quoy and Gaimard 1824

DESCRIPTION: The pigmy shark is recognized by its very small size (less than 30 cm or 12 in); its soft, slender body with a tiny spineless *first dorsal fin set far back on the trunk* with its rear tip slightly over the origin of the pelvic fins; and a *very long spineless second dorsal fin*, its base more than twice as long as the base of the first dorsal fin. The upper teeth are narrow, triangular, smooth-edged, and needle-pointed, with teeth from adjacent rows set in alternate arrangement. The lower teeth have strongly oblique, pointed cusps and overlapping bases, forming a continuous cutting edge. Teeth number U 10–1–10, L 9 to 11–1–9 to 11. The denticles are low and square, with a depression in the center, and of two sizes, the smaller being the more numerous. Color varies from light brown to brownish black above, slightly lighter below, with clear fin margins. The undersides are luminescent in live specimens. Average size is about 20 cm (8 in). The largest specimen on record measured almost 27 cm (11 in) and weighed 70 grams (2½ oz).

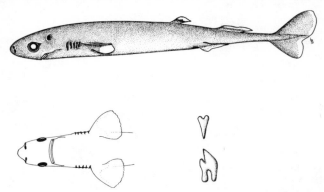

SIMILAR SPECIES: The cookie-cutter shark and *Isistius plutodus* have the base of the second dorsal fin only slightly longer than the base of the first dorsal fin.

RANGE: The pigmy shark inhabits subtropical and warm-temperate central waters of the North and South Pacific, South Indian, and South Atlantic oceans. North American records are from deep water several hundred miles off the California coast. It is rare in our area.

BIOLOGY: This dwarf shark inhabits the surface layers of the central areas of warm and warm-temperate oceans; it is usually found where the surface temperature is 16–27°C (61–81°F) and the depth is 1,600–3,300 fathoms. It makes considerable vertical migrations, probably congregating in schools and spending the daylight hours at depths of several hundred fathoms (although schools have not been observed, and it has not been caught in midwater), coming to the surface and scattering to feed during the night hours. It feeds on bathypelagic fishes (hatchetfishes, lightfish), squid, and minute crustaceans. Like many deep-water fishes, this shark is luminescent. The ventral surfaces are covered with thousands of tiny light organs, which combine to produce a bluish green glow.

REPRODUCTION: Development is ovoviviparous. Males mature at about 17 cm (7 in); females at about 23 cm (9 in) or less. The number of pups per litter appears to be constant at eight pups, which are probably born at 7.0–9.5 cm (3–4 in).

RELATION TO MAN: None.

FISHING: It is taken on surface trawls in the open ocean and most often by dip-netting when it is attracted to light.

REFERENCES: Bigelow and Schroeder 1957; Hubbs and McHugh 1950; Hubbs, Iwai, and Matsubara 1967; King and Ikehara 1956; Parin 1964.

# Cookie-cutter shark
## *Isistius brasiliensis* (Quoy and Gaimard) 1824

DESCRIPTION: This very small shark has *two spineless dorsal fins of equal height set far back on the trunk,* the rear tip of the first dorsal over the pelvic fins, and the *base of the second dorsal fin only slightly longer than the base of the first dorsal fin.* The upper teeth are small, slender, thornlike, and increasingly curved towards the corners of the mouth. The lower teeth are much larger, with erect triangular, smooth-edged cusps and overlapping bases; the lower teeth are shed as a unit, insuring that the shark has a full cutting edge at all times. Teeth number U 15 to 18–1–15 to 18, L 12 to 15–1–12 to 15; their number increases with age, the larger specimens having the larger numbers. The denticles are roughly square in shape, with a square depression in the center and raised points at the corners. Color is dark brown above and lighter below, *with a dark collar across the throat;* the body fins have pale margins, and the *caudal fin has dark tips.* The undersides may be luminescent. Specimens usually range from 14 to 50 cm (6–20 in); the largest on record measured 50 cm (20 in).

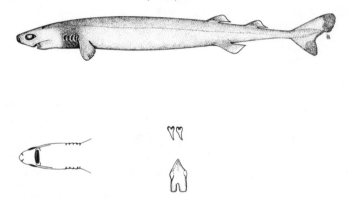

SIMILAR SPECIES: *I. plutodus* has fewer and larger teeth (U 14–1–14, L 9–1–9); it lacks the dark collar and the caudal fin with dark tips. The pigmy shark has a very long second dorsal fin, its base over twice as long as the base of the first dorsal.

RANGE: The cookie-cutter shark inhabits the deep waters of the tropical and subtropical belts of the Atlantic, Pacific, and Indian oceans. The only reports from our area are from north of the Bahamas. Beaked whale carcasses examined by the author in Ascension Island were covered by healed and fresh wounds presumably caused by the cookie-cutter shark, suggesting that it (or a species with similar feeding habits) may be common in that area.

BIOLOGY: This small shark inhabits the upper layers of warm, tropical, oceanic waters. Most catches occur between the surface and 300 fathoms during the night hours, indicating that it makes vertical migrations, probably spending the daylight hours in much deeper waters. It is believed to form schools. The cookie-cutter shark is known to feed extensively on large squid, but apparently it also attacks even larger prey. Available evidence indicates that it feeds by taking bites at large pelagic fishes (tunas, wahoo, dolphin, marlins, etc.) as well as porpoises and whales. Its very sharp cutting teeth allow it to effectively bite off a plug of flesh from large prey. How this slow-moving dwarf shark can approach and attack fast-moving prey such as squid and pelagic fishes is an interesting mystery at present. It has been suggested that the shark is approached by predators, which, after the initial approach, reject it as food and veer off; at that instant the shark may be able to make a quick dash and effect a quick bite. The ventral surface of the head and body (except for the dark collar around the gill area), as well as the ventral fin surfaces, are luminescent, emitting a bright greenish glow. The number of light organs is highly variable; some specimens may have very few or emit no light at all.

REPRODUCTION: Development is presumably ovoviviparous. A 31-cm (12-in) male was still immature, while another 37 cm (15 in) was mature. Females mature at about 40 cm (16 in). Six or seven large eggs have been reported from females, but the embryos have not been reported. This shark may have nursery areas near oceanic islands, but this needs confirmation.

RELATION TO MAN: This little shark has been accused of biting the rubber parts of nuclear submarines, which it probably mistakes for whales.

FISHING: It is caught on surface and midwater trawls during the night hours. It does not appear to be attracted to lights.

REFERENCES: Bigelow and Schroeder 1957; Garrick and Springer 1964; Hubbs, Iwai, and Matsubara 1967; Johnson 1978; Jones 1971; King and Ikehara 1956; Parin 1964; Seigel 1978; Strasburg 1963.

## *Isistius plutodus* Garrick and Springer 1964

DESCRIPTION: This small shark has *two spineless dorsal fins set far back on the trunk*, the first dorsal with its rear tip over the pelvic fins; *the second dorsal* is *higher than the first*, and its base is only slightly larger than the base of the first dorsal fin. The teeth are small, narrowly triangular, smooth-edged, erect near the center of the mouth, and slightly oblique at the sides. The lower teeth are very large, with broadly triangular cusps and high rectangular bases; those at the center of the jaw are erect and symmetrical, those at the sides have slightly oblique cusps with their points toward the center of the mouth. Teeth number U 14–1–14, L 9–1–9. The denticles are low and squarish, with a depression at the center. Color is uniform dark brown above and below, except for a band of paler brown on the underside of the head from mouth to gill slits. The undersides are probably luminescent. The type specimen measured 42 cm (17 in).

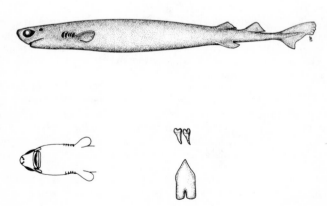

SIMILAR SPECIES: The cookie-cutter shark has dorsal fins of equal size, a dark collar around the throat, and a black-tipped caudal fin. The pigmy shark has a long second dorsal fin, whose base is more than twice as long as the base of the first dorsal.

RANGE: Specimens have been reported from the Gulf of Mexico and off Okinawa.

BIOLOGY: Its habits are probably similar to those of the cookie-cutter shark.

REPRODUCTION: No data available.

RELATION TO MAN: None.

FISHING: The type specimen was caught in a midwater trawl.

REFERENCES: Garrick and Springer 1964.

## *Squaliolus laticaudus* Smith and Radcliffe 1912

DESCRIPTION: This *minute* shark has a cigar-shaped body, a *long and pointed snout*, a large, nearly round eye, *a first dorsal fin with a spine at its origin* located forward on the trunk, and a *very long, spineless second dorsal fin*, its base over twice as long as that of the first dorsal fin. The upper teeth are long, pointed, and smooth-edged. The lower teeth have oblique cusps and overlapping bases. The number of teeth in the upper jaw is variable, with several series of teeth being functional at the same time; the lower teeth number 8 to 10–1–8 to 10. The dermal denticles are four-pointed, with a depression at the center, and of variable size. Color is black or blackish brown above and below, with white or white-margined fins. The undersides possess numerous light organs, but their luminescence has not been observed. Average size is 15–22 cm (6–9 in). Maximum size is about 27 cm (11 in). This is the smallest shark known.

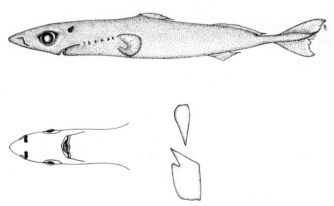

SIMILAR SPECIES: The cookie-cutter shark, the pigmy shark, and *Isistius plutodus* have spineless dorsal fins set far back on the trunk.

RANGE: It has been reported from the western and eastern North Atlantic, the western South Atlantic, the western Indian Ocean, and the western Pacific Ocean. It is probably cosmopolitan in deep waters near continents; however, there are no reports of its presence near North American coasts.

BIOLOGY: This tiny shark inhabits productive waters near continental masses at depths of 110–275 fathoms. It undertakes vertical migrations, spending the day at about 275 fathoms and migrating up to about 110 fathoms at night; it has not been caught at the surface. It is known to feed on squid, lanternfishes, and lightfishes.

REPRODUCTION: Development is presumably ovoviviparous. Males mature at 15–22 cm (6–9 in), females at 17–20 cm (7–8 in). The embryos have not been reported.

RELATION TO MAN: None.

FISHING: It is caught in midwater trawls at depths of 110–275 fathoms.

REFERENCES: Bigelow and Schroeder 1957; Fowler 1941; Hubbs, Iwai, and Matsubara 1967; Seigel 1978; Seigel et al. 1977; Smith and Radcliffe 1912.

# Family Pristiophoridae—Sawsharks

The Pristiophoridae are a small family of deep-water sharks characterized by having the snout produced into a long flat blade with teeth on each side and by having long barbels on the ventral side of the snout. Other characteristics include large spiracles behind the eyes, five or six lateral gill slits situated ahead of the pectoral fins, two large dorsal fins, and no anal fin. Small fishes, they measure less than 152 cm (60 in) and inhabit depths greater than 200 fathoms. They are probably cosmopolitan in deep water. Development is ovoviviparous. Six species are presently recognized; only one has been reported in the Western Hemisphere.

The sawsharks resemble the sawfishes (of the batoid family Pristidae), which are sharklike rays that attain lengths up to 610 cm (20 ft) and live in shallow water throughout tropical and subtropical waters. In contrast to the sawsharks, the sawfishes have ventral gill slits, lack the barbels on the underside of the snout, and have the pectoral fins joined to the head.

### American sawshark
*Pristiophorus schroederi* Springer and Bullis 1960

DESCRIPTION: The American sawshark is recognized by its *snout prolonged into a long flat blade with "teeth" on each side* and by the presence of *two* long *barbels on the underside of the snout*. It has large spiracles behind the eyes, five *lateral* gill slits, and two equally large dorsal fins. The "teeth" of the saw are en-

larged dermal denticles, and, unlike those of the sawfishes, they are replaced when lost. The teeth (mouth) are very small, with one smooth conical cusp, number U 36, L 32, and are alike in both jaws. Color is light gray to brownish gray above and whitish below. The largest specimen known measured 81 cm (32 in).

SIMILAR SPECIES: It is the only shark with a sawlike snout known from the waters of the Western Hemisphere. The sawfishes have ventral gill slits, lack the barbels on the underside of the snout, and have the pectoral fins joined to the head.

RANGE: The limits of its distribution are unknown. The only known specimens have come from off southeast Florida and from Bahamian waters. It appears to be locally common in deep water around Cay Sal Bank.

BIOLOGY: This is a poorly known deep-water species. It probably uses its saw to stun and disable prey just as sawfishes do. Specimens have been caught at depths of 350–520 fathoms.

REPRODUCTION: Development is probably ovoviviparous. The young measure about 30 cm (12 in) at birth.

RELATION TO MAN: None.

FISHING: It is caught in deep-water trawls.

REFERENCES: Bass, D'Aubrey, and Kistnasamy 1975d; Slaughter and Springer 1968; Springer and Bullis 1960.

# Family Squatinidae—Angel Sharks

This is a family of flattened sharks with a terminal mouth, eyes on top of the head, large spiracles behind the eyes, greatly expanded pectoral fins, two equally small dorsal fins near the tail, and no anal fin. Angel sharks greatly resemble skates and can be considered intermediate forms between sharks and the batoid fishes (skates and rays). They differ from the batoids in that their pectoral fins are not attached to the head, their five gill slits are ventrolateral instead of ventral, and they have movable eyelids. Angel sharks are small to medium-sized bottom dwellers found in shallow coastal waters throughout tropical and warm-temperate seas. Development is ovoviviparous. Eleven species are presently recognized, all of which resemble each other very closely. Only two species inhabit our coasts.

1. Inner nasal barbel tapering .... *Squatina dumerili* (p. 72)
   Inner nasal barbel broadly spatulate .... *Squatina californica* (p. 71)

## Pacific angel shark
### *Squatina californica* Ayres 1859

DESCRIPTION: The Pacific angel shark is characterized by its *flattened body, terminal mouth, eyes on top of the head*, large spiracles behind the eyes, and *greatly expanded pectoral fins*. It has two equally small dorsal fins located near the tail. The teeth are conical, pointed, smooth-edged, broad-based, and similar in both jaws and number U 9–9, L 10–10, with a broad gap at the symphysis. Color is sandy gray to reddish brown, speckled with darker spots, above; the undersides are white. Average size is about 100 cm (39 in) and 10 kg (22 lb). This species is said to reach 155 cm (61 in) and 27 kg (60 lb).

SIMILAR SPECIES: The skates and rays have the pectoral fins joined to the head and have ventral gill slits. The flattened body and the terminal mouth distinguish this species readily from other sharks in the area.

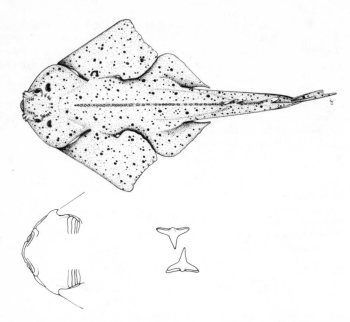

RANGE: The Pacific angel shark inhabits the Pacific coast of North America from southern Alaska to Baja California. It is extremely abundant around the California Channel Islands.

BIOLOGY: The Pacific angel shark is often found buried in the mud or sand, with only the eyes and upper parts exposed, near rocks or ledges. It is most common at depths of 8 fathoms or less but often wanders into depths of 100 fathoms. It is a nocturnal fish, cruising about at night and returning to rest to the same area by day. Reported prey includes California halibut, corbina, and queen fish.

REPRODUCTION: Development is ovoviviparous. Its reproductive processes have not been described, but they are probably similar to those of the Atlantic angel shark.

RELATION TO MAN: Its flesh is edible. It is harmless unless provoked.

FISHING: It is often taken by spearing or caught in gill nets, but it also takes baited hooks.

REFERENCES: Bigelow and Schroeder 1948; Feder, Turner, and Limbaugh 1974; Standora and Nelson 1977.

## Atlantic angel shark
*Squatina dumerili* Lesueur 1817

DESCRIPTION: The Atlantic angel shark is characterized by its *flattened body, terminal mouth, eyes on top of the head,* large spiracles behind the eyes, *greatly expanded pectoral fins,* and two equally small dorsal fins located near the tail. The teeth are conical, smooth-edged, broad-based, alike in both jaws, and number U 10–10, L 9–9, with a broad gap at the symphysis. Color varies from light gray to reddish brown above, often with irregular dark brown splotches; the undersides are whitish. Average size is 90–122 cm (34–48 in) and 10–27 kg (22–60 lb). Maximum size is about 155 cm (61 in).

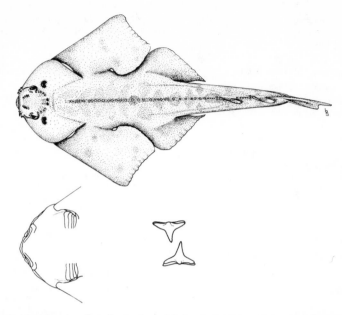

SIMILAR SPECIES: The skates have the pectoral fins joined to the head and have ventral gill slits. The angel shark's flattened shape and eyes on top of the head readily distinguish it from all other sharks in the area.

RANGE: The Atlantic angel shark inhabits the Atlantic coast of the United States from Massachusetts to the Florida Keys, the Gulf of Mexico, and the Caribbean. It is locally common from southern New England to the Maryland coast.

BIOLOGY: This is a little-known bottom dweller often found buried in the sand or mud in shallow water in northern parts of the range and in deeper waters (about 70 fathoms) of the continental shelf in southern parts. It feeds on mollusks, crustaceans, flounders, skates, and other bottom fishes. It apparently migrates seasonally from shallow to deep water. Its habits are poorly known.

REPRODUCTION: Development is ovoviviparous. Maturity is probably reached at a length of 90–105 cm (35–41 in). The pups measure 28–30 cm (11–12 in) at birth. Up to sixteen pups in one litter have been observed, and it is said that gravid females may contain up to twenty-five pups. Birth usually occurs at depths of 10–15 fathoms during the spring or early summer months.

RELATION TO MAN: Its flesh is edible but seldom marketed. This shark can inflict a nasty bite with its sharp teeth and should be handled with caution.

FISHING: It is usually an accidental catch in trawls.

REFERENCES: Bigelow and Schroeder 1948; Gordon 1956; Hoese 1962.

## Family Heterodontidae—Bullhead Sharks

The bullhead sharks, also known as Port Jackson sharks, are distinguished by the presence of two dorsal fins, each with a strong spine at the origin, a first dorsal fin originating over the pectoral fin base, and an anal fin. Other characteristics include short blunt snouts, ridges above the eyes, and conspicuous upper and lower lip grooves. They possess two types of teeth (*Heterodontus* = "different tooth"); the front teeth have sharp cusps for seizing prey, while the teeth in the rear of the jaw have round, blunt cusps ("molariform" teeth) and are used to crush the hard shells of their crustacean prey. They are considered to be primitive sharks because of their hybodont dentition and the presence of spines on the dorsal fins. These sharks are confined to the Pacific and Indian oceans. Presently eight species are recognized; at least two are found in North American waters. For a review of the family, see Taylor 1972*b*.

1. Body and sides with small dark spots smaller than one-third the eye diameter; no pale bar across top of head .... *Heterodontus francisci* (p. 74)
   Body and sides with large dark spots equal or larger than one-half the eye diameter; pale bar across top of head .... *Heterodontus mexicanus* (p. 75)

## Horn shark
*Heterodontus francisci* (Girard) 1854

DESCRIPTION: The horn shark is characterized by a short and blunt head with high ridges above the eyes. The frontal teeth are tricuspid, with the central cusp the largest; the lateral teeth are modified into flat molars. Teeth number about U 20 to 29, L 17 to 29, and are similar in both jaws. In young specimens 20 cm (8 in) or less all the teeth are similar and bear up to seven cusps. Color is light to dark brown above, with small, scattered black spots over the body and fins. All or most of the spots are *smaller than one-third the eye diameter*, and may be faded or absent in adults. The undersides are pale yellow. Average size is 90 cm (35 in). A 98-cm (39-in) specimen weighed 10 kg (22 lb). The species is said to reach 120 cm (47 in).

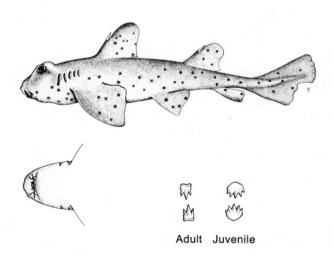

Adult Juvenile

SIMILAR SPECIES: The dogfish sharks have dorsal fins with spines but lack the anal fin. The Mexican horn shark has spots larger than one-half the eye diameter, lower ridges above the eyes, a slightly pointed snout, a faint white bar across the top of the head, and larger dermal denticles (about 125 denticles/cm$^2$ in the anterior area of the first dorsal fin, compared with 200 denticles/cm$^2$ in the horn shark).

RANGE: The horn shark inhabits shallow and deep waters from central California to the Gulf of California. It is common south of Point Conception.

BIOLOGY: The horn shark is a sluggish, solitary bottom dweller. It is nocturnal, and it spends the day among rocks, where it is often found resting with the head in a crevice. It is most abundant around kelp beds in 4–6 fathoms, although some have been caught in 100 fathoms or deep in caves. It feeds on small fishes, crustaceans, and mollusks. It is believed to migrate from shallow to deeper water at certain times of the year.

REPRODUCTION: Development is oviparous. Egg case is screw-shaped with a broad flange spirally twisted around it. The egg case measures about 12 cm (5 in) in length; it is pale brown when freshly laid but turns dark after a few days. Egg cases are scattered among the rocks and hatch six to nine months later. The hatchlings measure 15–17 cm (6–7 in).

RELATION TO MAN: This is one of the few sharks that can be kept in captivity. It is often used as an experimental shark or exhibited in aquaria, where it has survived up to twelve years. It has no other economic importance.

FISHING: It is occasionally caught with small hooks.

REFERENCES: Beebe and Tee-Van 1941; Dempster and Herald 1961; Kato, Springer, and Wagner 1967; Myers 1977; B. G. Smith 1942; Taylor 1972*b*.

## Mexican horn shark
*Heterodontus mexicanus* Taylor and Castro-Aguirre 1972

DESCRIPTION: The Mexican horn shark is characterized by a slightly pointed and short snout with low ridges above the eyes. The anterior teeth are tricuspid,

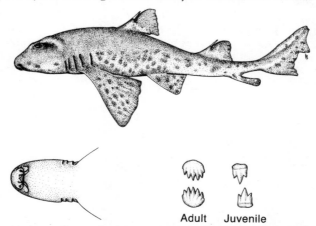

Adult    Juvenile

with the central cusp being the largest; the lateral teeth are modified into flat molars. Teeth number U 19 to 25, L 15 to 21, and are similar in both jaws. In specimens of less than 20 cm (8 in) all the teeth are similar, each tooth having eight to nine cusps. Color is grayish brown with a slight bronze iridescence above, and grayish white to white below, with a *pale bar across the top of the head* and scattered dark spots over the body. The spots are *about one-half the eye diameter.* The species grows to about 70 cm (28 in).

SIMILAR SPECIES: The horn shark has a broader snout, higher ridges above the eyes, smaller body spots, and larger dermal denticles. The dogfish sharks have dorsal fins with spines but lack the anal fin.

RANGE: The Mexican horn shark has been reported from the waters off Baja California to off Peru. The limits of its distribution are not well known.

BIOLOGY: Its diet and habits have not been described; they are probably similar to those of the horn shark.

REPRODUCTION: Development is oviparous. Males reach maturity at lengths of 55 cm (22 in) or less. The egg case is screw-shaped with a thick ridge spirally twisted around it. This ridge bears wide flanges, which lie parallel to the axis of the case. The tip of the egg case bears a pair of short tendrils. The egg case measures 6–8 cm (2–3 in) in length. The hatchlings measure about 14 cm (6 in). The shallow waters and lagoons around Bahía Magdalena are some of its nursery areas.

RELATION TO MAN: None.

FISHING: It is commonly caught in shrimp trawls in the Gulf of California.

REFERENCES: Mathews and Guardado France 1975; Taylor 1972*b*; Taylor and Castro-Aguirre 1972.

# Family Ginglymostomatidae—Nurse Sharks and Carpet Sharks

The nurse and carpet sharks are sluggish, bottom-dwelling sharks of shallow tropical waters. They are characterized by the presence of fleshy nasal barbels or feelers just anterior to the mouth and a deep groove connecting the nostril with the mouth. Other characteristics include short snouts with rectangular mouths and small eyes; slightly dorsoventrally flattened bodies, broadest in the pectoral region but quickly tapering to a tail in line with the body; five gill slits, the fifth one being very small and almost covered by the fourth; spiracles present just behind the eye; and multicuspid teeth. Their diet consists of invertebrates and small fishes. This family includes oviparous and ovoviviparous species. The number of species recognized varies between twelve and twenty-four, most of which inhabit Indo-Pacific waters or the Red Sea. Only one species is found in the Atlantic.

## Nurse shark
*Ginglymostoma cirratum* (Bonnaterre) 1788

DESCRIPTION: The nurse shark has conspicuous *nasal barbels* and a first dorsal fin originating *over or posterior* to the pelvic fin origin. The mouth is full of minute teeth, which number U 30 to 36, L 28 to 31, and are similar in both jaws. The teeth have one large cusp flanked on each side by two or three denticles. Color is dark brown above and slightly lighter below. Juveniles often have black spots. Average size is 230–300 cm (7–10 ft), but it is believed to reach 425 cm (14 ft). The average weight of a 240-cm (94-in) specimen is 150 kg (330 lb).

SIMILAR SPECIES: The nurse shark is the only Atlantic shark with long tapering nasal barbels. The Pacific cat sharks lack both the barbels and the groove connecting the nostrils to the mouth.

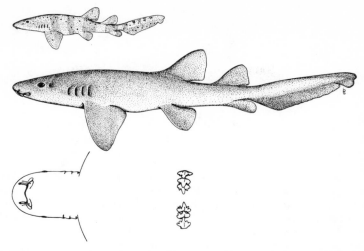

RANGE: In the Atlantic, the nurse shark is found from off Cape Hatteras to off Brazil in the west, and off West Africa and the Cape Verde Islands in the east. There are reports of strays from Rhode Island and Chesapeake Bay. In the Pacific, it is found from the Gulf of California to Peru. It is locally very common in shallow waters throughout the West Indies, South Florida, and the Keys.

BIOLOGY: The nurse shark is usually found lying motionless on the bottom, often with the head in a cave or under coral formations. It frequently congregates in schools of twenty to thirty individuals in shallow water. It feeds on lobster, shrimp, crabs, squid, short-spined sea urchins, and small fish.

REPRODUCTION: The nurse shark is ovoviviparous. Maturity is reached at about 150 cm (59 in). In Florida, mating occurs all year in shallow water. Females produce twenty to thirty pups in each brood, although very young or small females (less than 230 cm, or 91 in) produce fewer pups. Pups measure 30 cm (12 in) at birth. Off Florida, the young are found year-round.

RELATION TO MAN: The nurse shark is considered a nuisance in many places throughout the Antilles because it raids fish traps. However, its hide is the best for the production of leather, and its flesh is edible. The shark has been involved in provoked and unprovoked attacks on divers. Unwary divers often attempt to capture small nurse sharks by picking them up by their tails as the sharks lie motionless on the bottom; these sharks quickly turn on their tormentors and are capable of inflicting serious injury with their tenacious biting.

FISHING: The nurse shark will bite on almost any bait, but it is too sluggish to offer the sportsman any challenge.

REFERENCES: Applegate 1972; Beebe 1941; Bigelow and Schroeder 1948; Böhlke and Chaplin 1970; Moss 1972.

# Family Rhiniodontidae—Whale Shark

The whale shark, the largest living fish, is the only member of this family.

## Whale shark
### *Rhiniodon typus* Smith 1828

DESCRIPTION: The whale shark is easily recognized by its *usually huge size* and its striking mottled appearance. It has a very short snout with a very *wide terminal mouth*. Its nostrils have short, blunt nasal barbels. It has *three pronounced longitudinal ridges* on each side of the trunk, the lowermost ridges becoming strong caudal keels near the lunate tail. Teeth are minute, extremely numerous, forming about 300 rows with hundreds of teeth each, with a single cusp curved backward, and similar in both jaws. Color is dark gray, reddish, or greenish gray above, *with white to yellow spots and transverse stripes*, and white to yellow below. This is the largest fish known; specimens 550–1,060 cm (18–35 ft) and weighing thousands of kilograms are common. A 1,158-cm (38-ft) specimen was estimated to weigh 12,088 kg (26,594 lb), but reliable weights for these fishes are not available. The largest known specimen measured 1,210 cm (39.7 ft), but the species is said to grow much larger.

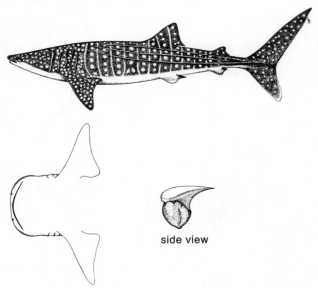

side view

SIMILAR SPECIES: The striking markings and its usual huge size easily distinguish it from all other sharks.

RANGE: The whale shark is found throughout all tropical seas, usually far offshore. In North American waters it has been reported from New York to Florida and the Gulf of Mexico, and from California southward. It is occasionally seen off Florida and the Keys.

BIOLOGY: This is a huge, sluggish, pelagic filter feeder, often seen swimming slowly on the surface. It appears most common in waters 20–25°C (68–78°F). Its food consists of crustaceans, squid, and small schooling fishes. It often forms schools, which are occasionally seen feeding on the surface. While feeding, the whale shark often maintains a vertical position in the water, with its head raised, often emerging out of the water, and the tail straight downward.

REPRODUCTION: Development is oviparous. Very little is known about its reproductive processes. All available information comes from a pregnant female captured off Sri Lanka earlier this century, said to have contained sixteen eggs, and from one huge egg case trawled from 31 fathoms off Mexico in 1953, which contained a fully developed embryo. This egg case measured 30×14×9 cm (12×6×4 in); the embryo measured 35.5 cm (14 in) and apparently was very close to hatching. Juveniles are very seldom seen or captured.

RELATION TO MAN: It is commercially fished in India, but it is of no commercial importance elsewhere. Although there are reports of its ramming small boats, it is more often rammed by boats. It is generally docile enough to be ridden by divers, who hold on to its fins or skin ridges.

FISHING: It is taken by harpoon because it is indifferent to baited hooks. Once harpooned, it often tows small boats for hours. These docile and sluggish fishes should be observed rather than pursued.

REFERENCES: Bass, D'Aubrey, and Kistnasamy 1975c; Bigelow and Schroeder 1948; Compagno 1978; Garrick 1964; Gudger 1941; Hubbs 1976; Penrith 1972; S. Springer 1957.

# Family Odontaspididae—Sand Tiger Sharks

These are large sharks of warm and temperate waters throughout the world. They are characterized by five gill slits anterior to the origin of the pectoral fins, a first dorsal fin placed far back on the trunk, and a second dorsal fin about as large as the first. Their teeth are long, slender, smooth-edged, and often with lateral denticles. They are voracious fish eaters, which usually live on or close to the bottom, often near shore. Presently eight species are recognized; some of them are strikingly similar, and future research may reduce their number. Two species are found in our area.

1. Teeth with one lateral denticle on each side, first upper tooth almost as large as the second, fourth tooth much smaller than fifth, and with a gap between fourth and fifth teeth . . . . *Odontaspis taurus* (p. 80)

    Teeth with two lateral denticles on each side, first upper tooth much smaller than second, fourth tooth larger than fifth, without a gap between fourth and fifth teeth . . . . *Odontaspis ferox* (p. 79)

## Ragged-tooth shark
*Odontaspis ferox* (Risso) 1810

DESCRIPTION: The ragged-tooth shark is characterized by *gill slits set anterior to the origin of the pectoral fins*, a stout body, and *a large second dorsal fin*, about three-quarters the height of the first dorsal fin. The teeth have long, narrow, *smooth-edged cusps with two or more lateral denticles on either side*. Teeth number U 23 to 27–23 to 27, L 18 to 24–18 to 24, and are similar in both jaws. The first tooth in the upper jaws is much smaller than the second, and there is no gap between the fourth and fifth teeth. Color is gray above and slightly lighter below. Average size is 152–212 cm (60–83 in). The species reaches 360 cm (11.8 ft) and 311 kg (684 lb).

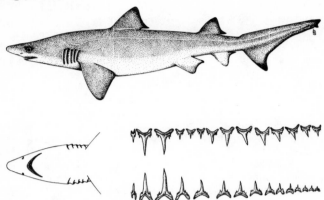

SIMILAR SPECIES: The sand tiger shark has one (occasionally two) lateral denticles on each side of the teeth and a very small fourth upper tooth followed by a gap.

RANGE: The ragged-tooth shark is probably cosmopolitan in warm and temperate waters, but its distribution is not well known. It has been reported from Mediterranean, Atlantic, and Pacific waters. It appears to be common in Japanese waters. The only North American records come from the California coast, where it is rare.

BIOLOGY: Most specimens have been caught in gill nets in 7–50 fathoms. It is believed that this species usually lives in much deeper water. Its diet and habits have not been reported.

REPRODUCTION: No data available.

RELATION TO MAN: In Japan it is utilized for fish oil, and its flesh is considered of poor quality. It is too rare in our area to be of economic importance.

FISHING: Most specimens have been accidental catches in gill nets set close to the bottom.

REFERENCES: Abe et al. 1968; Bass, D'Aubrey, and Kistnasamy 1975c; Garrick 1974; Kato, Springer, and Wagner 1967; Maul 1955.

NOTE: Some confusion exists regarding the identity of ragged-tooth sharks from North America. In the past they were considered to be *O. ferox* Risso 1810, a species originally described from the Mediterranean. More recently they have been attributed to *O. herbsti* Whitley 1950, a species originally described from Australia. The only apparent difference between these two species is coloration (dull red with darker blotches for *ferox*, plain gray for *herbsti*). Further research is needed to clarify this matter. For details see Garrick 1974.

## Sand tiger shark
*Odontaspis taurus* (Rafinesque) 1810

DESCRIPTION: The sand tiger shark is characterized by *gill slits anterior to the origin of the pectoral fins*, a first dorsal fin placed far back on the trunk, and *a second dorsal fin that is almost as large as the first*. The teeth have *long, narrow,* smooth-edged *cusps with one (occasionally two) small lateral denticle on either side*; they are similar in both jaws and number U 44 to 48, L 41 to 46. The teeth on the corners of the mouth are very minute and numerous. Color is light greenish gray above and grayish white below. Juveniles often have yellowish brown spots. Average size is 122–275 cm (48–108 in). A 268-cm (106-in) specimen was reported to weigh 114 kg (250 lb). The species reaches 315 cm (10.4 ft).

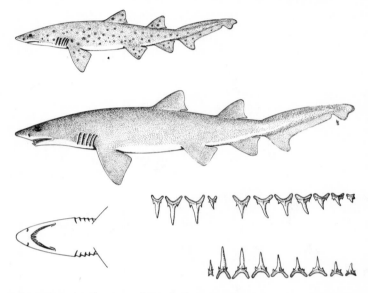

SIMILAR SPECIES: The ragged-tooth shark has two or more small lateral denticles on each side of the teeth instead of one; its first upper tooth is much smaller than the second and lacks a gap between the fourth and fifth teeth.

RANGE: The sand tiger shark inhabits the western Atlantic from the Gulf of Maine to Argentina, the Atlantic coast of Europe to North Africa, and the Mediterranean Sea. It is represented in Japanese and Australian waters by very closely related forms. Off North America it ranges from the Gulf of Maine to Florida and the Gulf of Mexico. It is common from Cape Cod to Delaware Bay during the warmer months.

BIOLOGY: This is a sluggish shark, usually found close to the bottom near shore, often in very shallow water (1–2 fathoms). It is a voracious fish eater, feeding on many species (alewives, bluefish, eels, flatfishes, mackerel, menhaden, mullet, redfish, speckled trout, and many others). It also eats crabs, lobsters, and squid. Its teeth are adapted for grasping small prey, and it is not believed to seek larger prey. This species has been observed resting motionless off the bottom, and an interesting buoyancy control mechanism has been reported: by swallowing air at the surface and holding it in the stomach, it appears to achieve neutral buoyancy. It is most active by night. It is a migratory species common in inshore waters during the summer months, moving southward or to deeper waters in winter.

REPRODUCTION: Development is ovoviviparous. Maturity is reached at about 215 cm (85 in). The embryos are oviphagous; usually only one embryo survives in each oviduct, having eaten its smaller siblings. The pups measure about 100 cm (39 in) at birth. In Florida waters the birth season is November through February.

RELATION TO MAN: It is of little, if any, economic importance. Although it inhabits shallow waters, it is generally not considered dangerous to swimmers or divers. It is a popular aquarium shark because of its fierce look and because it may survive up to ten years in captivity.

FISHING: Best fishing is accomplished with live bait in shallow waters at night.

REFERENCES: Bass and Ballard 1972; Bass, D'Aubrey, and Kistnasamy 1975c; Bigelow and Schroeder 1948, 1953; Clark 1963; Compagno 1978; S. Springer 1948.

# Family Alopiidae—Thresher Sharks

The thresher sharks are characterized by their enormously long caudal fins, which comprise about half the total length. These sharks use their long and powerful caudal fins for stunning prey with sharp blows. Their teeth are single-cusped and smooth-edged. Threshers are cosmopolitan in warm and temperate waters. Although they are most common in the open ocean, they are also found in cool inshore waters, where they occasionally become entangled in fishing nets. Development is ovoviviparous; the embryos are known to be oviphagous in two species. Presently three species are recognized.

1. Free rear tip of the first dorsal fin located far ahead of the origin of
   the pelvic fins; head smooth, lacking a groove . . . . . . . . . . . . . . . . . .     2
   Free rear tip of the first dorsal fin located over or slightly ahead of
   the origin of the pelvic fins; a marked groove on top of the head,
   running from above the eyes to the gill slits . . . . *Alopias superciliosus* (p. 83)
2. Teeth with erect or slightly oblique cusps, lacking denticles on their
   outer sides . . . . *Alopias vulpinus* (p. 84)
   Teeth with strongly oblique cusps, with one or more denticles on
   their outer sides . . . . *Alopias pelagicus* (p. 82)

## Smalltooth thresher
*Alopias pelagicus* Nakamura 1935

DESCRIPTION: This is a rare shark characterized by a *moderate-size eye*, a free rear tip of the first dorsal fin *located far ahead* of the level of the pelvic fins, and an enormous caudal fin, which measures about 55 percent of the total length. The teeth are small and have oblique cusps with *lateral denticles* on their outer sides. Teeth number U 21 or 22–21 or 22, L 21–21. Color is slaty gray with metallic hues above and grayish or white below. Average size is about 300 cm (10 ft). The largest specimen on record measured about 500 cm (16.4 ft).

SIMILAR SPECIES: The thresher shark lacks the teeth with lateral denticles. The bigeye thresher has an enormous eye, a free rear tip of the first dorsal fin over or behind the origin of the pelvic fins, and fewer teeth.

RANGE: The smalltooth thresher has been recorded from the western Pacific (off Taiwan and Japan), the western Indian Ocean, and the eastern North Pacific. The only specimen reported in our area was caught near Islas Marías off the western coast of Mexico. Its range is probably wider. Many specimens probably go unreported because of confusion with the thresher shark.

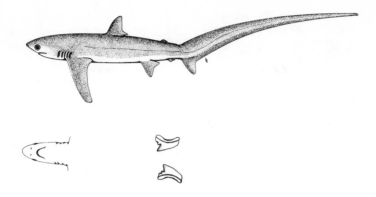

BIOLOGY: Almost nothing is known about the biology and behavior of the smalltooth thresher. It is said to inhabit surface waters.

REPRODUCTION: Development is ovoviviparous. A female 264 cm (104 in) long was reported carrying two pups, indicating that this species reaches maturity at a smaller size than other thresher sharks. The embryos are oviphagous; consequently the litters consist of two pups, one in each uterus. A 96-cm (38-in) embryo has been recorded.

RELATION TO MAN: None.

FISHING: Most specimens are caught on longlines, except some accidentally caught in nets.

REFERENCES: Bass, D'Aubrey, and Kistnasamy 1975c; Castro-Aguirre and Lachica-Bonilla 1973; Nakamura 1935; Otake and Mizue 1981.

## Bigeye thresher
### *Alopias superciliosus* (Lowe) 1840

DESCRIPTION: The bigeye thresher is characterized by an *enormous upward-looking eye*, a *marked groove on top of the head*, running from above the eye to the gill slits, a free rear tip of the first dorsal fin located *over or slightly ahead* of the origin of the pelvic fins, and an enormous caudal fin, which reaches about 50 percent of the total length. The teeth have slender, slightly curved cusps with smooth edges and are similar in both jaws. Teeth number U 11 or 12–11 or 12, L 10 to 12–10 to 12. Color is dark purplish brown or grayish brown with metallic hues above, somewhat lighter below, occasionally with pale cream undersides. Most specimens captured measure 335–400 cm (11–13 ft) and weigh about 160 kg (350 lb), but some bigeye threshers probably reach 450 cm (18 ft).

SIMILAR SPECIES: Both the thresher shark and smalltooth thresher lack the large eye and the grooves on the head and have twice as many teeth.

RANGE: This species was first reported from Madeira in 1840. Not until 1941 was another specimen recorded, when one was captured off Florida. However, it is considered now to be cosmopolitan in warm and temperate waters. In North American waters it has been recorded from New York to Florida and from California to the Gulf of California. It has been reported to be locally common off Cape Hatteras from April to June.

BIOLOGY: The nearly uniform coloration of most specimens and the large eye clearly indicate that this is a deep-water species. Catches at 20–85 fathoms indi-

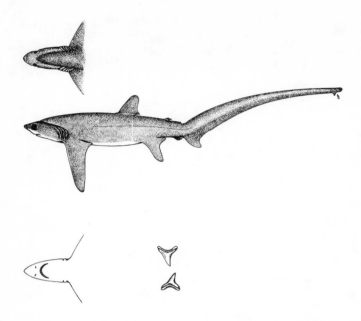

cate that it ascends in the water column at night. It is known to feed on squid, small tunas, lancetfishes, hake, herring, and other small fishes. It occasionally approaches land, even entering shallow waters. This shark maintains an elevated body temperature, several degrees higher than the ambient temperature; this is probably an adaptation for penetrating deeper and colder waters.

REPRODUCTION: Development is ovoviviparous. Males probably mature at about 290 cm (9.5 ft), females at about 350 cm (11.5 ft). The embryos are oviphagous. Embryos measuring 63–100 cm (25–39 in) have been recorded; birth probably occurs when they reach about 100 cm (39 in). The usual number of pups is two per litter.

RELATION TO MAN: The bigeye thresher is generally too scarce to be of economic importance, except as a local nuisance in swordfish fisheries, where it takes baits set for swordfish. A shark will often dislodge several baits from their hooks before impaling or hooking itself.

FISHING: It is often caught in swordfish longlines or by fishermen trolling deep for swordfish. Chemical lights (Cyalume lures) are often used as attractants. Best catches are at night with baits set deeper than 20 fathoms in depths greater than 125 fathoms. Many specimens are foul-hooked on their caudal fins, and they often escape capture because of their great size and strength.

REFERENCES: Bass, D'Aubrey, and Kistnasamy 1975c; Bigelow and Schroeder 1948; Fitch and Craig 1964; Gruber and Compagno 1981; Gubanov 1978; Nakamura 1935; S. Springer 1943; Stillwell and Casey 1976.

## Thresher shark
### Alopias vulpinus (Bonnaterre) 1788

DESCRIPTION: The thresher shark is characterized by a moderate-size eye, a first dorsal fin free rear tip located *ahead* of the origin of the pelvic fins, and an enormous caudal fin, which reaches about 50 percent of the total length. The teeth are small, with curved, smooth-edged cusps, and similar in both jaws. Teeth number U 20–20, L 21–21. Color varies from brown to black above, with metallic hues; the undersides are white. Specimens 300–500 cm (10–16 ft) and 230 kg (500 lb) are common. Exceptional specimens may reach 610 cm (20 ft) and 450 kg (1,000 lb).

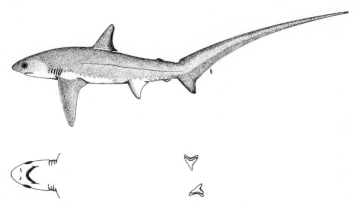

SIMILAR SPECIES: The smalltooth thresher has teeth with one or more lateral denticles on the outer side. The bigeye thresher has an enormous eye and fewer teeth, and the free rear tip of its first dorsal fin reaches over or behind the origin of the pelvic fins.

RANGE: The thresher shark is cosmopolitan in warm and temperate waters. Off North America it ranges from British Columbia to California, and from the Gulf of Saint Lawrence to Florida and the Gulf of Mexico. It is common in offshore waters and in cold inshore waters off New England.

BIOLOGY: This is essentially a pelagic species, usually seen far offshore, although it often wanders close to shore while pursuing schools of fish. While it is often seen on the surface, most longline catches occur at about 100 fathoms. The thresher shark feeds mainly on small schooling fishes, which it stuns with blows from its powerful tail. Its most common prey are bluefish, menhaden, shad, mackerel, and other schooling fishes. It is also known to feed on squid.

REPRODUCTION: Development is ovoviviparous. The females mature at about 300 cm (10 ft). Litters consist of four to six pups, which measure 137–155 cm (54–61 in) and weigh 5–6 kg (12 lb) at birth.

RELATION TO MAN: The thresher shark is often a nuisance to mackerel fishermen because it becomes entangled in their nets. Although it is not common in United States fish markets, it is fished with longlines in other parts of the world. It is considered harmless to humans, although two boat attacks have been reported. It is classed as a gamefish.

FISHING: Most specimens are caught on longlines at depths of about 100 fathoms. A few are caught by sports fishermen using trolled baits and lures as well as drifting baits. Hooks should be small because thresher sharks have small mouths. Most specimens are hooked on the upper lobe of the caudal fin, and only a few are hooked in the mouth. They impale themselves while trying to stun live bait with their long caudal fins. Once hooked, thresher sharks put up an energetic resistance and quite often succeed in tearing off the hook.

REFERENCES: Bass, D'Aubrey, and Kistnasamy 1975c; Bigelow and Schroeder 1948; Gubanov 1972, 1978; Hart 1973; Hixon 1979; Joseph 1954; Leim and Scott 1966; Morrow 1955; Whitley 1940.

# Family Cetorhinidae—Basking Shark

The basking shark is the only member of this family, although the southern hemisphere forms are considered by some specialists to be a different species. Others place the basking shark with the Lamnidae.

## Basking shark
*Cetorhinus maximus* (Gunnerus) 1765

DESCRIPTION: The basking shark is recognized by its conical snout, subterminal mouth, *enormous gill slits*, which extend from the back to the midline of the throat, dark *bristlelike gill rakers* inside the gills (rakers present most of the year), strong *caudal keels* on the caudal peduncle, and a *lunate tail*. Teeth are minute and very numerous, about one hundred per row, with a single conical cusp often curved backward, and similar on both jaws. Color is grayish brown to slaty-gray or black above, uniformly throughout or with irregular lighter patches; the undersides are paler, often with white patches under the snout and mouth or along the ventral side. Two albino specimens from the North Atlantic have been recorded. It is the second-largest fish, surpassed only by the whale shark. Average size is 700–900 cm (22–29 ft). A 920-cm (30-ft) specimen was reported to weigh 3,900 kg (8,600 lb). Largest measured specimen was 980 cm (32 ft). Basking sharks 1,220–1,370 cm (40–45 ft) have often been reported without supporting evidence.

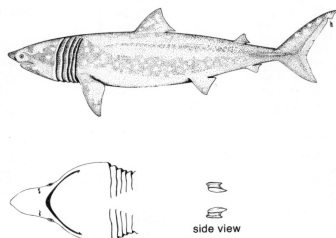

side view

SIMILAR SPECIES: The mackerel sharks have fewer and much larger teeth and smaller gill slits without gill rakers. Large white sharks in the water can be confused with basking sharks (divers beware!); white sharks usually appear uniformly colored, while basking sharks usually present a mottled appearance. The whale shark has a terminal mouth and spots and stripes on the dorsal side.

RANGE: It is found in subpolar and temperate seas throughout the world, occasionally straying into warmer seas in winter. In North America it ranges in waters off Newfoundland to North Carolina, straying south off Florida and very rarely into the Gulf of Mexico, and from the Gulf of Alaska to Baja California. It is common from Nova Scotia to the Gulf of Maine in summer and in the coastal bays of central and southern California in winter.

BIOLOGY: It is often seen swimming slowly near the surface, with the dorsal fin and the tip of the caudal fin exposed, hence the name basking shark. It appears to subsist entirely on plankton (primarily crustaceans), which is abundant in subpolar and temperate waters during most of the year. To capture food, the basking shark simply swims with its mouth wide open; the stiff gill rakers strain plankton from the water as the water passes from the mouth to the gill slits.

This is a migratory species, although its seasonal movements are not well known. In the North Atlantic it appears to move to the northern parts of its range in summer while the plankton is abundant there, moving south as the abundance of plankton decreases with the onset of the boreal winter. Although the basking shark is an oceanic species, large schools of these sharks appear close to shore off Iceland and northern Europe during the summer months. Their presence near shore and their basking habit are probably related to their reproductive cycle, because they show evidence of mating activity at these times. During autumn they disappear and are not seen again until the subsequent summer, when they return after having given birth. The nursery areas are unknown.

The apparent absence of these sharks from the North Atlantic in winter and the fact that they shed their gill rakers have engendered the belief that they do not feed in winter, when there is little plankton around, but instead that they shed their rakers and hibernate in deep water until the following summer. However, it has not been determined whether the gill rakers are necessary for feeding and whether basking sharks actually hibernate. It is possible that they may be active below the surface in areas where they are not available to fisheries or observation.

Off California the seasonal pattern is reversed; these sharks are present throughout the year, being most numerous from September to May and being very scarce in summer.

REPRODUCTION: Development is believed to be ovoviviparous. There are no modern reports of females with embryos, the only report dating back to 1776. Consequently, almost nothing is known about the species' reproductive processes. Females mature at 400–500 cm (13–16 ft). Embryos are believed to measure 150–180 cm (59–71 in) at birth. A free-swimming juvenile of 165 cm (65 in) has been recorded.

RELATION TO MAN: The basking shark supported small fisheries throughout the North Atlantic for centuries. It was fished for its liver oil, which was burned in lamps until replaced by petroleum products. A single shark yields 200–400 gallons of oil. More recently this species has been used for fish meal and animal feed. Because it is a very slow-growing shark that produces few young, it cannot support intensive fisheries. Consequently, most fisheries have died out as a result of overfishing.

In some areas it is considered a nuisance, because its habit of swimming on the surface causes it to become entangled in floating nets, to which it causes great damage in its efforts to escape. There are a few reports of basking sharks ramming small boats, although those encounters are probably accidental.

FISHING: It is taken by harpoon. Equipment consists of a metal harpoon connected to 200–400 feet of three-quarter-inch rope attached to a fifty-gallon drum. The harpoon is thrust between the gills and the dorsal fin. The fish usually sounds when struck and attempts to roll out the harpoon against the bottom, as evidenced by many bent harpoon shafts. The drum is used to slow down the fish and to bring it to the surface after it has tired. It often takes several hours to land one of these great fishes. Because the basking shark has been threatened by overfishing, it should not be killed for sport.

REFERENCES: Bass, D'Aubrey, and Kistnasamy 1975c; Bigelow and Schroeder 1948, 1953; Fitch 1948; Frøiland 1975; Gudger 1948a; Matthews 1950, 1962; Matthews and Parker 1950; Phillips 1948; Springer and Gilbert 1974.

## Family Lamnidae—Mackerel Sharks

The Lamnidae are a small family of large, fast-swimming sharks known as the lamnids, isurids, or mackerel sharks. These sharks share certain adaptations for high-speed swimming: a conical snout, very large gills for more efficient gas exchange, a streamlined fusiform body, a very reduced second dorsal fin, a caudal peduncle that is dorsoventrally flattened forming prominent *keels* on both sides (which strengthen the tail), and a *lunate tail* with two nearly symmetrical lobes. Some lamnids have been shown to maintain an elevated body temperature 7–10°C higher than the water temperature. The rise in temperature is achieved through a highly developed system of countercurrent heat exchangers through the circulatory system, which prevents heat from being dissipated by the circulating blood and the gills. Further research will probably show elevated temperature to be a characteristic of all lamnids. The adaptation for high-speed swimming allows these sharks to occupy a niche at the top of oceanic food chains by feeding on other fast-moving predators such as sharks, swordfish, tunas, seals, sea lions, etc. Some lamnids may follow seasonal migration patterns in pursuit of their prey, but very little is known about these movements. They are ovoviviparous, and in some species the embryos probably feed on unfertilized eggs in the oviduct. Five species are recognized, all of wide distribution.

1. Teeth broadly triangular in shape, with serrated edges .... *Carcharodon carcharias* (p. 88)
   Teeth long and slender, with smooth edges ...................... 2
2. Teeth with small lateral denticles ............................... 3
   Teeth without lateral denticles .................................. 4
3. Distance from the tip of the snout to the front of the eye less than one-half the distance from the back of the eye to the first gill slit; inhabiting Pacific waters .... *Lamna ditropis* (p. 93)
   Distance from the tip of the snout to the front of the eye more than one-half the distance from the back of the eye to the first gill slit; inhabiting Atlantic waters .... *Lamna nasus* (p. 94)
4. Underside of the snout and area around the mouth white .... *Isurus oxyrinchus* (p. 90)
   Underside of the snout and area around the mouth bluish black or dusky .... *Isurus paucus* (p. 91)

**White shark**
*Carcharodon carcharias* (Linnaeus) 1758

DESCRIPTION: The white shark can be recognized by its *large, triangular teeth with serrated edges*. Teeth number U 13–13, L 11 or 12–11 or 12, and are alike in both jaws. Color varies from leaden white to slaty brown or black above, shading to dirty white below. Often there is a black spot around the axil of the pectoral fin. Average specimens measure 460 cm (15 ft) and weigh more than 680 kg (1,500 lb). The largest recorded specimens measured from 580 to 640 cm (19–21 ft) and weighed more than 2,000 kg (4,800 lb). The maximum size of the white shark has been erroneously reported at 1,110 cm (36 ft), based on a set of jaws in the British Museum. Detailed analysis of those jaws has revealed that that shark probably measured 540 cm (17.8 ft). Relatively little data and much controversy exist regarding the maximum size attained by the white shark. The paucity of data reflects the problems of hooking, landing, and weighing such powerful and large specimens. Even when such specimens are obtained, the proper scales for weighing are usually not available. Judging from reported sightings and the size of bites on whale carcasses, it is probable that white sharks 750–800 cm (24–26 ft) exist. However, until one of those formidable specimens is captured and measured, the existence of white sharks over 640 cm (21 ft) must remain unproven.

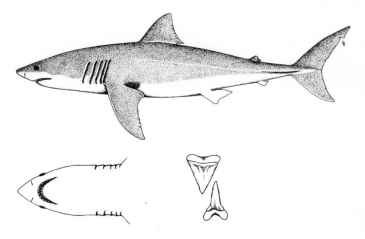

SIMILAR SPECIES: The makos and porbeagles have similar snouts and tails, but their teeth are smooth-edged.

RANGE: The white shark is found throughout temperate, subtropical, and tropical waters. In North American waters, it has been recorded from Newfoundland to Florida and the Gulf of Mexico and from southeastern Alaska to California. It is rare in Alaskan and Canadian waters and usually restricted to the summer months there; it is also rare south of Cape Hatteras and in the Gulf of Mexico and is found in these waters only in winter. Its presence is always sporadic, and nowhere can it be considered common.

BIOLOGY: The white shark is an inhabitant of the cool waters of the continental shelves and strays into warmer waters in winter. It frequently wanders into shallow water and even into the surf. Like the other lamnids, the white shark is a strong-swimming species that preys on large animals. Its usual prey includes seals, sea lions, porpoises, tuna, sturgeon, sea turtles, and other sharks. It is also known to consume small prey, and it is probably the most polyphagous of the lamnids. The stomach contents of one west-coast specimen yielded 150 crabs, 4 salmon, 2 hides of hair seals, and rockfish and hake remains. The white shark has been characterized as the most voracious of fishlike vertebrates and has been known to attack bathers, divers, and even boats. By contrast, some divers have reported it as a shy creature, fleeing upon visual contact with divers. Once its feeding behavior is initiated, its approach is very swift and determined. A direct and fast approach may be an adaptation to overcoming highly intelligent and fast-moving prey such as seals, sea lions, and porpoises. White sharks of the western North Atlantic may act as scavengers, feeding extensively on whale carcasses.

REPRODUCTION: Development is ovoviviparous. Very little is known about the reproductive processes of the white shark, because pregnant females have seldom been captured. Females are believed to reach maturity at 400–430 cm (13–14 ft). The few embryos recorded measured 60 cm (24 in), but they are believed to reach 120 cm (47 in) prior to birth. The smallest known free-swimming white shark measured 130 cm (51 in) and weighed 16 kg (36 lb).

RELATION TO MAN: Many fatalities have been attributed to the white shark, and it is a confirmed man-biter. White sharks have attacked bathers in shallow water and divers and boats in deeper waters. It is one of the most dangerous sharks, because of its large size, feeding habits, aggressiveness, and the fact that it enters shallow waters.

FISHING: The white shark is classed as a gamefish, and it is probably the world's largest. The pursuit of this shark as a sport requires highly specialized tackle and methods; since it is never plentiful and will often ignore the bait, it also requires substantial amounts of funds and patience. Sport fishing for white sharks is pursued only in a few places off South Africa, South Australia, and New York. It involves a great deal of chumming in waters known to be frequented by these sharks. The wire leaders used are very long, usually about 600 cm (20 ft), and are composed of several strands of heavy wire. These long leaders are a must since these sharks have the habit of rolling up on the leader and then abrading or biting through the line. Large reels such as 12/0 and 130-lb test line are also required. Most white sharks are caught in the upper water layers, but some have been caught as deep as 700 fathoms. When hooked, adult specimens put up a savage and determined resistance, and few are captured because of their formidable nature.

REFERENCES: Bass, D'Aubrey, and Kistnasamy 1975c; Bigelow and Schroeder 1948, 1953; Fitch 1949; Leim and Scott 1966; Pratt, Casey, and Conklin 1982; Randall 1973; Templeman 1963.

## Shortfin Mako
*Isurus oxyrinchus* Rafinesque 1810

DESCRIPTION: The shortfin mako has *moderately short pectorals* (usually less than 70 percent of the head length) and the origin of the first dorsal fin *posterior* to the free rear tips of the pectoral fins. The teeth have *long, slender, smooth-edged cusps*; they number U 12 or 13–12 or 13, L 12 or 13–12 or 13, and are alike in both jaws. The first two teeth on each jaw are much longer and slenderer than the rest. The color of living or fresh specimens is deep metallic blue above and snow-white below. The *underside of the snout and the area around the mouth are white*. Average size is 180–250 cm (71–98 in) and 60–135 kg (135–300 lb). Exceptional females may reach 380 cm (12.5 ft) and weigh 570 kg (1,250 lb).

SIMILAR SPECIES: The longfin mako has much longer pectoral fins, and the underside of its snout and the area around its mouth are dusky or blue-black. The porbeagle sharks have teeth with lateral denticles. The white shark has triangular teeth with serrated edges.

RANGE: The shortfin mako is found in warm and warm-temperate waters throughout all oceans. In North America it ranges from California in the Pacific

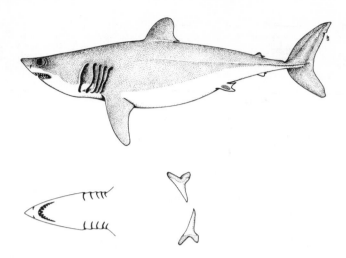

and the Grand Banks in the Atlantic southward to the tropics, including the Gulf of Mexico. It is very common in offshore waters from Cape Cod to Cape Hatteras.

BIOLOGY: This is an oceanic species at the top of the food chain, feeding on other fast-moving fishes such as swordfish, tunas, and other sharks. It is known to maintain an elevated muscle temperature, 7–10°C above the water temperature.

REPRODUCTION: Development is ovoviviparous. Males mature at about 200 cm (6.5 ft), while females mature at a larger size, greater than 260 cm (8.5 ft). Very little is known about reproduction in the shortfin mako, because females apparently abort embryos during capture. Litters are large, eight to ten pups, and the pups are probably born at 68–70 cm (27–28 in). Juveniles have more broadly rounded dorsal fins than the adults.

RELATION TO MAN: The shortfin mako is considered to be one of the great gamefishes of the world. Its flesh is quite flavorful and palatable, and small quantities are found in United States markets. There are numerous reports of the shortfin mako's attacking boats and anglers, but generally it is not considered a problem for divers and swimmers because of its oceanic nature. However, one attack on a swimmer has been documented.

FISHING: Shortfin makos are caught with trolled baits and lures as well as with live or dead baits from boats drifting or at anchor. Once hooked, they put up a fierce resistance, often leaping high into the air. They often cause injury to anglers and damage to boats. Great caution should be exercised while gaffing these fishes.

REFERENCES: Bass, D'Aubrey, and Kistnasamy 1975c; Bigelow and Schroeder 1948; Compagno 1978; Gubanov 1974; Randall and Levy 1976; Scattergood 1962.

## Longfin mako
### Isurus paucus Guitart 1966

DESCRIPTION: The longfin mako has *a large eye* and *very large pectoral* fins (almost as long as the head), the origin of the first dorsal fin *posterior* to the free rear tip of the pectoral fins, and a lunate tail with a *subterminal notch* on its upper lobe. The teeth have *long slender, smooth-edged cusps*; they are similar in both jaws and number U 12 or 13–12 or 13, L 11 to 13–11 to 13. Color is dark blue to bluish black above, bluish gray or dusky below, with some white patches. The *underside of the snout and the area around the mouth are dusky or bluish black.* A 218-cm (86-in) specimen was reported to weigh 70 kg (154 lb); the largest recorded measured 417 cm (13.7 ft).

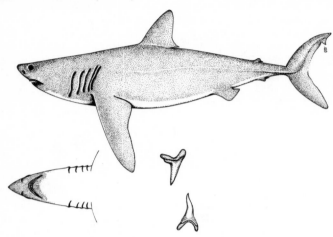

SIMILAR SPECIES: The shortfin mako has much shorter pectoral fins, and the underside of its snout and the area around its mouth are white. The white shark has triangular teeth with serrated edges. The porbeagle shark has teeth with lateral denticles.

RANGE: The longfin mako has been reported from the tropical Pacific Ocean and the western North Atlantic from Georges Bank to the Gulf of Mexico. It probably has wider distribution in deep, warm waters. It is common in Gulf Stream waters from the northern coast of Cuba to southeastern Florida.

BIOLOGY: The large eye indicates that this is a deep-dwelling shark. Off northern Cuba many longfin makos are hooked at depths of 60–120 fathoms, infrequently at 10–50 fathoms, off the continental shelf. Although this is an oceanic species, it is suspected that females approach land to give birth, and there is a report of a female from a Florida beach. Its diet probably consists of squid and schooling fishes. Very little is known about this species, which was not described until 1966.

REPRODUCTION: Development is ovoviviparous. The embryos have been described as having a greatly swollen stomach, and only two pups are produced in each litter, suggesting possible oviphagy. The pups measure about 100 cm (39 in) at birth.

RELATION TO MAN: It is fished off Cuba for animal feed and fish meal.

FISHING: It is usually caught on longlines in deep tropical waters, usually by people fishing for swordfish. Chemical lights (Cyalume lures) may be effective in attracting it to bait.

REFERENCES: Compagno 1978; Dodrill and Gilmore 1979; Garrick 1967; Guitart-Manday 1966.

## Salmon shark
### *Lamna ditropis* Hubbs and Follett 1947

DESCRIPTION: This lamnid of the *North Pacific Ocean* is characterized by a first dorsal fin originating *over or anterior* to the axil of the pectoral fin, and a *tail with a secondary keel.* The distance from the tip of the snout to the front of the eye is *less* than one-half the distance from the back of the eye to the first gill slit. The awllike teeth have smooth edges and *lateral denticles.* Teeth number U 15 to 16–15 to 16, L 13 to 15–13 to 15, and are alike in both jaws. Color is dark bluish gray to bluish black above, changing abruptly to snow white on ventral surface. Adults over 150 cm (59 in) have the *ventral surface coarsely blotched with black.* Length is up to 300 cm (10 ft).

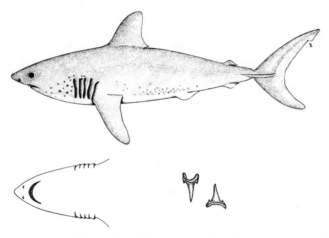

SIMILAR SPECIES: The makos lack the secondary keel on the caudal fin and the lateral denticles on the teeth. The white shark has triangular teeth with serrated edges. The porbeagle shark lacks the dark blotches on the ventral side and has a longer snout. The relationship of the salmon shark to similar species of the southern hemisphere has not been determined and needs clarification.

RANGE: The salmon shark inhabits the subarctic waters of the Bering Sea, the Sea of Japan south to Vladivostok and Niigata, and the northern Pacific south to Honshu in Japan and San Diego in California. It is not found south of 35°N latitude.

BIOLOGY: This is a pelagic species of subarctic and cold-temperate waters, a fast-moving predator at the top of the food chain. It migrates along the coasts following schools of salmon, often forming schools of thirty to forty individuals. In the northern parts of its range, it feeds on salmon, tomcod, mackerel, and pollack; in the southern parts, it feeds chiefly on squid, lantern fishes, and saury.

REPRODUCTION: Development is ovoviviparous. The yolk sac and umbilical cord are soon absorbed and thereafter the embryos feed on unfertilized eggs in the oviduct. The embryos acquire expanded throats and enormous stomachs due to the large amounts of yolk they consume. Usually two to four young are produced per litter. The young have asymmetrical tails at birth and measure 65–70 cm (26–28 in).

RELATION TO MAN: The salmon shark is considered an important predator on salmon and causes considerable damage to salmon nets and gear.

FISHING: The salmon shark is not classed as a gamefish, although it is pursued by sports fishermen in parts of the Strait of Georgia. It takes both surface and bottom baits.

REFERENCES: Gudger 1940; Hart 1973; Hubbs and Follett 1947; Nakaya 1971; Neave and Hanavan 1960; Roedel and Ripley 1950.

## Porbeagle shark
### *Lamna nasus* (Bonnaterre) 1788

DESCRIPTION: The porbeagle shark has a first dorsal fin originating *over or anterior* to the axil of the pectoral fin, and a *tail with a secondary keel*. The distance from the tip of the snout to the front of the eye is *at least* half as long as the distance from the back of the eye to the first gill slit. The teeth have *lateral denticles* and smooth edges, number U 24 to 32, L 23 to 26, and are alike on both jaws. The teeth of very young specimens may lack the lateral denticles. Color is dark bluish gray to brown above, changing abruptly to white below. *There is a patch of white at the trailing edge of the first dorsal fin.* Average size is 150–180 cm (59–71 in) and 135 kg (300 lb). It is reported to reach 365 cm (12 ft) and over 230 kg (500 lb); however, specimens over 250 cm (98 in) are rare.

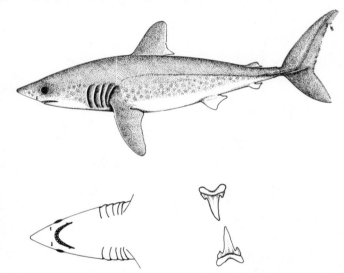

SIMILAR SPECIES: The white shark has triangular teeth with serrated edges. The makos lack the secondary keel on the caudal fin and the lateral denticles on the teeth. The salmon shark has a shorter snout and is confined to the northern Pacific Ocean. Specimens from New Zealand waters have been described as a different species, *Lamna whitleyi*, whose status is doubtful.

RANGE: The porbeagle shark inhabits the cold-temperate waters of the North Atlantic, South Atlantic, and South Pacific oceans. It is common in the continental waters of the North Atlantic, but it is seldom reported from the Southern Hemisphere. Its distribution in the South Pacific is uncertain due to the doubtful status of *Lamna whitleyi*. In North America it ranges from Newfoundland to New Jersey. It is locally common from southwest of the Grand Banks to Massachusetts Bay.

BIOLOGY: The porbeagle shark inhabits inshore and offshore waters colder than 19°C (66°F) from surface to bottom; only rarely is it found off the continental shelf. It is a strong and fast-swimming shark. Its food consists of mackerel, cod, squid, hake, cusk, flounder, and other fishes. It is a warm-bodied shark, keeping its body temperature 7–10°C higher than the water temperature.

REPRODUCTION: Development is ovoviviparous. The embryos are oviphagous. Gestation is believed to last about eight months. Litters consist of three to four pups (usually two in each oviduct). The pups have asymmetrical tails at birth and average 70 cm (28 in) and 9 kg (20 lb) at birth. In the North Atlantic the pups are born in the spring.

RELATION TO MAN: During the early nineteenth century, the porbeagle shark was in great demand for its liver oil, which was used for tanning purposes. During the 1960s, it was actively fished in Canadian waters by Norwegian fishermen, who took about nine million pounds yearly, destined for European food markets. That fishery has decreased considerably due to overfishing. Only two attacks on humans have been attributed to this species, since swimmers do not frequent the cold, deep waters that the porbeagle shark prefers.

FISHING: Usually it is hooked on lines put out for cod. It is classed as a gamefish because it puts up a determined fight, although it does not leap like the shortfin mako. It should be fished with deeply set baits. Wire leaders should be very long, 450–550 cm (15–18 ft), because of the fish's habit of rolling up on the wire, which often causes the line to abrade and break.

REFERENCES: Aasen 1963; Bass, D'Aubrey, and Kistnasamy 1975c; Bigelow and Schroeder 1948, 1953; Kato, Springer, and Wagner 1967; Leim and Scott 1966; Nakaya 1971; Svetlov 1978; Templeman 1963.

# Family Scyliorhinidae—Catsharks

The catsharks comprise a large family of small, bottom-dwelling sharks that inhabit the deep, cool waters of the continental slopes. They are characterized by: two dorsal fins (one exception has only one), the origin of the first dorsal fin located posterior to the origin of the pelvic fins (over or slightly ahead in a few exceptions), short and broad pectoral fins, an anal fin, and large oval eyes. Their teeth are small, multicuspid, and similar in both jaws. Often they are strikingly marked by spots, bars, stripes, or dark blotches. Their development is usually oviparous, but a few species are ovoviviparous. Egg cases are distinguished from those of other cartilaginous fishes by having a posterior end whose diameter is greater than that of the anterior end.

Because most species live on the bottom or near the bottom in very deep waters not exploited by fisheries, most specimens are caught in trawls or dredges operated by scientific survey ships. Consequently many species are poorly known and are known from only one or very few specimens. Presently eighty-six species are recognized, most of localized distribution; eighteen species have been reported from our area or are likely to stray into it. As the exploration of the continental slopes continues the number of species will undoubtedly increase.

NOTE: Juveniles cannot always be identified to species; the descriptions that follow are for adult specimens. In doubtful cases the excellent monograph by Springer (1979) should be consulted.

# Pacific Coast Species

1. First dorsal fin originating well ahead of the origin of the pelvic fins, head very wide and flattened .... *Cephalurus cephalus* (p. 103)
   First dorsal fin originating over or behind the origin of the pelvic fins ............................................................. 2
2. Dorsal surfaces with dark saddlelike blotches, numerous dark spots scattered over the body .... *Cephaloscyllium ventriosum* (p. 102)
   Color uniform, lacking dark blotches or spots ..................... 3
3. Having a row of enlarged dermal denticles on the upper margin of the anterior half of the upper caudal lobe...................... 4
   Lacking a row of enlarged dermal denticles on the upper margin of the anterior half of the upper caudal lobe...................... 5
4. Lining of mouth white .... *Parmaturus xaniurus* (p. 111)
   Lining of mouth dusky or black .... *Galeus piperatus* (p. 105)
5. Anal fin long, reaching base of caudal fin .... *Apristurus brunneus* (p. 97)
   Anal fin short, not reaching base of caudal fin .... *Apristurus kampae* (p. 98)

# Atlantic Coast Species

1. Crest of enlarged dermal denticles along upper margin of caudal fin .. 2
   Lacking crest of enlarged dermal denticles along upper margin of caudal fin .............................................. 4
2. Dorsal surface with complex pattern of dark blotches and spots .... *Galeus arae* (p. 104)
   Dorsal surface unmarked, of uniform color........................ 3
3. First dorsal fin originating over or slightly anterior to pelvic fins origin .... *Parmaturus campechiensis* (p. 110)
   First dorsal fin originating posterior to pelvic fin origin .... *Parmaturus manis* (p. 111)
4. Dorsal surface with light or dark markings, spots, or lines........... 5
   Dorsal surface uniform in color, lacking light or dark markings....... 9
5. Dorsal surface with numerous yellowish or white spots ............. 6
   Dorsal surface lacking yellowish or white spots .................... 7
6. Second dorsal fin as large as, or larger than, first dorsal fin .... *Schroederychthys maculatus* (p. 106)
   Second dorsal fin smaller than first dorsal fin .... *Scyliorhinus torrei* (p. 109)
7. Dorsal surface with large, solid, dark saddle blotches without additional spots, lines, or markings .... *Scyliorhinus meadi* (p. 107)
   Dorsal surface with dark reticulating lines or dark spots ........... 8
8. Dorsal surface with dark reticulating lines outlining dark saddle blotches .... *Scyliorhinus retifer* (p. 108)
   Dorsal surface with dark spots outlining dark saddle blotches .... *Scyliorhinus boa* (p. 106)
9. First dorsal fin origin over space between pelvic and anal fins .... *Apristurus parvipinnis* (p. 99)
   First dorsal fin origin over pelvic fin base......................... 10

10. Snout with narrow band of four rows of pores along its ventral surface .... *Apristurus riveri* (p. 101)

Snout with a band of eight to nine rows of pores along its ventral
surface ................................................................. 11

11. Rear tips of pelvic fins reaching to anal fin origin .... *Apristurus
laurussonii* (p. 99)

Rear tips of pelvic fins not reaching to anal fin origin .... *Apristurus
profundorum* (p. 100)

## Brown catshark
### *Apristurus brunneus* (Gilbert) 1892

DESCRIPTION: The brown catshark is characterized by a long snout with a
*conspicuous band of four rows of pores along its ventral surface, a first dorsal fin
originating posterior to the origin of the pelvic fins*, pectoral fins longer than the
length of the snout, and a *long anal fin that reaches to the base of the caudal fin*.
The teeth usually have five smooth-edged cusps, with the central cusp being the
largest; they number U 29 to 31, L 30 to 34, and are similar in both jaws. Color is
brown above and below, often with black-edged fins. Average size is about 55 cm
(22 in). The largest specimen on record measured 68 cm (27 in).

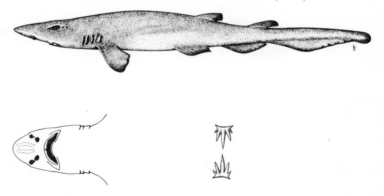

SIMILAR SPECIES: The longnose catshark has a shorter anal fin, whose posterior tip does not reach the base of the caudal fin. The filetail catshark and the
peppered catshark lack the enlarged pores on the snout, and they have enlarged
dermal denticles on the upper lobes of their caudal fins.

RANGE: The brown catshark inhabits the waters of the eastern Pacific from
British Columbia to southern California. The southern limits of its range are uncertain because of confusion with a very similar, perhaps identical, catshark, *Apristurus nasutus*. The brown catshark is common along the Strait of Georgia and
off the coast of Washington, becoming uncommon along the California coast.

BIOLOGY: The brown catshark has been caught in 95–196 fathoms off British
Columbia and Washington. It inhabits deeper waters in the southern parts of the
range, some specimens having been trawled from 400–520 fathoms. It feeds on
shrimp and small fishes.

REPRODUCTION: Development is oviparous. The egg case has a truncated anterior end, a rounded posterior end, and a rounded flange running along its lateral
edge and extending anteriorly and posteriorly into long coiled tendrils. The egg

case measures 5.4 cm (2 in) long and 2.3 cm (0.9 in) wide; it is translucent brown. An 8-cm (3.1-in) free-swimming specimen has been reported.

RELATION TO MAN: None.

FISHING: It is caught on longlines or in deep-water trawls.

REFERENCES: Cox 1963; DeLacy and Chapman 1935; Garman 1913; Hart 1973; Roedel 1951; Roedel and Ripley 1950; S. Springer 1979.

## Longnose catshark
*Apristurus kampae* Taylor 1972

DESCRIPTION: The longnose catshark has a slender body, a long *snout with a narrow band of four rows of pores along its ventral surface*, a *first dorsal fin originating posterior to the origin of the pelvic fins*, pectoral fins shorter than the length of the snout, and *a short anal fin* that does not reach to the base of the caudal fin (the interspace between the anal fin and caudal fin is greater than one-third the anal base length). Teeth are smooth-edged, multicuspid with three to four cusps in front and five to seven in the sides of the jaws, and similar in both jaws. Teeth number U 20 to 26–20 to 26, L 18 to 25–18 to 25, depending on size of the specimen. Color is uniformly dark gray or black. The inside of the mouth is bluish black. The only adult specimen recorded measured 36 cm (14 in).

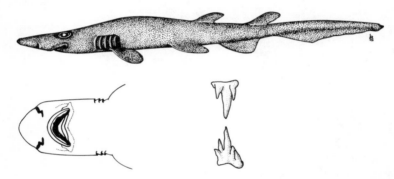

SIMILAR SPECIES: The brown catshark also has pores in the ventral midline of the snout, but it has a much longer anal fin, which reaches to the base of the caudal fin. The filetail catshark lacks the snout pores, the inside of its mouth is white, and its anal fin reaches to the base of the tail. The peppered shark lacks the snout pores, and its anal fin reaches to the base of the caudal fin.

RANGE: It has been reported from the Gulf of California and the Galapagos Islands. The limits of its distribution are unknown.

BIOLOGY: This is a rare deep-water shark. Only two specimens have been recorded; one from over 1,000 fathoms in the Gulf of California, the other from 250 fathoms off the Galapagos Islands. A deep-water shrimp was reported in the stomach of one of the specimens. Nothing is known about its habits.

REPRODUCTION: The type of development is unknown (but probably oviparous). Sexual maturity is reached at about 36 cm (14 in). Nothing else is known about its reproductive processes.

RELATION TO MAN: None.

FISHING: It is caught by trawling in very deep waters.

REFERENCES: S. Springer 1979; Taylor 1972*a*.

## Apristurus laurussonii (Saemundsson) 1922

DESCRIPTION: This small shark is characterized by a *broad snout* with a band of eight to nine rows of conspicuous pores along its ventral surface, by *two dorsal fins of nearly equal size*, by the *origin of the first dorsal fin over or slightly behind the middle of the pelvic fin base*, and by a *long anal fin* that extends from the rear tips of the pelvic fins to the base of the tail. The teeth are small, mostly tricuspid, and smooth-edged and number U 70 to 90, L 54 to 64. Color is uniform grayish brown above and below. Average size is 55–65 cm (22–26 in).

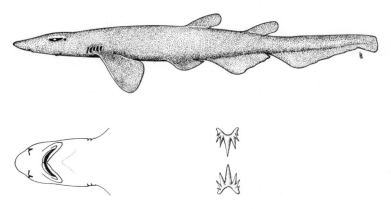

SIMILAR SPECIES: *A. profundorum* has much shorter pelvic fins, their rear tips not reaching the origin of the anal fin. In *A. parvipinnis* and *A. riveri* the first dorsal fin is smaller than the second dorsal fin. *Parmaturus manis* has enlarged dermal denticles along the upper edge of the caudal fin.

RANGE: *A. laurussonii* has been reported off Iceland, the New England coast, the Gulf of Mexico, and the Caribbean. The limits of its distribution are unknown, but evidently it is widespread in deep water. It is common in deep water in the Gulf of Mexico.

BIOLOGY: It has been taken in 300 fathoms off Iceland, but Gulf of Mexico and Caribbean specimens have come from depths of 500–800 fathoms. Its habits and diet are unknown.

REPRODUCTION: No data available.

RELATION TO MAN: None.

FISHING: It is caught only in deep-water trawls.

REFERENCES: Bigelow, Schroeder, and Springer 1953; Hureau and Monod 1973; S. Springer 1966, 1979.

## Apristurus parvipinnis Springer and Heemstra 1979

DESCRIPTION: This small shark is characterized by a *long snout* with a band of eight to nine rows of conspicuous pores along its ventral surface, by a *second dorsal fin two to four times larger than the first dorsal fin*, and by *the origin of the first dorsal fin located over the space between the pelvic and anal fins*. The teeth are small, with three to six cusps (usually four), and similar in both jaws and number about U 50, L 50. Color is black throughout. Average size is 45–50 cm (18–20 in).

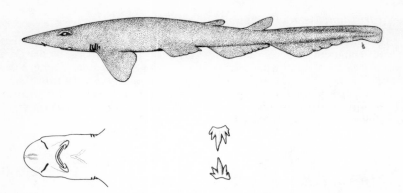

SIMILAR SPECIES: *A. riveri* has the origin of the first dorsal fin located over the rear half of the pelvic fin base. In *A. profundorum* and *A. laurussonii* the dorsal fins are of equal size. *Parmaturus manis* has a row of enlarged dermal denticles along the upper edge of the caudal fin.

RANGE: *A. parvipinnis* inhabits the Gulf of Mexico and the Caribbean. It is common in deep water in the Gulf of Mexico.

BIOLOGY: Specimens have been collected at depths of 350–600 fathoms. Nothing else is known of its habits.

REPRODUCTION: No information available.

RELATION TO MAN: None.

FISHING: It is caught in deep-water trawls.

REFERENCES: S. Springer 1966, 1979.


## *Apristurus profundorum* (Goode and Bean) 1896

DESCRIPTION: This small shark is characterized by a broad *snout with a band of eight to nine rows of conspicuous pores along its ventral surface,* by *two dorsal fins nearly equal in size,* by a *first dorsal fin that originates over the middle of the pelvic fin base,* and by *pelvic fins whose rear tips do not reach to the origin of the anal fin.* The teeth are tricuspid and smooth-edged, with a long, sharp central cusp flanked by smaller cusps on both sides, number U 25–25, L 25–25, and are similar in both jaws. Color is dark grayish brown or black throughout. Average size is probably 50 cm (20 in).

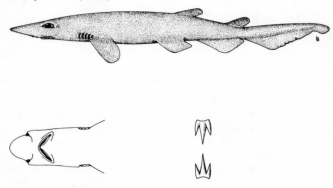

Shortfin mako (*Isurus oxyrinchus*). Howard Hall

Nurse shark (*Ginglymostoma cirratum*). Kenneth Highfill, Nat'l. Audubon Soc.
Coll., Photo Researchers

Sandbar shark (*Carcharhinus plumbeus*). Tom Stack/Tom Stack & Associates

Tiger shark (*Galeocerdo cuvieri*). Ron and Valerie Taylor/Tom Stack & Associates

White shark (*Carcharodon carcharias*). Ron and Valerie Taylor/Tom Stack & Associates

Caribbean reef shark (*Carcharhinus perezii*). V. Farley Sonnier

Dusky shark (*Carcharhinus obscurus*). Dr. Carleton Ray, Nat'l. Audubon Soc. Coll., Photo Researchers

Pacific angel shark (*Squatina californica*). Howard Hall

SIMILAR SPECIES: *A. laurussonii* has a much larger anal fin that extends from the rear tip of the pelvic fins to the base of the caudal fin; however, it may prove to be identical (synonymous) to *A. profundorum*. In *A. parvipinnis* and *A. riveri* the first dorsal fin is smaller than the second dorsal. *Parmaturus manis* has enlarged dermal denticles along the upper edge of the caudal fin.

RANGE: The only specimen positively identified was caught off Delaware Bay in 816 fathoms.

BIOLOGY: There is no information available, other than the fact that it is a deep-dwelling species.

REPRODUCTION: No data available.

RELATION TO MAN: None.

FISHING: It is caught in deep-water trawls.

REFERENCES: S. Springer 1966, 1979; Springer and Sadowsky 1970.

## *Apristurus riveri* Bigelow and Schroeder 1944

DESCRIPTION: This small shark is characterized by a *long snout with a narrow band of four rows of conspicuous pores along its ventral surface*, by a *first dorsal fin originating over the pelvic fins*, and by a *second dorsal fin much larger than the first dorsal fin*. Females and immature males have teeth with three smooth-edged cusps, with the central cusp being much larger than the others. Adult males have teeth with a single, cone-shaped cusp. Teeth number U 24 to 29–24 to 29, L 19 to 22–19 to 22, and are similar in both jaws. Color is dark brown above and below. Average size is 42 cm (17 in). Largest recorded specimen measured 48 cm (19 in).

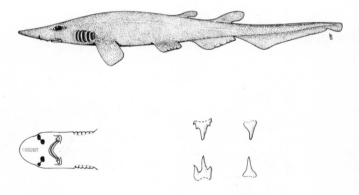

SIMILAR SPECIES: Similar catsharks in the area have eight rows of pores on the ventral side of the snout instead of four rows. Furthermore, *A. parvipinnis* has the origin of the first dorsal fin located over the space between the pelvic and anal fin; *A. laurussonii* and *A. profundorum* have dorsal fins of nearly equal size.

RANGE: *A. riveri* inhabits the deep waters of the Gulf of Mexico and the Caribbean.

BIOLOGY: Specimens have been collected at depths of 350–600 fathoms. Nothing else is known of its habits.

REPRODUCTION: Development is oviparous. Females are believed to mature at about 40 cm (16 in), males at a slightly larger size. The egg cases are smooth-surfaced, translucent, and greenish with indistinct bands of lighter color and measure about 5.5 cm (2 in) long by 1.3 cm (0.5 in) wide.

RELATION TO MAN: None.

FISHING: It is caught in deep-water trawls.

REFERENCES: Bigelow and Schroeder 1944, 1948; S. Springer 1966, 1979.

## Swell shark
*Cephaloscyllium ventriosum* (Garman) 1880

DESCRIPTION: The swell shark has a stout body, a flattened head with a very short snout and a very wide mouth, and a *first dorsal fin originating behind the origin of the pelvic fins*. The teeth are small and numerous, usually with three smooth-edged cusps but occasionally with four or five cusps, and with the central cusp much larger than the others. Teeth number U 55 to 60, L 55 to 60, and are similar in both jaws. Color is yellowish brown above, with seven to eight dark brown *saddlelike areas over the dorsal surfaces and numerous round, dark brown spots* scattered over the body; the undersides are brownish. Average size is about 90 cm (35 in); maximum size is about 110 cm (43 in).

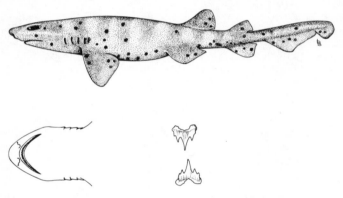

SIMILAR SPECIES: A closely related species may inhabit waters around Santa Catalina, Guadalupe, and other offshore islands. This shark, if a different and valid species, remains undescribed; it has egg cases with short tendrils 2 cm (0.8 in) or less, instead of the typically long tendrils of the swell shark. The leopard shark has similar saddlelike markings, but its first dorsal fin originates well ahead of the pelvic fins.

RANGE: The swell shark inhabits the tropical eastern Pacific from California to Chile. It is common in California waters from Monterey southward.

BIOLOGY: This is a common bottom dweller usually found in 5–20 fathoms, which occasionally strays into depths of 120–160 fathoms. It prefers the rocky, algae-covered areas of kelp beds. It is active by night only, spendinig the day hiding in crevices or caves in a very lethargic state. Although the swell shark is generally solitary, many may congregate in particular areas. It has the remarkable ability to distend its stomach by swallowing water or air, swelling the loose skin of the trunk into a nearly spherical shape; hence the name. It feeds on small fishes but is capable of swallowing relatively large prey.

REPRODUCTION: Development is oviparous. Egg cases are rectangular, 3–6 cm by 9–13 cm (1–2 in by 3–5 in), with short, tapering horns and long tendrils,

80–200 cm (31–79 in). Freshly laid egg cases are light tan in color, darkening after a short time but remaining translucent throughout development. Eggs hatch in 7½ to 10 months, depending on temperature. Hatching usually occurs at night, and the pups measure 14–15 cm (6 in).

RELATION TO MAN: The swell shark, a nuisance to fishermen, often enters lobster traps, attracted by the decomposing fish used for bait. It is often exhibited in aquaria, where it usually survives a few months. Its flesh is of poor quality.

FISHING: It is usually captured in lobster traps or by divers, who can approach this shark very easily.

REFERENCES: Cox 1963; Edwards 1920; Garman 1913; Grover 1972a, 1972b, 1974; S. Springer 1979.

## Head shark
*Cephalurus cephalus* (Gilbert) 1892

DESCRIPTION: The head shark is recognized by its *very wide and flattened head*; by its *very short, rounded snout*, with a length about one-quarter the width of the mouth; and by the origin of the first dorsal fin *slightly ahead* of the origin of the pelvic fins. The teeth are small, usually tricuspid, smooth-edged, with three to five series of functional teeth in alternate arrangement, and similar in both jaws; teeth on the sides have more cusps, up to seven per tooth. Teeth number U 27 to 36–27 to 36, L 27 to 36–27 to 36. Color is dark gray, dark brown, or blackish above, slightly lighter below; the eye is iridescent green. Average size is 18–26 cm (7–10 in). Maximum recorded size is 32 cm (12 in), but it probably grows to 40 cm (16 in).

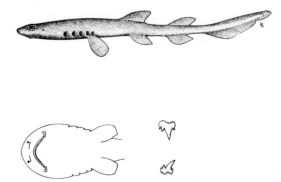

SIMILAR SPECIES: All the other catsharks in the area have the origin of the first dorsal fin over or behind the origin of the pelvic fins. The dogfish sharks lack the anal fin. The nurse shark has long nasal barbels.

RANGE: The head shark has been reported from the Gulf of California and the Revillagigedo Islands, but the limits of its distribution are not known. Specimens have also been reported from off Chile and Peru, but they may belong to a different species presently undescribed. The head shark is regularly caught in the Gulf of California.

BIOLOGY: This is a poorly known little shark from deep water, usually caught between 136–460 fathoms in continental slopes. It has the green eye and the soft body typical of deep-water sharks. Large numbers have been caught in a single trawl, indicating that it may congregate in large numbers in deep water. Nothing else is known of its habits.

REPRODUCTION: Development is ovoviviparous. Sexual maturity is reached at about 14–20 cm (6–8 in). The embryos are born at about 10 cm (4 in).

RELATION TO MAN: None.

FISHING: It is caught only by trawling in deep water, usually in depths greater than 150 fathoms.

REFERENCES: Bigelow and Schroeder 1941; Garman 1913; Mathews and Ruiz 1974; S. Springer 1979.

## Marbled catshark
*Galeus arae* (Nichols) 1927

DESCRIPTION: The marbled catshark is characterized by a slender body with a *first dorsal fin originating posterior to the pelvic* fins and the presence of a *row of enlarged scales along the upper edge of the caudal fin*. The teeth have three to five smooth-edged cusps with the central cusp being slenderer and larger than the others; they number U 36–36, L 35–35, and are similar in both jaws. Color is yellowish brown with a *striking color pattern of dark brown blotches and spots* along the back and sides; the undersides are lighter and unmarked. Average size is about 35 cm (14 in); this fish probably reaches 40 cm (16 in).

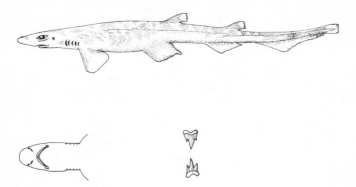

SIMILAR SPECIES: The striking color pattern and enlarged dermal denticles in the tail distinguish it from the other catsharks in the area.

RANGE: The marbled catshark inhabits the slopes of the continental shelf from the coast of Georgia southward to the eastern Gulf of Mexico and Colombia. It is common throughout its range. Several subspecies are recognized within its range.

BIOLOGY: This is a common catshark, which inhabits continental slopes at depths of 160–400 fathoms and temperatures of 6–11°C (43–52°F). The juveniles are found in the shallower parts of the depth range, while the adults inhabit the deeper parts. It is known to feed on various species of deep-water shrimp.

REPRODUCTION: The type of development has not been determined, but it is believed to be ovoviviparous because eggs without cases have been found inside a female. Maturity is reached at about 27cm (11 in). Gravid females are very seldom seen, although large numbers of females have been caught.

RELATION TO MAN: None.

FISHING: It is usually caught in deep-water shrimp trawls.

REFERENCES: Bigelow and Schroeder 1948; Bullis 1967; Nichols 1927; S. Springer 1966, 1979.

## Peppered shark
### *Galeus piperatus* Springer and Wagner 1966

DESCRIPTION: The peppered shark is a very small shark characterized by a *first dorsal fin originating posterior to the origin of the pelvic fins*, by the underside of the *snout lacking conspicuous pores,* and by the presence of a *row of enlarged dermal denticles on the upper margin of the anterior half of the upper caudal lobe.* The teeth have three to seven smooth-edged cusps, with the central cusp being the largest; they number U 29 to 32–29 to 32, L 29 to 32–29 to 32, and are similar in both jaws. Color is brown above, gray with bluish reflections below, *with tiny, black, pepperlike spots* (melanophores) *on the ventral and lateral surfaces. The lining of the mouth is dusky or black.* Juveniles have brown or black mottling on the back and silvery gray undersides. This shark is known to reach 36 cm (14 in).

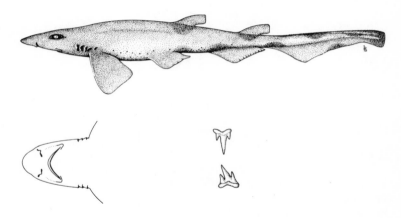

SIMILAR SPECIES: The filetail catshark also has enlarged denticles on the anterior margin of the tail, but the lining of its mouth cavity is white.

RANGE: All specimens reported were taken in the northern Gulf of California, where the peppered catshark is common.

BIOLOGY: It has been taken at depths of 220–725 fathoms. Most specimens have been caught on or near the bottom. Nothing else is known of its habits.

REPRODUCTION: Development is oviparous. Maturity is reached at about 18 cm (7 in). Females may carry ten or more eggs. Egg cases measure about 3.5 cm (1.4 in); they lack tendrils and are nearly elliptical and olive green in color when fresh. Pups hatch at about 4–5 cm (2 in).

RELATION TO MAN: None.

FISHING: It is caught only by trawling in deep waters.

REFERENCES: Hubbs and Taylor 1969; Mathews 1975; S. Springer 1979; Springer and Wagner 1966.

## Schroederychthys maculatus Springer 1966

DESCRIPTION: This small shark is characterized by a very slender body, a broad head, a *short trunk*, a *very long caudal region* (the distance from the origin of the first dorsal fin to the tip of the tail is much longer than the rest of the body), a *first dorsal fin originating posterior to the pelvic fins*, and a *second dorsal fin larger than the first*. The teeth have one large central cusp flanked by much smaller cusps on each side; they number U 48 to 53, L 36 to 42, and are similar in both jaws (except that the lower teeth have shorter central cusps). Color is tan or light brown above with scattered yellowish or white spots; the undersides are white and unmarked. Young or half-grown specimens have seven to nine dark saddle blotches, which fade or disappear in the adults. Average size is about 30 cm (12 in); maximum size is about 34 cm (13 in).

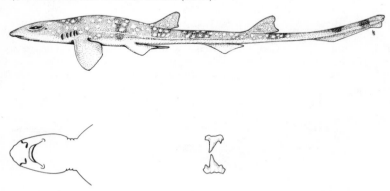

SIMILAR SPECIES: *Scyliorhinus torrei* has similar white or yellowish spots, but it has a shorter caudal region, and its second dorsal fin is smaller than the first.

RANGE: Most specimens have been caught off Rosalind and Quita Sueño banks in the western Caribbean. The limits of this species' distribution are not known.

BIOLOGY: This little-known shark is found at depths of 100–225 fathoms, where it appears to favor bottoms of fine white calcareous material. It feeds on octopus, squid, and small fishes.

REPRODUCTION: Development is oviparous. Males mature at about 38 cm (11 in); the size of females at maturity has not been determined. One female contained an opaque, greenish, longitudinally striated egg case, which measured 4.4 cm (1.7 in) by 1.4 cm (0.5 in) and had threadlike tendrils 22 cm (9 in) long.

RELATION TO MAN: None.

FISHING: It is caught in deep-water trawls.

REFERENCES: S. Springer 1966, 1979.

## Scyliorhinus boa Goode and Bean 1896

DESCRIPTION: This small catshark has a slender body, a wedge-shaped snout, and a *first dorsal fin originating posterior to the pelvic fins*. The teeth are triangular, smooth-edged, with a large central cusp flanked by a smaller cusp on either side, and alike in both jaws. Teeth number about U 24–24, L 23–23. Color is light brown above with *darker blotches outlined by rows of small black spots*, and with lighter undersides. It grows to at least 55 cm (22 in).

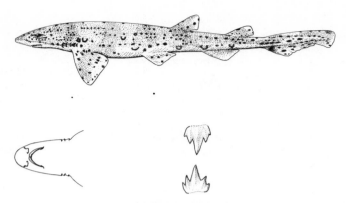

SIMILAR SPECIES: The chain dogfish has a pattern of solid black lines instead of spots.

RANGE: It is found from Hispaniola, through the Lesser Antilles, to the Venezuelan coast.

BIOLOGY: This is a poorly known catshark, which has been reported from 200 to 400 fathoms. Nothing else is known of its habits.

REPRODUCTION: No data available.

RELATION TO MAN: None.

FISHING: It is caught in deep-water trawls.

REFERENCES: Goode and Bean 1896; S. Springer 1979.

## *Scyliorhinus meadi* Springer 1966

DESCRIPTION: This very small shark has a stout body with a broad head and a very short snout, and a *first dorsal fin originating posterior to the pelvic fins*. The teeth have one large central cusp flanked by small side cusps; the frontal teeth have five cusps, and the others have three. They number U 25 to 28–25 to 28, L 23–23. Color is light gray above, with about *nine darker, grayish black saddle blotches spaced over the back and extending to the sides, without light or dark spots in the blotches or among the blotches*; the undersides are grayish white. The few specimens collected have all been immatures ranging from 18 to 49 cm (7 to 19 in).

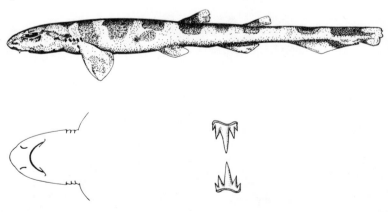

SIMILAR SPECIES: The color pattern of solid dark blotches without light or dark spots or lines distinguishes it from all the other catsharks in the area.

RANGE: It inhabits the western Atlantic from North Carolina to Cuba and the Bahamas. The limits of its distribution are not well known.

BIOLOGY: Specimens have been trawled from depths of 180–300 fathoms. One specimen with cephalopod beaks in the stomach has been reported.

REPRODUCTION: Development is probably oviparous. A specimen 49 cm (19 in) was still immature. The egg capsules have not been recorded.

RELATION TO MAN: None.

FISHING: It is caught only in deep-water trawls.

REFERENCES: Burgess, Link, and Ross 1979; S. Springer 1966, 1979.

## Chain dogfish
### Scyliorhinus retifer (Garman) 1880

DESCRIPTION: The chain dogfish is a small catshark with a slender body, a wedge-shaped snout, and a *first dorsal fin originating posterior to the pelvic fins*. The teeth are triangular, smooth-edged, with one large central cusp flanked by a smaller cusp on either side, and alike in both jaws. Teeth number U 21 to 26–0 to 2–21 to 26, L 20 to 22–0 to 4–20 to 22. Color is reddish brown above and yellowish below, with *distinctive black or dark brown lines forming a chainlike pattern over the back and sides*. Average size is about 38 cm (15 in); the largest recorded measured 47 cm (19 in).

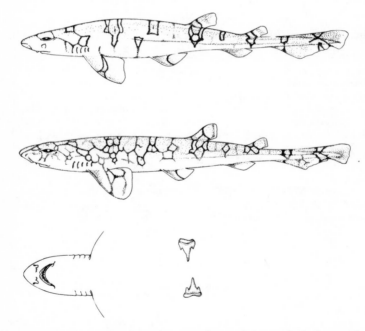

SIMILAR SPECIES: The distinctive markings distinguish it from other catsharks.

RANGE: It inhabits the continental slopes of the western Atlantic from

Georges Bank to Nicaragua, including the Gulf of Mexico. It appears to be most abundant in deep waters off Virginia and North Carolina.

BIOLOGY: This little shark is a bottom-dwelling species found in the deep waters of the continental shelf and slopes, usually in temperatures near 10°C (50°F). It is occasionally taken at depths of 20–125 fathoms in the northern parts of the range, but it inhabits deeper waters (250 fathoms or more) in the southern parts. Its diet is not known.

REPRODUCTION: Development is oviparous. Pregnant females have seldom been taken, but the egg cases are believed to be 5–6 cm (2 in) long by about 2 cm (0.9 in) wide, with a long tendril at each corner, and brownish amber in color. The pups measure about 10 cm (3.9 in) at hatching. One trawl off Cape Hatteras produced a large number of newly hatched or small chain dogfish, suggesting that the nursery areas may be highly localized.

RELATION TO MAN: None.

FISHING: This dogfish is taken by trawling in depths greater than 40 fathoms and at temperatures around 10°C (50°F).

REFERENCES: Bigelow and Schroeder 1948; Goode and Bean 1896; S. Springer 1966, 1979; Springer and Sadowsky 1970.

## *Scyliorhinus torrei* Howell-Rivero 1936

DESCRIPTION: This small shark has a slender body, a broadly rounded snout, and a *first dorsal fin that is larger than the second dorsal fin* and *originates posterior to the pelvic fins*. Teeth are triangular, smooth-edged, with one larger central cusp flanked on either side by a smaller cusp, and similar in both jaws. Teeth number U 20 to 23–20 to 23, L 19 or 20–19 or 20. Color is *pale brown* above, with about seven dorsal saddle blotches of slightly darker brown spaced over the back, and with *small, whitish spots evenly distributed over the back and sides*. Undersides are pale brown or white. Average size is 26 cm (10 in). The largest recorded of these sharks measured 29 cm (11 in).

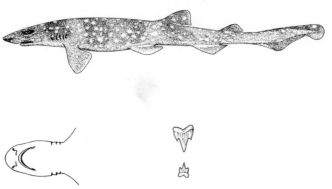

SIMILAR SPECIES: Another Caribbean catshark, *Schroederychthys maculatus*, has an identical color pattern but it has only been reported from the offings off Nicaragua. *Schroederychthys maculatus* differs from *Scyliorhinus torrei* in having an extremely long caudal section (the distance from the origin of its first dorsal fin to the tip of the tail is much longer than the rest of the body), and its second dorsal fin is slightly larger than the first. The other catsharks in the area lack the white spots.

RANGE: Specimens have been collected off the north coast of Cuba, the southeast coast of Florida, and the Virgin Islands. The limits of this shark's distribution are not known.

BIOLOGY: *S. torrei* has been collected in depths of 125–300 fathoms. Reported stomach contents are squid and possibly cuttlefish. Nothing else is known about its habits.

REPRODUCTION: Neither eggs nor newly hatched pups have been recorded.

RELATION TO MAN: None.

FISHING: It is caught only in deep-water trawls.

REFERENCES: Bigelow and Schroeder 1948; S. Springer 1966, 1979; Springer and Sadowsky 1970.

## *Parmaturus campechiensis* Springer 1979

DESCRIPTION: This shark is characterized by a slender body, a wide head with a rounded, short snout, a *first dorsal fin originating over or slightly ahead of the pelvic fin origin*, a *second dorsal fin larger than the first*, and *enlarged dermal denticles on the upper edge of the caudal fin*. The teeth have three cusps, a few with four cusps, are similar in both jaws, and number about U 60, L 60. Color is grayish above, with slightly darker undersides, gill slits, and the outer parts of the fins. The only known specimen, a juvenile, measured about 16 cm (6 in). The size at maturity is not known.

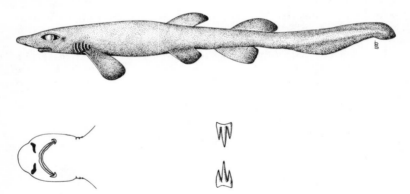

SIMILAR SPECIES: *Parmaturus manis* has a smaller and more posterior first dorsal fin.

RANGE: *P. campechiensis* is known only from the Bay of Campeche, Gulf of Mexico.

BIOLOGY: It is believed to live in midwater at depths greater than 200 fathoms. The only specimen known was caught in 600 fathoms.

REPRODUCTION: No data available.

RELATION TO MAN: None.

FISHING: It is caught in midwater trawls at depths greater than 200 fathoms.

REFERENCES: Springer 1979.

## Parmaturus manis Springer 1979

DESCRIPTION: This shark is characterized by a slender body, a long, flattened snout, a *first dorsal fin originating over the middle of the pelvic fin base*, a second dorsal fin larger than the first, and a *row of enlarged dermal denticles along the upper edge of the caudal fin*. The teeth are small with three to five cusps, with the central cusp the largest. Teeth number about U 30–30, L 26–26, and are similar in both jaws. Color is light gray throughout. Only five specimens, all juveniles, 23–33 cm (9–13 in) have been reported. The size at maturity is not known.

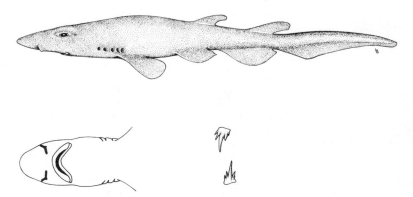

SIMILAR SPECIES: *P. campechiensis* has a more anterior and larger first dorsal fin.

RANGE: The only known specimens were caught off Massachusetts.

BIOLOGY: It has been caught in 360–460 fathoms. Nothing else is known of its habits.

REPRODUCTION: No data available.

RELATION TO MAN: None.

FISHING: It is caught in deep-water trawls.

REFERENCES: Bigelow and Schroeder 1954; S. Springer 1979.


## Filetail catshark
### Parmaturus xaniurus (Gilbert) 1892

DESCRIPTION: The filetail catshark is characterized by a short snout, a first dorsal fin originating *posterior* to the origin of the pelvic fins, and the presence of a *row of enlarged dermal denticles in the upper margin of the anterior half of the upper caudal lobe*. The teeth have three to five smooth-edged cusps, with the central cusp the largest; they number U 41 to 45–41 to 45, L 42–42, and are similar in both jaws. Color is brownish black above and slightly lighter below. *The lining of the mouth cavity is white.* Specimens up to 50 cm (20 in) are common. The largest specimen recorded measured 55 cm (22 in). This shark probably reaches 60 cm (24 in).

SIMILAR SPECIES: The peppered shark also has enlarged dermal denticles on the tail, but the lining of its mouth cavity is dusky or black. Other catsharks in the area lack enlarged dermal denticles on the tail.

RANGE: The filetail catshark is found from central California to the Gulf of California. It is common in deep water in the Santa Barbara basin.

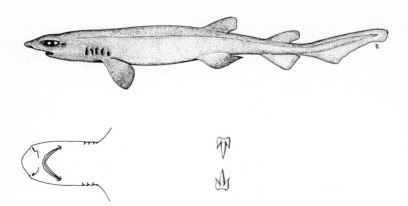

BIOLOGY: This is a common catshark off the west coast, often found in trawl catches. It has been reported from diverse deep-water habitats. Some have been observed at the bottom under low oxygen conditions in deep water; others have been caught in midwater at more than 250 fathoms above the sea bottom in waters slightly over 300 fathoms.

REPRODUCTION: Development is oviparous. Maturity is reached at about 41 cm (16 in). The egg case is long and slender, widest about the middle, tan colored, and has long tendrils. It measures 7–11 cm (3–4 in) long and about 3 cm (1 in) wide. The egg cases of the filetail catshark can be identified by the presence of a flange, T-shaped in cross section, that runs along the lateral edge.

RELATION TO MAN: None.

FISHING: It is caught in midwater and bottom trawls over deep waters.

REFERENCES: Garman 1913; Lee 1969; Roedel and Ripley 1950; S. Springer 1979.

## Family Proscyllidae—Ribbontail Catsharks

This is a family of very small deep-water sharks that comprises two species. The Cuban ribbontail catshark is the only one found in our area.

### Cuban ribbontail catshark
*Eridacnis barbouri* (Bigelow and Schroeder) 1944 (= *Triakis barbouri*)

DESCRIPTION: This little shark has a slender body, large oval eyes with a nictitating membrane, a noticeable spiracle behind the eye, short labial furrows, two equally large dorsal fins, the first dorsal *originating well ahead* of the pelvic fins, and a long and elongated caudal fin. The teeth are very small and numerous. The front teeth have *three needlelike* cusps with longitudinal striations, with the central cusp being much larger than the others; the rear teeth are low and comblike. Teeth number about U 60 to 62, L 60 to 62. The dermal denticles are three-pointed. Color is pale gray or tan above, with darker blotches along the anterior edge of the pectoral fins and on the caudal fin, and grayish white or paler below. Average size is about 28 cm (11 in). The species probably reaches 40 cm (16 in).

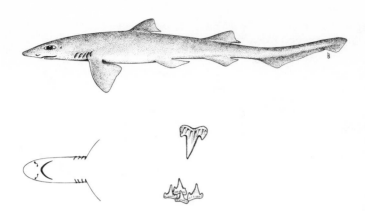

SIMILAR SPECIES: The catsharks have the first dorsal fin originating over or behind the origin of the pelvic fins. The smoothhounds have low, blunt teeth, and the first dorsal fin larger than the second. The requiem sharks have bladelike teeth and a well-defined caudal fin.

RANGE: The Cuban ribbontail catshark is known only from the Straits of Florida from south Florida to the northern coast of Cuba. It is common in deep water along the northern coast of Cuba.

BIOLOGY: This little shark has been caught at depths of 235–335 fathoms. Nothing else is known of its habits.

REPRODUCTION: Development is ovoviviparous. A 30-cm (12-in) female was reported to contain two pups 9–10 cm (4 in) in length, apparently ready for birth.

RELATION TO MAN: None.

FISHING: It is caught in deep-water trawls.

REFERENCES: Bigelow and Schroeder 1948; Compagno 1978.

# Family Pseudotriakidae—False Catsharks

The Pseudotriakidae are a small family of rare, large, deep-water sharks characterized by a very long and low first dorsal fin, which is as long as the caudal fin. Other characteristics include slender bodies, small gill slits, large spiracles, a poorly developed nictitating lower eyelid, and the presence of an anal fin. This family is often included within the catsharks (Scyliorhinidae), from which it differs in the shape and position of the first dorsal fin. Development is ovoviviparous. Two species are usually recognized, *Pseudotriakis acrales* (= *acrages*) of the western Pacific and *P. microdon* of the Atlantic; these two species are probably synonymous. Specimens from our area have been reported as *P. microdon*.

## False catshark
*Pseudotriakis microdon* Brito Capello 1867

DESCRIPTION: The false catshark is a rare, deep-water species characterized by a very short snout, its length about one-half the mouth width, and a *long and low first dorsal fin, which is as long as the caudal fin* (or five to seven times longer than high) and located anterior to the origin of the pelvic fins. The teeth are minute and extremely numerous, with three to five cusps (the central cusp the largest), and are arranged in perpendicular files in the upper jaws and in diagonal files in the lower jaws. Color is brownish gray throughout, with the tips of the fins slightly darker. Average size is 270 cm (106 in). The largest specimen reported measured 295 cm (116 in).

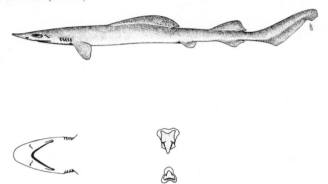

SIMILAR SPECIES: The catsharks have the first dorsal fin located over or posterior to the origin of the pelvic fins. The dogfishes lack an anal fin. The long and low first dorsal fin distinguishes the false catshark from all the other sharks in our area.

RANGE: It is found in deep water throughout the Atlantic, Pacific, and Indian oceans. The only North American records come from the waters off New York and New Jersey.

BIOLOGY: This is a rare deep-water species usually reported from 200–800 fathoms, although it may wander into shallow water, as many other deep-water fishes do. Nothing else is known about its habits. Fewer than a dozen specimens have ever been reported.

REPRODUCTION: Development is ovoviviparous. Males mature at about 240 cm (95 in), females at about 280 cm (110 in). It has been suggested that the embryos may be oviphagous, but this needs confirmation. A 274-cm (108-in) female was reported to contain two 85-cm (33-in) embryos. Size at birth is probably about 90 cm (35 in), since a 93-cm (37-in) free-swimming specimen has been reported.

RELATION TO MAN: None.

FISHING: Only accidentally caught on longlines in depths of 200 fathoms or greater.

REFERENCES: Bass, D'Aubrey, and Kistnasamy 1975a; Bigelow and Schroeder 1948; Forster et al. 1970.

## Family Triakidae—Smoothhound Sharks

The smoothhounds are small to medium-sized sharks, with slender bodies, large oval eyes, a variably developed nictitating membrane, a noticeable spiracle, low or blunt teeth, dorsal fins without spines, a large second dorsal fin about three-quarters the size of the first dorsal fin, no precaudal pits, and a short and broad caudal fin. Development is ovoviviparous or viviparous. These sharks inhabit shallow to moderately deep water over the continental shelves of all oceans; their diet consists primarily of crustaceans. Some are of local economic importance; others are a nuisance to fishermen.

This family is closely allied to the Carcharhinidae. There are sharks, such as the soupfin shark, that possess characteristics of both families and are considered transitional. Presently about thirty-six species are recognized; the number of species in the family depends on whether the transitional species are included or moved to the Carcharhinidae. Seven species inhabit our area. There may be undescribed smoothhounds in the southern limits of our area. For additional information see Compagno (1970) and Heemstra (1973).

## Pacific Coast Species

1. Numerous dark saddle bars and dark spots on dorsal surface . . . .
   *Triakis semifasciata* (p. 120)
   Lacking dark markings on dorsal surface. . . . . . . . . . . . . . . . . . . . . . . . . .  2
2. Second dorsal fin and anal fin equal in size . . . . *Galeorhinus zyopterus* (p. 121)
   Second dorsal fin much larger than anal fin . . . . . . . . . . . . . . . . . . . . . .  3
3. Trailing edge of dorsal fins frayed; teeth with short sharp points . . . .
   *Mustelus henlei* (p. 117)
   Trailing edges of dorsal fins not frayed, teeth with rounded blunt cusps . . . . . . . . . . . . . . . . . . . . . . . . . . . . . . . . . . . . . . . . . . . . . . .  4
4. First dorsal fin originating slightly posterior to the free rear tips of the pectoral fins, with the midpoint of its base closer to the origin of the pelvic fins than to the pectoral axil, caudal fin usually with an indistinct lower lobe . . . . *Mustelus californicus* (p. 115)
   First dorsal fin originating over the free rear tips of the pectoral fins, with the midpoint of its base closer to the pectoral axil than to the origin of the pelvic fins, caudal fin with a sharp-pointed lower lobe . . . . *Mustelus lunulatus* (p. 118)

## Atlantic Coast Species

1. Internostril distance 2.7–3.6 percent of total length, caudal fin with a rounded lower lobe . . . . *Mustelus canis* (p. 116)
   Internostril distance 1.2–2.4 percent of total length, caudal fin with a sharp-pointed lower lobe . . . . *Mustelus norrisi* (p. 119)

### Gray smoothhound
*Mustelus californicus* Gill 1864

DESCRIPTION: The gray smoothhound has a slender body with a noticeable spiracle behind the eye, a first dorsal fin originating *slightly posterior* to the free rear tips of the pectoral fins and with the midpoint of its base closer to the origin of the pelvic fins than to the pectoral axil, a second dorsal fin much larger than the anal fin, and a caudal fin with usually an indistinct lower lobe. The teeth are small and numerous, pavementlike, and have low, blunt cusps. Color is brown or dark gray above and white below. Albino specimens from Elkhorn Slough (Monterey Bay, California) have been reported several times. This shark grows to about 116 cm (46 in).

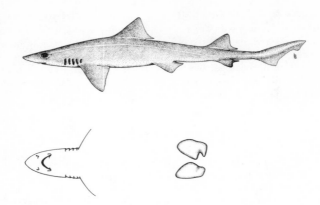

SIMILAR SPECIES: The brown smoothhound has a more anterior first dorsal fin, with the midpoint of its base about equidistant to the pectoral axil and the origin of the pelvic fins, and its teeth are pointed. The sicklefin smoothhound has a pointed lower caudal lobe tip.

RANGE: The gray smoothhound is found from northern California, where it is rare, to the Mexican coast. It is common in inshore waters off southern California.

BIOLOGY: This is a common shark of bays, sounds, and rocky shores. It is found at depths of 1–25 fathoms, usually in 3 fathoms or less. Its diet consists primarily of crabs. It is often seen with schools of leopard sharks in very shallow water. In inshore waters off central California it is very common during the winter months and rare during the rest of the year.

REPRODUCTION: Development is viviparous. Males mature at about 60 cm (24 in); females mature at about 74 cm (29 in). The gestation period probably lasts ten to eleven months. The litters range from three to sixteen pups, which measure 20–30 cm (8–12 in) at birth.

RELATION TO MAN: It is occasionally marketed in California.

FISHING: It is often caught in gill nets or shallow-water trawls.

REFERENCES: Cohen 1973; Heemstra 1973; Kato, Springer, and Wagner 1967; Limbaugh 1963; Miller and Lea 1972; Roedel and Ripley 1950; Talent 1973.

## Smooth dogfish
*Mustelus canis* (Mitchill) 1815

DESCRIPTION: The smooth dogfish has a very slender body, a prominent spiracle behind the eye, an internostril distance of 2.7–3.6 percent of the total length, a second dorsal fin much larger than the anal fin, and a caudal fin with a *rounded lower lobe*. The teeth are very *small, pavementlike, with low blunt cusps*, very numerous, and similar in both jaws. Color is olive gray to brown above, yellowish or grayish white below. It is capable of slowly changing shade by contraction of its melanophores (pigment cells). Average size is about 122 cm (48 in), but it is reported to reach 152 cm (60 in).

SIMILAR SPECIES: The Florida smoothhound has a narrower internostril distance (1.2–2.4 percent of total length), and the lower lobe of its caudal fin is pointed.

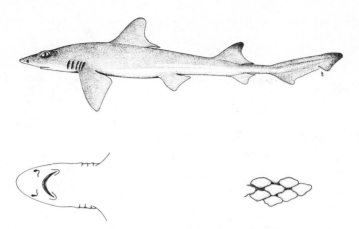

RANGE: It inhabits the western Atlantic from the Bay of Fundy to Uruguay. In North American waters it ranges from the Bay of Fundy (only as a very rare stray) to Florida and the Gulf of Mexico. It is common from Cape Cod to Charleston.

BIOLOGY: This is a common shark in bays and inshore waters, usually found at depths of less than 10 fathoms. It feeds primarily on crabs, lobsters, and shrimp, but it is an opportunistic feeder and a scavenger and will consume whatever prey is easily available. It is a migratory species, regularly moving north-south with the seasons; it summers from Cape Cod to Delaware Bay and winters from Chesapeake Bay to South Carolina. It is primarily nocturnal, which is probably related to the nocturnal habits of its crustacean prey.

REPRODUCTION: Development is viviparous. Maturity is reached at about 85 cm (33 in). The gestation period is believed to last about ten months. The pups measure 34–39 cm (13–15 in) at birth. Litters usually consist of ten to twenty pups. Birth usually occurs in early summer.

RELATION TO MAN: Because of its abundance, exceeded only by that of the spiny dogfish, it interferes with shrimp trawling operations and affects crab and lobster stocks. It is extensively used as a laboratory animal and often displayed in aquaria.

FISHING: It is easily taken with hook and line using squid or shrimp bait. It is often caught in large numbers by shrimp trawlers.

REFERENCES: Bigelow and Schroeder 1940, 1948; Casterlin and Reynolds 1979; Compagno 1978; Heemstra 1973; Leim and Scott 1966; S. Springer 1939a.


## Brown smoothhound
### Mustelus henlei (Gill) 1962

DESCRIPTION: The brown smoothhound has a slender body with a noticeable spiracle behind the eye; *a first dorsal fin with thin and frayed rear edges*, originating over the free rear tips of the pectoral fins, with the midpoint of its base about equidistant from the pectoral axil and the origin of the pelvic fins; and a second dorsal fin much larger than the anal fin. The teeth are small, numerous, and *pavementlike* and have *short, sharp points*. The upper teeth have a slightly oblique, median cusp flanked by a strong notch and a smaller cusp; the lower teeth have more erect cusps. Color is reddish brown above, silvery white below. Average size is about 65 cm (26 in); it grows to about 97 cm (38 in).

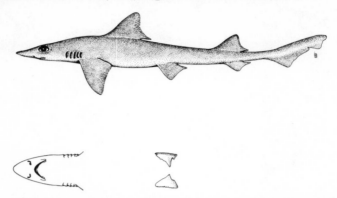

SIMILAR SPECIES: The gray smoothhound has a more posterior first dorsal fin, its origin lying posterior to the free rear tips of the pectoral fins; its teeth are round and blunt. The sicklefin smoothhound has a lower caudal lobe with a pointed tip. The soupfin shark has the second dorsal fin and the anal fin of the same size.

RANGE: The brown smoothhound is found from the Oregon coast to the coast of Peru. It is locally common in bays north of Monterey, with extensive populations in San Francisco, Tomales, and Humbolt bays. It is rarely reported south of the Gulf of California.

BIOLOGY: It inhabits shallow coastal waters, usually very close to shore. It is common in tidal flats and around oyster beds, where it feeds on crabs, shrimp, and small fishes.

REPRODUCTION: Development is viviparous. Maturity is reached at about 50 cm (20 in). The pups are born at about 21 cm (8 in).

RELATION TO MAN: Its flesh is of high quality and occasionally marketed in California.

FISHING: It provides bay fishermen with lively sport on light tackle with cut or squid bait.

REFERENCES: Bane and Bane 1971; Heemstra 1973; Kato, Springer, and Wagner 1967; Roedel and Ripley 1950; Russo 1975.


## Sicklefin smoothhound
*Mustelus lunulatus* Jordan and Gilbert 1882

DESCRIPTION: The sicklefin smoothhound has a slender body with a noticeable spiracle behind the eye, a first dorsal fin that originates over the free rear tips of the pectoral fins and has a non-frayed, nearly vertical posterior edge, a second dorsal fin much larger than the anal fin, and a lower caudal lobe with a *pointed tip*. The teeth are small and numerous, pavementlike, with rounded, blunt cusps (occasionally with a low, sharp cusp). Color is grayish or olive brown above, paler or yellowish below. The largest reported sicklefin smoothhound was 110 cm (43 in), but the species is said to reach 175 cm (69 in).

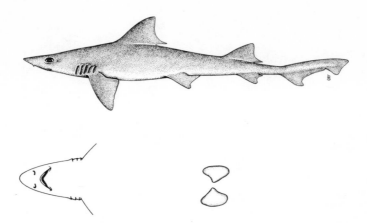

SIMILAR SPECIES: Other smoothhounds in the area, except in the Gulf of California, lack the lower caudal lobe with a pointed tip. Gray smoothhounds from the Gulf of California are said to have pointed lower caudal lobes. In doubtful cases check the number of precaudal vertebrae: eighty-nine to ninety-nine for the gray smoothhound; seventy-four to eighty-two for the sicklefin smoothhound.

RANGE: It inhabits inshore waters from southern California to the Gulf of Panama. It is common from southern California to the Gulf of California.

BIOLOGY: This is a coastal species that feeds on crustaceans. Its habits are poorly known.

REPRODUCTION: Development is probably ovoviviparous. Males mature at about 75 cm (30 in); the size of females at maturity has not been reported. The pups are born at about 33 cm (13 in).

RELATION TO MAN: It is often considered a nuisance by fishermen because of its habit of rolling up in nets.

FISHING: It is often caught in gill nets set close to shore.

REFERENCES: Heemstra 1973; Kato, Springer, and Wagner 1967; Miller and Lea 1972; Norris 1923; Roedel and Ripley 1950.


## Florida dogfish
*Mustelus norrisi* Springer 1939

DESCRIPTION:The Florida dogfish has a very slender body, a prominent spiracle behind the eye, an internostril distance of 1.2–2.4 percent of the total length, a second dorsal fin much larger than the anal fin, and the caudal fin with a *sharp-pointed lower lobe* directed rearward. Embryos and young pups may have a rounded lower caudal lobe. The teeth are very *small, pavementlike, with low blunt cusps*, very numerous, and similar in both jaws. Color is gray above and paler or dirty white below. Average size is about 75 cm (30 in) for males, and about 90 cm (35 in) for females. It reaches about 100 cm (39 in).

SIMILAR SPECIES: The smooth dogfish has a wider internostril distance (2.7–3.6 percent of total length) and has a caudal fin with a rounded lower lobe.

RANGE: It has been reported from the Florida west coast, the southern Caribbean, and the Western Atlantic south to Brazil. The limits of its distribution are not well known. It is common throughout the Florida west coast.

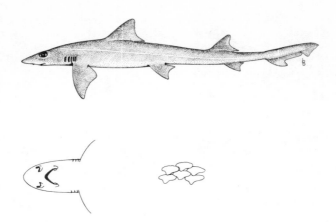

BIOLOGY: This is a species usually found in shallow coastal waters, 3–4 fathoms or less, during the winter months. A specimen caught in 50 fathoms has also been reported. This dogfish feeds on crabs, shrimp, and small fishes.

REPRODUCTION: Development is viviparous. Males reach maturity at about 58 cm (23 in), females at about 65 cm (26 in). The pups measure about 30 cm (12 in) at birth. Litters usually consist of seven to fourteen pups. The birth season appears to be in late winter or early spring.

RELATION TO MAN: None.

FISHING: It is often taken in fish nets, usually very close to shore.

REFERENCES: Bigelow and Schroeder 1948; Heemstra 1973; S. Springer 1939a.


## Leopard shark
### Triakis semifasciata Girard 1854

DESCRIPTION: The leopard shark is easily recognized by its striking color pattern of *numerous, well-defined, dark saddle bars interspaced with dark spots* (rare individuals have irregular dark streaks instead of bars), and by its *first dorsal fin originating far ahead of the pelvic fins*. The teeth are small and numerous; they have one long, oblique, central cusp flanked by one or two smaller cusps on each side, and they number about U 25–25, L 19–19. Color is variable, ranging from grayish brown with darker markings to metallic silver with almost black markings above, and paler undersides. An albino specimen has been reported. Average size is 150 cm (59 in) for males and 180 cm (71 in) for females. It grows to about 210 cm (83 in).

SIMILAR SPECIES: The swell shark has indistinct dark saddle markings, and its first dorsal fin originates behind the origin of the pelvic fins.

RANGE: The leopard shark ranges from the Oregon coast to the Gulf of California. It is common in inshore waters throughout its range from spring to midsummer.

BIOLOGY: This is a common shark in shallow inshore waters, usually found in 2–4 fathoms. It is a gregarious fish, often forming large schools. Small sharks, 90 cm (35 in) or less, feed mainly on crabs; larger sharks are opportunists that feed on echiuroid worms, shrimp, clams, octopuses, small fish, and fish eggs. The presence of mud-dwelling animals such as clams and echiuroid worms in many of the stomach contents analyzed suggests a groveling habit or perhaps suction feeding.

REPRODUCTION: Development is ovoviviparous. Females reach maturity at about 100–110 cm (39–43 in), and males at a somewhat smaller size. Gestation lasts approximately one year, with most females giving birth in May; by June they are carrying newly fertilized eggs. Pups measure 18–20 cm (7–8 in) at birth; litters range from seven to thirty pups, depending on the size of the female. San Francisco, Tomales, and Bodega bays are some of the nursery areas.

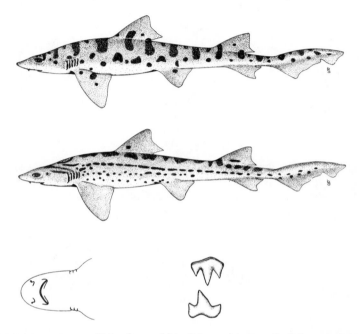

RELATION TO MAN: It is often sold in fish markets, its flesh being of excellent quality. It is often exhibited in aquaria, where it survives several years (one survived ten years in captivity). It is generally timid and harmless, usually fleeing from divers; however, one attack on a bleeding diver has been reported.

FISHING: It is easily caught with squid or sardine bait set on the bottom. Large numbers are taken by spearfishing, although it is a wary fish.

REFERENCES: Bane and Bane 1971; Feder, Turner, and Limbaugh 1974; Follett 1976; Roedel and Ripley 1950; Russo 1975; Talent 1976.

## Soupfin shark
*Galeorhinus zyopterus* Jordan and Gilbert 1883

DESCRIPTION: The soupfin shark has a prominent *spiracle behind the eye*, the origin of the *second dorsal fin located directly above the origin of the equal-sized anal fin*, and a *very wide terminal lobe of the caudal fin*. The teeth have *slightly oblique, smooth-edged cusps with a deep notch on their outer margins and four to five denticles from notch to base*; they are similar in both jaws and number about U 36, L 34. Color is dark bluish gray to dark gray above, fading to white below. Average size is 165 cm (65 in) for males and 175 cm (69 in) for females. Maximum size is about 200 cm (79 in).

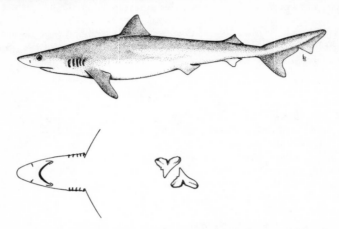

SIMILAR SPECIES: In the smoothhounds, the second dorsal fin is much larger than the anal fin, and it originates well ahead of the origin of the anal fin. The Pacific sharpnose shark has the origin of the second dorsal fin well behind the origin of the anal fin, and its teeth lack the basal denticles.

RANGE: It inhabits the western coast of North America and the western coast of South America (Chile and Peru). In North American waters it extends from British Columbia to Baja California. It is common off the California coast.

BIOLOGY: This is a coastal species usually found in 10–40 fathoms, except in the nursery areas, where females are found in less than 10 fathoms. It often strays into deeper waters, and there are recorded catches in 225 fathoms. It is an opportunistic feeder, often preying on sardines, flounders, rockfish, mackerel, and squid. It migrates north in summer and south in winter, but its movements are not well-defined. Off northern California males are most abundant, while females are most abundant off southern California.

REPRODUCTION: Development is ovoviviparous. Males mature at abut 155 cm (61 in) and females at about 170 cm (67 in). Mating takes place in the spring, and gestation lasts about twelve months. The pups measure about 35 cm (14 in) at birth. Litters range from six to fifty-two pups, the average being thirty-five pups. Some pups are found in Tomales and San Francisco bays, but the most important nursery areas appear to be south of Point Conception.

RELATION TO MAN: This is the most economically important of the west-coast sharks. In California there is a long-established market for fresh fillets and dried fins. Around 1940 an intensive fishery developed from British Columbia to California to take the soupfin shark for their vitamin A–rich livers, which brought as much as thirteen dollars a pound. Due to the taking of pregnant females and young in the nursery areas, the fishery was depleted by 1946.

FISHING: During the heyday of the shark liver fishery, gill nets of twenty-inch mesh were used in less than 80 fathoms. Best fishing is in areas 10–20 fathoms, with baits set on the bottom.

REFERENCES: Bane and Bane 1971; Ripley 1946; Roedel and Ripley 1950; Walford 1935.

NOTE: The soupfin shark possesses characteristics of both the Triakidae and the Carcharhinidae, demonstrating that these two families are closely related. It is often included in the Carcharhinidae.

## Family Carcharhinidae—Requiem Sharks

The requiem sharks, also known as carcharhinids, whaler sharks, or gray sharks, comprise one of the largest shark families. These are small to large sharks characterized by a flattened but not laterally expanded snout, eyes with a well-developed nictitating membrane, the fifth gill slit over or behind the origin of the pectoral fin, the first dorsal fin originating well ahead of the pelvic fins, well-developed precaudal pits, and a caudal fin measuring less than one-third the total length, its upper lobe about twice as long as the lower lobe. Their teeth are usually bladelike; characteristically, the upper teeth are broadly triangular with serrated edges, while the lower teeth are narrow and smooth-edged. In spite of the name "gray sharks," some are brown, bronze, blue, or olive. A few species are ovoviviparous but most are viviparous.

Most requiem sharks are voracious predators, feeding on crustaceans, mollusks, smaller sharks, rays, and numerous bony fishes. Usually the smaller species are found close to shore while the larger ones are found well offshore.

This is the most economically important shark family, as many species are utilized for food, oil, leather, shagreen, fish meal, and many other uses; others cause great losses to the longline fisheries by their predations on hooked fishes and to trawl fisheries with damage to nets. A few species are dangerous to man. Presently about sixty species are recognized, and about twenty-two are found in our area. For additional information on Carcharhinus see the excellent monograph by Garrick (1982).

1. Spiracles present .......................................................... 2
   Spiracles absent ........................................................... 3
2. Dorsal surfaces with dark blotches or bars, a prominent ridge on caudal peduncle sides .... *Galeocerdo cuvieri* (p. 125)
   Dorsal surfaces lacking markings or uniformly colored, lacking ridges on caudal peduncle sides .... *Paragaleus pectoralis* (p. 127)
3. Second dorsal fin at least three-fourths as high as first dorsal fin .... *Negaprion brevirostris* (p. 146)
   Second dorsal fin less than one-half as high as first dorsal fin......... 4
4. Midpoint of first dorsal fin base closer to pelvic fin origin than to pectoral axil (color bright blue in life, fading to gray after death) .... *Prionace glauca* (p. 147)
   Midpoint of first dorsal fin base closer to pectoral axil than to pelvic fin origin ............................................................... 5
5. First dorsal fin only slightly tapered toward its apex, which is broadly rounded; fins white-mottled (adults) or black-tipped (juveniles); if black-tipped, there are also black saddle blotches on caudal peduncle .... *Carcharhinus longimanus* (p. 137)
   First dorsal fin with a pointed or acutely rounded apex; not white-mottled; if black-tipped, without black saddle blotches on caudal peduncle ................................................................ 6

6. Interdorsal ridge present...................................... 7
   Interdorsal ridge absent ....................................... 13
7. Upper frontal teeth with strongly oblique cusps, a notch on outer margin and two to five coarse serrations from notch to base; snout much longer than mouth width (large green eyes in life) .... *Carcharhinus signatus* (p. 144)
   Upper frontal teeth without strongly oblique cusps, snout shorter or not much longer than mouth width ........................... 8
8. First dorsal fin origin over or anterior to pectoral axil, or at least closer to axil than to pectoral fin free rear tip.................... 9
   First dorsal fin origin over or posterior to pectoral fin free rear tip; if anterior, it is closer to free rear tip than to axil .................. 10
9. Usually fourteen teeth on each side of upper jaw, first dorsal fin almost twice as high as snout length (adults only), precaudal vertebrae 82 to 97 .... *Carcharhinus plumbeus* (p. 141)
   Usually 15 or more teeth on each side of upper jaw, first dorsal fin only slightly higher than snout length, precaudal vertebrae 101 to 110 .... *Carcharhinus altimus* (p. 128)
10. Inner margin of second dorsal fin free rear tip more than twice as long as height of fin, first dorsal fin origin posterior to pectoral fin free rear tip .... *Carcharhinus falciformis* (p. 132)
    Inner margin of second dorsal fin free rear tip less than twice as long as height of fin, first dorsal fin origin over or slightly anterior to pectoral fin free rear tip........................................ 11
11. Upper teeth with narrow cusps well delimited from their bases, not more than thirteen upper teeth and twelve lower teeth on each side of the jaw .... *Carcharhinus perezii* (p. 140)
    Upper teeth with broadly triangular cusps not well delimited from their bases, usually at least fourteen upper teeth and thirteen lower teeth on each side of the jaw .......................... 12
12. Height of second dorsal fin 1.5–2.3 percent of total length and 1.6–2.1 percent in length of rear tip, precaudal vertebrae 86 to 97 (inhabiting continental waters) .... *Carcharhinus obscurus* (p. 139)
    Height of second dorsal fin 2.1–3.3 percent of total length and 1.6–2.1 percent in length of rear tip, precaudal vertebrae 103–109 (inhabiting waters around oceanic islands) .... *Carcharhinus galapagensis* (p. 133)
13. Labial furrows present, at least three-fourths of eye diameter in length............................................... 14
    Labial furrows absent, or if present, less than one-half of eye diameter in length ......................................... 16
14. Total number of teeth on outer row of upper jaw twenty-seven to thirty, inhabiting eastern Pacific waters .... *Rhizoprionodon longurio* (p. 148)
    Total number of teeth on outer row of upper jaw twenty-three to thirty-seven, inhabiting western Atlantic waters................. 15
15. Precaudal vertebrae 58 to 66, inhabiting Atlantic and Gulf coasts of the U.S. and Mexico .... *Rhizoprionodon terraenovae* (p. 150)
    Precaudal vertebrae 66 to 75, inhabiting Caribbean waters south of 24° north latitude .... *Rhizoprionodon porosus* (p. 149)

16. Second dorsal fin originating over or posterior to the midpoint of anal fin base . . . . *Carcharhinus porosus* (p. 143)

Second dorsal fin originating well ahead of the midpoint of anal fin base . . . . . . . . . . . . . . . . . . . . . . . . . . . . . . . . . . . . . . . . . . . . . . . . . . 17

17. Upper teeth broadly triangular, lacking a notch on their outer margins, snout much shorter than mouth width . . . . *Carcharhinus leucas* (p. 135)

Upper teeth narrow, or, if of moderate width, with a notch on their outer margins, snout as long or longer than mouth width . . . . . . . . . 18

18. Fins conspicuously black-tipped . . . . . . . . . . . . . . . . . . . . . . . . . . . . . . 19

Fins unmarked or with only slightly dusky tips, not black-tipped . . . . . 20

19. First dorsal fin originating about the midpoint of pectoral fin inner margin; anal fin white . . . . *Carcharhinus limbatus* (p. 136)

First dorsal fin originating over or posterior to pectoral fin free rear tip; anal fin black-tipped (on specimens larger than 70 cm) . . . . *Carcharhinus brevipinna* (p. 130)

20. Upper and lower teeth similar, narrow, erect, and smooth-edged . . . . *Carcharhinus isodon* (p. 134)

Upper and lower teeth dissimilar; upper teeth oblique, with curved or notched outer margins, with serrated edges; lower teeth with finely serrated edges . . . . . . . . . . . . . . . . . . . . . . . . . . . . . . . . . . . . . . . . 21

21. Nostrils transversely located, snout tip with a small black spot surrounded by white (inhabiting the Gulf of California) . . . . *Carcharhinus velox* (p. 145)

Nostrils obliquely located, snout tip plain-colored or with a dark or dusky blotch . . . . . . . . . . . . . . . . . . . . . . . . . . . . . . . . . . . . . . . . . . . . . 22

22. Only eleven teeth on each side of lower jaw, snout tip with a dusky or black blotch . . . . *Carcharhinus acronotus* (p. 127)

Usually not less than thirteen teeth on each side of lower jaw, snout tip plain-colored . . . . *Carcharhinus brachyurus* (p. 129)

## Tiger shark
### *Galeocerdo cuvieri* (Lesueur) 1822

DESCRIPTION: The tiger shark is the easiest to identify of all the requiem sharks, because of its many diagnostic characteristics. It has a snout much shorter than the width of the mouth, *long labial furrows* around the corners of the mouth, *a visible but small spiracle* behind the eye, and a very long and pointed caudal fin with reinforcing ridges on the sides. The shape of the teeth is the best diagnostic characteristic; they have *curved cusps with finely serrated edges, a deep notch on the outer margin*, and are similar in both jaws. Teeth number U 9 to 12–0 or 1–9 to 12, L 9 to 12–0 or 1–9 to 12. Color varies from bluish or greenish gray to black above and from light gray to dirty yellow or white below. Juveniles and specimens up to 150–180 cm (59–71 in) have a mottled appearance; *their dorsal surfaces are covered with dark spots* on a lighter background. In larger sharks, the spots fuse together, forming vertical bars or *stripes producing a tigerlike appearance*, hence the name. In older sharks the bars tend to fade but often persist on the flanks or in the caudal region. A race from the southeastern Caribbean has been described as being shiny black above and immaculate white below. This is one of the largest sharks; adults 335–425 cm (11–14 ft) and 385–635 kg (850–1,400 lb) are common. The largest specimens are believed to exceed 550 cm (18 ft) and 900 kg (2,000 lb).

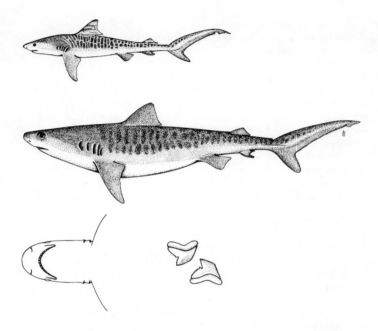

SIMILAR SPECIES: The characteristic teeth and markings distinguish the tiger shark from other requiem sharks.

RANGE: The tiger shark has worldwide distribution in tropical and warm-temperate waters. Off North America it is found from Cape Cod to Florida and the Gulf of Mexico and from southern California southward. It is common off the Carolinas, Georgia, Florida, and the Gulf of Mexico. It is one of the most abundant large sharks in the Caribbean region. Reports of tiger sharks straying far from their normal range are not uncommon.

BIOLOGY: This shark inhabits warm waters in both deep oceanic and shallow coastal regions. It is proverbially voracious and probably the most polyphagous of all sharks. The reported stomach contents of tiger sharks include: conchs, crabs, horseshoe crabs, spiny lobsters, squid, many species of bony fishes, smaller sharks, skates, rays, porpoises, turtles, marine birds, human remains, garbage, offal, and artifacts of all kinds. Although it appears to be a sluggish fish, it becomes very active and vigorous when stimulated by food.

REPRODUCTION: Development is ovoviviparous. Maturity is reached at about 290 cm (114 in). Gestation is believed to last slightly more than a year. The pups measure 68–85 cm (27–33 in) at birth. Litters are large, often comprising from thirty-five to fifty-five pups.

RELATION TO MAN: The tiger shark is of commercial value in the West Indies, where the flesh is eaten either fresh or salted. The skin can be processed into very high quality leather. This is considered one of the most dangerous sharks and is believed to be responsible for many casualties, especially in the West Indies.

FISHING: It is classed as a gamefish, and it affords the angler a lively sport because of its great size and strength. Large hooks and baits are usually used.

REFERENCES: Bigelow and Schroeder 1948; Compagno 1978; Dodrill and Gilmore 1978; Gudger 1948*b*, 1949; S. Springer 1949, 1963.

*Paragaleus pectoralis* (Garman) 1906

DESCRIPTION: This shark is characterized by a snout longer than the width of the mouth, *labial furrows* around the mouth, a visible spiracle behind the eye, and a first dorsal fin originating over the free rear tips of the pectoral fins. The upper teeth are oblique and smooth-edged, with straight inner margins and notched outer margins; *the outer margins have three to four denticles from notch to base*. The frontal lower teeth are erect and symmetrical; the rest are similar to the upper teeth. Teeth number U 12 or 13–3–12 or 13, L 13 to 15–3–13 to 15. Color is olive gray above, paler below. Average size is about 65 cm (26 in); it grows to about 100 cm (39 in).

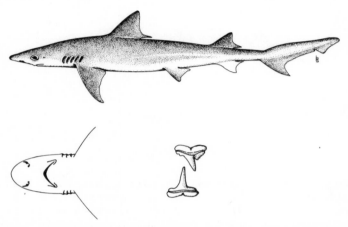

SIMILAR SPECIES: The night shark lacks the pronounced labial furrows and the visible spiracle.

RANGE: This species has been reported from the west coast of Africa between latitudes of 16°N and 9°S including the Cape Verde Islands, the east coast of Africa, and the New England coast. There is only one American record; consequently it must be considered a very rare visitor or a rare stray in our area.

BIOLOGY: This small shark inhabits shallow tropical waters. Nothing else is known of its habits.

REPRODUCTION: No data available.

RELATION TO MAN: None.

FISHING: No data available.

REFERENCES: Bass, D'Aubrey, and Kistnasamy 1975*b*; Bigelow and Schroeder 1948; Garman 1913; Krefft 1968*b*.

## Blacknose shark
*Carcharhinus acronotus* (Poey) 1860

DESCRIPTION: The blacknose shark has a snout as long as, or longer than, the width of the mouth and a first dorsal fin originating over or behind the free rear tips of the pectoral fin. The *upper teeth have narrow, oblique cusps strongly notched on their outer margins*, with *serrated edges* that become progressively coarser towards the bases. The lower teeth have narrow, erect, symmetrical cusps, with more finely serrated edges than the upper teeth. Teeth number U 12 or 13–1 or 2–12 or 13, L 11 or 12–1–11 or 12. Color is yellowish or greenish gray, yellowish brown, or brown above; undersides are yellowish or paler. The tip of the second dorsal fin is dusky or black. There is a *dusky blotch at the tip of the snout*, distinct and dark in the young, diffuse and dusky in adults. Average size is 125 cm (49 in) and 10 kg (22 lb). It grows to about 140 cm (55 in).

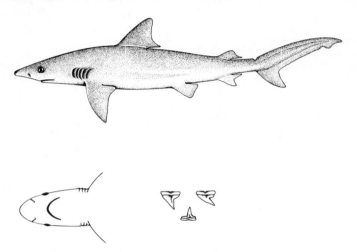

SIMILAR SPECIES: The bull shark has a shorter snout, and its teeth are not deeply notched. The smalltail shark has a second dorsal fin originating farther back, over or slightly behind the midpoint of the anal fin base, and lacks the dusky blotch on the nose. Other similar requiem sharks have an interdorsal ridge or lack the strongly notched teeth.

RANGE: It inhabits the western Atlantic from North Carolina to southeastern Brazil, including the Gulf of Mexico. It is abundant in coastal waters from the Carolinas to Florida and the Gulf of Mexico during the summer and fall.

BIOLOGY: It is a coastal species that feeds on small fishes. It is often preyed upon by larger sharks. Nothing else is known about its habits.

REPRODUCTION: Development is viviparous. Sexual maturity is reached at about 100 cm (39 in). Litters consist of three to six pups, which measure about 50 cm (20 in) at birth. Off Florida its birth season is January through April; off the Carolinas it gives birth in the summer; in the Gulf in May and early June.

RELATION TO MAN: It is occasionally marketed throughout its range.

FISHING: It is often caught in gill nets set close to the shore.

REFERENCES: Bigelow and Schroeder 1948;Böhlke and Chaplin 1970; Clark and von Schmidt 1965; Compagno 1978; Nichols 1917.


## Bignose shark
*Carcharhinus altimus* (Springer) 1950

DESCRIPTION: The bignose shark has a *snout as long as*, or longer than, the width of the mouth, a first dorsal fin originating over the pectoral axil, or behind it almost to the midpoint of the inner pectoral margin, and a marked interdorsal ridge. The upper teeth have broadly triangular, overlapping cusps with serrated edges; the front teeth are large and erect, while those on the sides become progressively oblique. The lower teeth have narrow, erect cusps with finely serrated edges and broad bases. Teeth number U 14 to 16–1 or 2–14 to 16, L 14 or 15–1–14 or 15. Color is gray above and whitish below, with the lower sides of the pectoral tips being darker. Average size is about 240 cm (94 in); it grows to at least 282 cm (111 in).

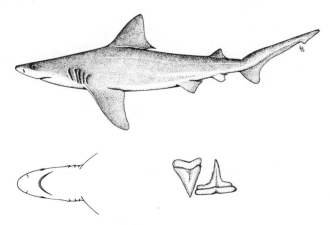

SIMILAR SPECIES: The sandbar shark has a shorter snout and a higher first dorsal fin. The Galapagos shark has a shorter snout. The silky and dusky sharks have the origin of the first dorsal fin over the free rear tips of the pectoral fins. The oceanic whitetip shark has pectorals and first dorsal fin with broadly rounded tips.

RANGE: The bignose shark inhabits tropical and subtropical waters of the Atlantic, Pacific, and Indian oceans. It is common around the Bahamas and the West Indies and an unusual catch off South Florida.

BIOLOGY: This is a bottom-dwelling shark found in the deeper waters of the continental shelf in tropical and subtropical areas. It is usually caught at depths of 50–235 fathoms, but it occasionally visits the upper layers at night. It is known to feed on chimaeras, smaller sharks, squid, and octopuses.

REPRODUCTION: Development is viviparous. Maturity is probably reached at about 200 cm (79 in). The pups are born in the summer and may reach 75 cm (30 in) at birth. The litters range from three to eleven pups, with seven being the usual number.

RELATION TO MAN: It is extensively used for oil, fish meal, and animal feed throughout the Caribbean region.

FISHING: It is usually caught in longlines.

REFERENCES: Bass, D'Aubrey, and Kistnasamy 1973; Compagno 1978; S. Springer 1950b.

## Narrowtooth shark

*Carcharhinus brachyurus* (Günther) 1870

DESCRIPTION: The narrowtooth shark has a snout about as long as the width of the mouth, a first dorsal fin originating over or slightly anterior to the free rear tips of the pectoral fins, and a second dorsal fin originating slightly behind the origin of the anal fin, and it lacks an interdorsal ridge. Small specimens have upper teeth with erect symmetrical cusps with finely serrated edges; large specimens have narrowly triangular to scythe-shaped, finely serrated cusps, which become increasingly oblique toward the mouth corners. The lower teeth have erect or slightly oblique cusps with very fine serrated edges. Teeth number about U 14 to 16–1 to 3–14 to 16, L 14 or 15–1 to 3–14 or 15. Color is brownish gray above, with a band of the upper color extending downward into the lighter sides. The fins may have darker edges or slightly dusky tips but *lack conspicuous black markings*. The species is known to reach 292 cm (115 in).

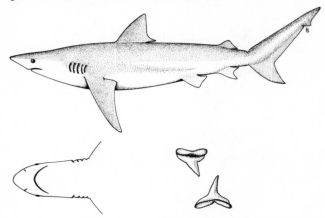

SIMILAR SPECIES: The blacktip shark and the spinner shark have fins with conspicuous black markings and longer gill slits. The characteristic teeth of the narrowtooth shark distinguish it from other sharks lacking an interdorsal ridge.

RANGE: This shark has worldwide distribution in subtropical to warm-temperate coastal waters. It has been reported from the South Atlantic, the Indian Ocean, and the eastern Pacific. It appears to be absent from the western North Atlantic. In our area it has been reported only off southern California, where it is rare.

BIOLOGY: It is believed to be a coastal species. It has been reported to feed on bottom fishes. Its habits are poorly known.

REPRODUCTION: Development is viviparous. Males mature at about 210 cm (82 in); the size of females at maturity has not been reported. Pups are born at 60–70 cm (23–27 in). Litters usually range from thirteen to twenty pups.

RELATION TO MAN: It is too scarce to be of economic importance. It has been implicated in attacks on swimmers.

FISHING: It is usually caught in shallow-water trawls.

REFERENCES: Bass, D'Aubrey, and Kistnasamy 1973; Bigelow and Schroeder 1948; Garrick 1982; Kato, Springer, and Wagner 1967.

### Spinner shark
*Carcharhinus brevipinna* (Müller and Henle) 1841

DESCRIPTION: The spinner shark is characterized by a snout as long as, or longer than, the width of the mouth, the first dorsal fin originating over or posterior to the free rear tips of the pectoral fin, and short upper labial furrows. The teeth have narrow, triangular, erect cusps and broad bases in both jaws; the *upper teeth have finely serrated edges*, and the *lower teeth have smooth edges*. Young specimens may have smooth-edged upper teeth. Teeth number U 16–2 or 3–16,

L 15 or 16–1–15 or 16. Color is gray or bronze above and white below, with a band of gray extending downward over the lighter undersides from the level of the pectoral fins to over the pelvic fins. Young specimens of less than 70 cm (28 in) have unmarked fins. Older ones have the second dorsal, anal, pectorals, and the lower lobe of the caudal fin *black-tipped*; the other fins may or may not be black-tipped. Average size is 196 cm (77 in) and 56 kg (123 lb). Maximum recorded size is 278 cm (109 in).

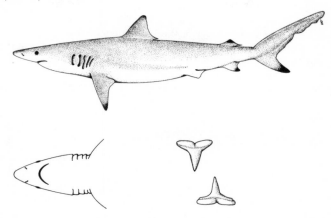

SIMILAR SPECIES: This species is often confused with the blacktip shark, which has a stouter body, lower teeth with finely serrated edges, a more anterior first dorsal fin origin, and a white anal fin. The finetooth shark has a shorter snout, smooth-edged upper teeth, the first dorsal fin originating over the axil of the pectoral fin, and unmarked fins.

RANGE: The spinner shark has almost circumtropical distribution, having been reported from the Atlantic, Indian, and western Pacific oceans and the Mediterranean Sea. It has not been reported from the eastern Pacific. In North American waters it ranges from North Carolina to Florida and the Gulf of Mexico, being common throughout its range during the warmer months.

BIOLOGY: This is a fast-moving shark common in inshore and offshore waters. It is often seen in schools, leaping out of the water while spinning. The reasons for the leaping behavior are not known, but it is said that a feeding shark charges a school of small fish from below and with a spinning motion, often breaking the surface. Its food consist of small schooling fishes, squid, small sharks, and rays. It appears to migrate to offshore waters in winter.

REPRODUCTION: Development is viviparous. Males mature at about 170 cm (67 in) and females at about 180 cm (71 in). The pups measure 60–75 cm (24–30 in) at birth; litters usually consist of six to twelve pups, which are born in early summer.

RELATION TO MAN: It is often marketed fresh. Although one attack on a swimmer has been attributed to it, it is not usually considered dangerous to man because it feeds on small fishes.

FISHING: It is generally caught on longlines and rod and reel. It offers some challenge to the sports fisherman by putting up a determined fight.

REFERENCES: Bass, D'Aubrey, and Kistnasamy 1973; Bigelow and Schroeder 1948; Branstetter 1981; Clark and von Schmidt 1965; Compagno 1978; Garrick 1982.

# Silky shark
## *Carcharhinus falciformis* (Bibron) 1841

DESCRIPTION: The silky shark is characterized by a snout shorter than the width of the mouth, a low sloping first dorsal fin originating behind the free rear tips of the pectoral fins, an interdorsal ridge, and a *second dorsal fin with a very long posterior free rear tip* (about 2¼ times the vertical height of the fin). The upper teeth are broadly triangular, with serrated edges and weakly *notched outer margins* and become increasingly oblique toward the corners of the mouth; their *serrations are larger at the bases* of the teeth than at the tips. The lower teeth have narrow cusps and broad bases and are symmetrical, erect, and smooth-edged. Teeth number U 14 to 16–1 to 3–14 to 16, L 14 to 17–1–14 to 17. Color is brown or bronze above and lighter below, fading to gray after death. Average size is 200–240 cm (79–94 in); maximum size is about 330 cm (10.8 ft).

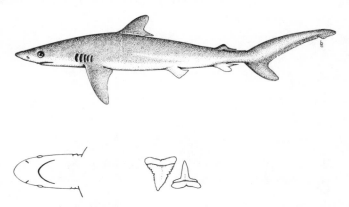

SIMILAR SPECIES: The dusky shark has a blunter snout, the free rear tip of its second dorsal is never more than twice the height of the fin, and its upper teeth are uniformly serrated. The night shark has a much longer snout.

RANGE: It inhabits warm-tropical and subtropical waters throughout the world, although it is not restricted to oceanic waters. Off North America it ranges from Delaware to Florida and the Gulf of Mexico and from Baja California southward. It is common from South Carolina to Florida and the Gulf of Mexico.

BIOLOGY: The silky shark is found in warm waters of the continental slopes and beyond, often straying into coastal waters. It is a fast-moving, surface-dwelling species, which feeds on squid and small fishes. Small specimens are sometimes found with schools of small tuna.

REPRODUCTION: Development is viviparous. Maturity is probably reached at about 230 cm (91 in). The gestation period is unknown. Litters range from six to fourteen pups, which measure 75–80 cm (30–31 in) at birth.

RELATION TO MAN: It is edible and occasionally marketed.

FISHING: It is caught on longlines or by fishing on the surface.

REFERENCES: Bane 1966; Bass, D'Aubrey, and Kistnasamy 1973; Bigelow and Schroeder 1948; Compagno 1978; Garrick 1982; Garrick, Backus, and Gibbs 1964; Gilbert and Schlernitzauer 1966.

# Galapagos shark
## *Carcharhinus galapagensis* (Snodgrass and Heller) 1905

DESCRIPTION: The Galapagos shark has a snout shorter than the width of the mouth, a first dorsal fin that is shorter than twice the snout length and that originates over or posterior to *the midpoint* of the inner margin of the pectoral fins, and a marked interdorsal ridge. The upper teeth have broadly triangular cusps with serrated edges; the lower teeth are symmetrical and erect, with microscopically fine serrations. Teeth usually number U 14–1–14, L 14–1–14. Color is dark gray above and white below, without any fin markings. It grows to at least 300 cm (117 in).

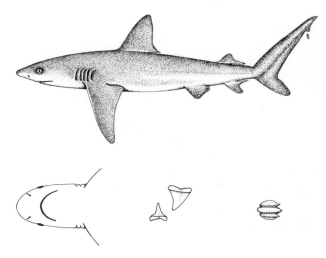

SIMILAR SPECIES:The dusky shark is very similar and very difficult to separate from the Galapagos shark without direct comparison. The dusky shark has a more sloping first dorsal fin and a lower second dorsal fin 1.5–2.3 percent of total length (2.1–3.3 percent of total length in the Galapagos shark) and fewer precaudal vertebrae (86 to 97 in the dusky shark, 103 to 109 in the Galapagos shark). The silky shark has a first dorsal fin with a more rounded apex; this fin originates behind the free rear tip of the pectoral fin. The sandbar shark has a higher first dorsal fin originating farther forward. The reef shark has a more sloping first dorsal fin, and its second dorsal fin has a much shorter free rear tip. The bignose shark has a longer snout.

RANGE: The Galapagos shark appears to be circumtropical around oceanic islands, as it has been reported from the islands of the tropical Pacific (Hawaii, Revillagigedo, Clipperton, Cocos, and Galapagos), the tropical Atlantic (Bermuda, Virgin Islands, Ascension, and Saint Helena), and the Indian Ocean (Walters Shoal), with large adults occasionally being found in the high seas or straying into continental shores. The limits of its distribution are not well-defined due to confusion with similar species. It probably strays into our area.

BIOLOGY: This shark inhabits the waters around tropical oceanic islands, with large adults also found in the high seas and occasionally straying into continental shores. It is usually very abundant around oceanic islands, but it appears to be replaced in continental waters by other species, such as the dusky shark. It feeds on groupers, triggerfishes, moray eels, flounders, octopuses, and squid. It generally stays in deep water during daytime, entering shallow rocky shores at dusk or night.

REPRODUCTION: Development is viviparous. The size at maturity is not known; specimens 240 cm (94 in) are still immature. An 80-cm (31-in) specimen shows an unhealed umbilical scar, indicating a recent birth. Litters of nine to sixteen pups have been reported.

RELATION TO MAN: The Galapagos shark is of no economic importance because of its usually remote habitat. The flesh is of excellent quality. One fatal attack in the Virgin Islands has been attributed to it. It has been described by divers in the eastern Pacific as being very aggressive; however, in Ascension Island it is not regarded as dangerous by divers, who leave the water only when the really large ones appear.

FISHING: Juveniles are very easily taken with hook and line around rocky shores at night.

REFERENCES: Bass, D'Aubrey, and Kistnasamy 1973; Garrick 1982; Kato, Springer, and Wagner 1967; Limbaugh 1963; Snodgrass and Heller 1905; Tester 1969.

## Finetooth shark
### *Carcharhinus isodon* (Valenciennes) 1839

DESCRIPTION: The finetooth shark has a snout shorter than the width of the mouth and a first dorsal fin originating over the free rear tips of the pectoral fin. The teeth have *slender, erect, smooth-edged cusps* and broad bases; they number U 13 to 15–1–13 to 15, L 13 to 15–1 to 3–13 to 15, and are *similar in both jaws.* Color is bluish gray or bronze above and white below; the *fins are unmarked.* Average size is 150 cm (59 in) and 14 kg (31 lb). Maximum reported size is 189 cm (74 in).

SIMILAR SPECIES: The lemon shark has a second dorsal fin that is almost as large as the first. The blacktip shark has finely serrated teeth and black-tipped fins. The spinner shark has upper teeth with finely serrated bases and black-tipped fins.

RANGE: The finetooth shark inhabits the Atlantic coast of North America from New York to Florida and the Gulf of Mexico. It is common off South Carolina in late summer.

BIOLOGY: This is a coastal species that inhabits shallow waters 2–3 fathoms or less and feeds on small fishes. Gill net catches suggest schooling behavior.

REPRODUCTION: Development is viviparous. Males reach maturity at about 120 cm (47 in); females mature at about 140 cm (55 in). Litters consist of one to six pups, which measure about 48 cm (19 in) at birth.

RELATION TO MAN: It is of local economic importance, as large numbers are caught in gill nets set close to shore. It is marketed fresh.

FISHING: It is caught in gill nets or accidentally in shrimp trawls in shallow water. Specimens are taken occasionally by rod and reel in coastal waters of the northern Gulf of Mexico.

REFERENCES: Bigelow and Schroeder 1948; Branstetter and Shipp 1980; Compagno 1978.

## Bull shark
### *Carcharhinus leucas* (Valenciennes) 1841

DESCRIPTION: The bull shark has an *extremely short snout* (much shorter than the width of the mouth), a first dorsal fin with a pointed apex, and a second dorsal fin much smaller than the first. The upper teeth have broadly triangular, *heavily serrated cusps*; the lower teeth have narrow, triangular, finely serrated cusps on a broad base. The anterior teeth are erect and symmetrical, while those on the sides are slightly oblique. Teeth number U 12 to 14–1–12 to 14, L 12 or 13–1 or 2–12 or 13. Color is pale to dark gray above and white below. The fins are black-tipped in the young. Average size for males is 225 cm (88 in) and 95 kg (209 lb); average size for females is 240 cm (94 in) and 130 kg (285 lb). The species is said to grow to 350 cm (11.5 ft) and 230 kg (500 lb).

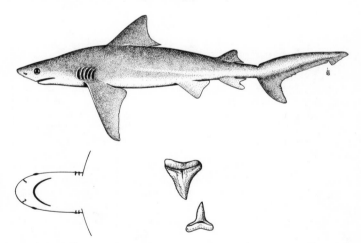

SIMILAR SPECIES: The oceanic whitetip shark has similar snout and teeth, but the tips of the first dorsal and pectoral fins are broadly rounded. The lemon shark has a second dorsal fin that is almost as large as the first and has a yellowish color. The tiger shark has notched teeth. The so-called Lake Nicaragua shark (*C. nica-*

*raguensis*) and the majority of recorded specimens of Ganges shark (*C. gangeticus*) are now considered synonymous with the bull shark.

RANGE: The bull shark is cosmopolitan throughout warm seas. In North American waters it ranges from New York to Florida and the Gulf of Mexico and from southern California to the Gulf of California. It is rare off New York and along the California coast. It is common off southeastern Florida and in the Gulf of Mexico.

BIOLOGY: This is a sluggish shallow-water species commonly found in estuaries, harbors, and creeks. It enters fresh water, rarely penetrating hundreds of miles upstream. It feeds on other sharks, rays, numerous bony fishes, mollusks, and crustaceans. It is one of the most common requiem sharks in the Gulf of Mexico, preying heavily on small sandbar sharks.

REPRODUCTION: Development is viviparous. Maturity is reached at about 200 cm (79 in). In the Gulf of Mexico mating takes place in June and July; gestation probably lasts ten to eleven months, and the pups are born in April, May, and June. In warmer waters mating and parturition occur year-round. Pups measure 75 cm (29 in) at birth. The low-salinity estuaries of the Gulf Coast are important nursery areas for the bull shark.

RELATION TO MAN: The flesh is edible but is primarily used for fish meal; the hide is of good quality. This is a dangerous shark, responsible for many attacks on bathers; most freshwater attacks are attributed to it. It is often kept in aquaria, surviving at most one or two years in captivity.

FISHING: Primarily caught on longlines. It will take almost any bait, but it seems to prefer fresh shark or ray.

REFERENCES: Bass, D'Aubrey, and Kistnasamy 1973; Bigelow and Schroeder 1948, 1961; Compagno 1978; Garrick 1982; N. H. Jensen 1976; Kritzler and Wood 1960; Schwartz 1959, 1960; Thornson 1976; Thornson, Watson, and Cowan 1966; Vorenberg 1962.


## Blacktip shark
*Carcharhinus limbatus* (Valenciennes) 1841

DESCRIPTION: The blacktip shark has a snout about as long as the width of the mouth and a first dorsal fin originating about the midpoint of the inner margin of the pectoral fin. The teeth have narrow, triangular, erect cusps with *finely serrated edges* and broad bases; they number U 14 to 16–1 to 3–14 to 16, L 13 to 16–1 to 3–13 to 16, and are similar in both jaws. Color is dark gray, bluish gray, or dusky bronze above, white or yellowish below, with a well-marked *band of the upper gray extending downward along the lighter sides* from the level of the pectoral fins to the pelvic fins. The dorsal and pectoral fins and the lower lobe of the caudal fin are *black-tipped*, although sometimes these markings may fade with growth. The *anal fin is white*. Average size is about 150 cm (59 in) and 18 kg (40 lb). Specimens from our area seldom reach 180 cm (71 in); specimens from other areas have been reported to reach 255 cm (100 in).

SIMILAR SPECIES: The lack of an interdorsal ridge and the presence of black-tipped fins and erect, symmetrical teeth with finely serrated edges distinguish the blacktip shark from the other requiem sharks in the area, except for the spinner shark. The spinner shark has the origin of the first dorsal fin over or posterior to the free rear tips of the pectoral fins, smooth-edged teeth in the lower jaw, and a black-tipped anal fin in specimens larger than 70 cm (28 in).

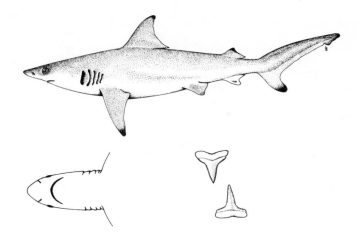

RANGE: The blacktip shark is circumtropical. In North America it ranges from New England, where it is rare, to Florida and the Gulf of Mexico and from Baja California southward. It is very abundant off South Carolina, Georgia, Florida, and the northern Gulf Coast in summertime.

BIOLOGY: This species inhabits shallow coastal waters and surface offshore waters. It is a fast-moving shark often seen leaping and spinning out of the water. It feeds on squid, menhaden and other schooling fishes, and rays. It migrates to deeper water in winter, often in schools. Although it is a common species, relatively little is known about its habits.

REPRODUCTION: Development is viviparous. Males reach maturity at about 135 cm (53 in) and females at about 155 cm (61 in). Gestation lasts ten to eleven months. The young are born in late spring or early summer and measure 55–70 cm (22–28 in) at birth. Litters usually consist of four to six pups. Young pups are common in the surf zone in summer.

RELATION TO MAN: It is used for fish meal and marketed fresh, and its skin is used for leather. It has been implicated in attacks on swimmers. It is mainly fished for sport.

FISHING: It takes both surface and bottom baits and provides spectacular sport on light tackle, often leaping out of the water. In spite of its sporting qualities, it is not classified as a gamefish.

REFERENCES: Bass, D'Aubrey, and Kistnasamy 1973; Bigelow and Schroeder 1948; Compagno 1978; Garrick 1982.


## Oceanic whitetip shark
*Carcharhinus longimanus* (Poey) 1861

DESCRIPTION: The oceanic whitetip shark is characterized by a snout shorter than, or long as, the width of the mouth, a *first dorsal fin* with a *broad and evenly rounded apex, very long pectoral fins* (as long as, or longer than, the distance from the tip of the snout to the last gill slit), the free rear tip of the anal fin that almost reaches to the base of the caudal fin, and a weak (occasionally absent) interdorsal ridge. The upper teeth are broadly triangular with serrated edges and mostly erect; the lower teeth have narrow, serrated cusps and broad bases. Teeth number U 13 or 14–1 or 2–13 or 14, L 13 to 15–1 to 3–13 to 15. Color varies from olive gray to brown above and from dirty white to yellow below. Usually, the dorsal fins, pectorals, and caudal lobes are *white-tipped*, hence the name. The amount of white pigmentation is highly variable and occasionally completely absent. Embryos and juveniles have the pectoral, dorsal, and pelvic fins black-tipped. Average size is 150–250 cm (59–98 in) and 35–70 kg (80–150 lb). Unusual specimens may reach 350 cm (11.5 ft); exceptional females are said to grow even larger.

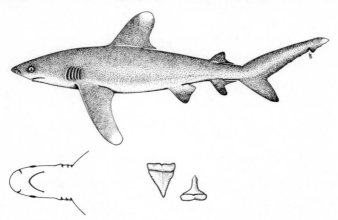

SIMILAR SPECIES: The bull shark has a similar rounded snout, but it lacks the evenly rounded fins and an interdorsal ridge.

RANGE: The oceanic whitetip shark is circumtropical. In North America it ranges from Georges Bank to Florida and the Gulf of Mexico and from southern California to the tropics. It is common in the warm, deep waters of the Gulf Stream and rare off the west coast.

BIOLOGY: This is a strictly pelagic species, found wherever the temperature exceeds 22°C (72°F) and the depth exceeds 100 fathoms, very seldom straying into shallower areas. It is one of the most common sharks in warm oceanic water. Although it appears to be a sluggish shark, it is known to feed on squid, tunas, barracuda, white marlin, and other fast-moving fishes. It appears equally active by day or night. There seems to be segregation of the sexes in certain areas.

REPRODUCTION: Development is viviparous. Maturity is probably reached at about 180 cm (71 in). The pups are born at a length of 65–75 cm (26–30 in) during spring and summer. Litters consist of five to fifteen pups.

RELATION TO MAN: This shark often causes considerable damage to the catch in swordfish and tuna longline fisheries. The meat is marketed in the Caribbean. The species is considered dangerous to man.

FISHING: The oceanic whitetip is a very cautious fish, being suspicious of baited hooks, making many passes at the bait before taking it. When hooked, it puts up a feeble resistance and can be boated with relative ease.

REFERENCES: Backus, Springer, and Arnold 1956; Bass, D'Aubrey, and Kistnasamy 1973; Bigelow and Schroeder 1948; Bullis 1961; Compagno 1978; Garrick 1982; Gubanov 1978; Hubbs 1951; Schuck and Clark 1951.

## Dusky shark
*Carcharhinus obscurus* (Lesueur) 1818

DESCRIPTION: The dusky shark has a snout shorter than, or as long as, the width of the mouth; a sloping first dorsal fin originating over or slightly anterior to the free rear tips of the pectoral fins, and a marked interdorsal ridge. The upper teeth are broadly triangular with serrated edges; the front teeth are nearly erect, the others slightly oblique. The lower teeth have narrow, nearly erect cusps with more finely serrated edges than the upper teeth. Teeth number U 14 or 15–1 or 2–14 or 15, L 13 to 15–1 or 2–13 to 15. Color is gray or bluish gray above, white below. Average size is 305 cm (10 ft) and 160–180 kg (352–396 lb). Maximum size is about 364 cm (11.9 ft).

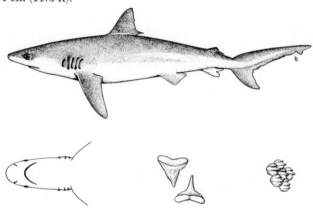

SIMILAR SPECIES: The sandbar shark, with which the dusky is often confused, has a much higher and anteriorly placed first dorsal fin, with its origin over the pectoral axil. The bull shark lacks an interdorsal ridge. The silky shark has the origin of the first dorsal fin posterior to the free rear tips of the pectoral fins, and a second dorsal fin free rear tip twice as long as the fin height. The cusps of its teeth are delimited from the bases. The oceanic whitetip shark has the first dorsal fin and the pectoral fins with broadly rounded tips; its second dorsal fin reaches almost to the base of the caudal fin. The bignose shark has a more anterior origin of the first dorsal fin, over the pectoral axil. The Caribbean reef shark has a more anterior origin of the first dorsal fin over the pectoral axil and has narrower upper teeth.

The very similar Galapagos shark has not been reported from the continental waters of North America. It inhabits waters off oceanic islands, while the dusky inhabits continental coastlines. Large adults found in the open ocean should be examined carefully. The Galapagos shark has an erect, higher second dorsal fin (2.1–3.3 percent of the total length, compared with 1.5–2.3 percent of total length in the dusky shark) and a higher number of precaudal vertebrae, usually 103 to 109 (86 to 97 in the dusky shark).

RANGE: The dusky shark has been reported from numerous localities throughout the world. It is probably cosmopolitan in warm and temperate continental waters. In North America it ranges from Georges Bank, where it is rare, to Florida and the Gulf of Mexico and from southern California to the Gulf of California.

BIOLOGY: This is one of the larger species inhabiting continental waters; it is found from inshore waters to the outer reaches of the continental shelf. It is a polyphagous shark; reported stomach contents include flatfishes, groupers, jacks, barracudas, other sharks, rays, mullet, eels, squid, octopods, starfishes, and numerous reef fishes. The dusky shark is known to move southward in winter and northward in summer along the east coast.

REPRODUCTION: Development is viviparous. Males reach sexual maturity at about 290 cm (114 in); females at about 300 cm (118 in). It gives birth throughout its range and over a long season. Litters usually consist of six to fourteen pups, which measure 85–100 cm (33–39 in) at birth. The gestation period is believed to be about sixteen months.

RELATION TO MAN: This shark is often marketed fresh throughout its range. Its hide is often used for leather. Its size, habits, and abundance make it potentially dangerous to swimmers or divers, although only a few attacks on man have been attributed to it. It is sought by sportsmen for its fighting qualities, although it is not classed as a gamefish.

FISHING: It is most often caught with baits set in deep water. Because of its large size and endurance it will give the sportsman a hard fight.

REFERENCES: Bass, D'Aubrey, and Kistnasamy 1973; Bigelow and Schroeder 1948; Garrick 1982; Huish and Benedict 1977; S. Springer 1946; Tibbo and Mc-Kenzie 1963.

## Caribbean reef shark
*Carcharhinus perezii* (Poey) 1876 (= *C. springeri*)

DESCRIPTION: The Caribbean reef shark has a snout shorter than the width of the mouth, a first dorsal fin originating over the free rear tips of the pectoral fins, a second dorsal fin with a *very short free rear tip* (its inner margin is shorter than or equal to the height of the fin), and an interdorsal ridge. The upper teeth have *narrow cusps with serrated edges and broad bases*; the front two to four teeth on each side of the jaw are erect; the others are increasingly oblique. The lower teeth have narrow, erect, triangular cusps with serrated edges and broad bases. Teeth number U 12 or 13–1 or 2–12 or 13, L 12 or 13–1–12 or 13. Color is grayish brown to olive gray above, and white to yellow below. Average size is 160 cm (63 in); it grows to 295 cm (115 in).

SIMILAR SPECIES: The dusky shark has broadly triangular, anterior upper teeth, and the free rear tip of its second dorsal fin is much longer (nearly twice the fin height). The silky shark has teeth with larger serrations at the bases than at the cusps, and the free rear tip of its second dorsal fin is much longer (about twice the height of the fin). The sandbar shark has the first dorsal fin originating more anteriorly, over the pectoral axil. The bignose shark has a longer snout (its length greater than the width of the mouth) and has broadly triangular teeth. The Galapagos shark has a more erect first dorsal fin, a second dorsal fin with a longer free rear tip, and more symmetrical upper teeth.

RANGE: The Caribbean reef shark inhabits the southeast coast of Florida, the Caribbean Sea, and the western Atlantic south to Brazil. There are few reliable records from the Gulf of Mexico, perhaps because of confusion with similar species. It is one of the most abundant sharks around the Bahamas and the Antilles.

BIOLOGY: This is a bottom-dwelling species that inhabits shallow coastal waters, usually being found around coral reef areas in less than 15 fathoms. Its diet is not known, but it probably feeds on fishes and rays. It is capable of lying motionless on the bottom like a nurse shark. Under certain conditions it also enters caves, lying motionless or "sleeping" on the bottom for a few hours. This behavior is not fully understood.

REPRODUCTION: Development is viviparous. The pups are probably born at 60–75 cm (24–30 in). Litters of four to six pups have been reported. Very little is known about the species' reproductive processes.

RELATION TO MAN: It is marketed throughout its range, usually salted. It is also used for fish meal, oil (liver), and leather. It has been implicated in shark attacks on humans.

FISHING: It is caught mainly on longlines throughout its range.

REFERENCES: Bigelow and Schroeder 1944, 1948; Böhlke and Chaplin 1970; Compagno 1978; Garrick 1982; Randall 1968.

## Sandbar shark
*Carcharhinus plumbeus* (Nardo) 1827 (= *C. milberti*)

DESCRIPTION: The sandbar shark is characterized by a snout shorter than the width of the mouth; by a *large first dorsal* fin originating *over* the axil of the pectoral fin, its height equal to or greater than twice the snout length (embryos and young specimens have slightly lower first dorsal fins); and by the presence of an interdorsal ridge. The upper teeth have broadly triangular cusps with finely serrated edges; the frontal teeth are erect, and the others are oblique with curved margins. The lower teeth have narrow, triangular, erect cusps with more finely serrated edges than the upper teeth. Teeth number U 14 to 16–1 or 2–14 to 16, L 14 to 16–1 or 2–14 to 16. Its *widely spaced, non-overlapping dermal denticles without definite teeth on their free edges are also diagnostic* (similar species have dermal denticles with definite teeth on their free edges). Color is bluish gray, brownish gray, bronze, or brown above and paler or whitish below. Average size is about 200 cm (78 in) and 52 kg (114 lb) for males, and 208 cm (82 in) and 66 kg (145 lb) for females. Maximum recorded size is 240 cm (94 in).

SIMILAR SPECIES: The dusky shark has the origin of the first dorsal fin placed farther back over the free rear tips of the pectoral fins. The bignose shark has a longer snout (its length is equal to or greater than the width of the mouth) and has a smaller first dorsal fin (its height is less than 10 percent of the shark's total length). The bull shark has a similar snout but lacks the interdorsal ridge, and its dermal denticles have definite teeth on their free edges.

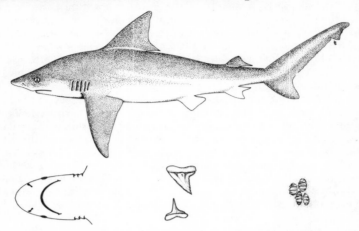

RANGE: The sandbar shark has been reported from widely spaced areas throughout the world, indicating a cosmopolitan distribution. In North America it ranges from New England to Florida and the Gulf of Mexico. It is common from South Carolina to northern Florida and in the eastern Gulf of Mexico.

BIOLOGY: This is a common inhabitant of shallow coastal waters and estuaries. It is a bottom-dwelling species most common in 10–30 fathoms but occasionally found in 100–135 fathoms. It is seldom seen at the surface except in nursery areas. Although it lives in estuarine areas, it does not penetrate fresh water. It is an opportunistic feeder, preying on numerous species of crustaceans, mollusks, and small fishes. It tends to segregate by sex; large females are abundant in shallow water along the nursery areas in summer. It is a migratory species, moving to the northern parts of the range in summer and to the southern parts in winter. Young sandbar sharks are heavily preyed upon by tiger sharks and bull sharks.

REPRODUCTION: Development is viviparous. Maturity is reached at about 183 cm (72 in). Mating takes place in spring or early summer. Gestation is believed to last about nine to twelve months. The primary nursery areas in North America are shallow coastal waters and estuaries from Long Island to Cape Canaveral, with a secondary nursery area along the northern coast of the Gulf of Mexico. The young are born from March to early August and measure about 60 cm (24 in) at birth, being somewhat smaller in the northern parts of the range. Litters range from one to fourteen pups, with nine the usual number. The young remain in estuarine or shallow coastal waters until the onset of cooler weather, when they move to deeper water (50–75 fathoms), often forming schools.

RELATION TO MAN: This is one of the most economically important species on the east coast, because it is very abundant and its flesh is quite palatable. Because it stays away from beaches, does not feed on the surface, and seeks small prey, it has seldom been implicated in shark attacks. However, its large size makes it potentially dangerous.

FISHING: The sandbar shark prefers fresh fish, and cut bait is more effective than the entire fish. Best fishing is at night in 15–30 fathoms, with baits set on the bottom. The young offer lively sport on light tackle in shallow estuarine waters in summertime.

REFERENCES: Bigelow and Schroeder 1948; Bass, D'Aubrey, and Kistnasamy 1973; Compagno 1978; Garrick 1982; S. Springer 1960; Wass 1973.

## Smalltail shark
### *Carcharhinus porosus* (Ranzani) 1840

DESCRIPTION: This shark has a slender body, a long snout (its length is much greater than the width of the mouth), a first dorsal fin originating over the midpoint of the inner margin of the pectoral fin, the origin of the second dorsal fin *over or slightly behind the midpoint of the base of the anal fin*, and a caudal fin measuring about one-fourth of the total length. The upper teeth have broadly triangular, increasingly oblique cusps with *serrated margins* and a notch on the outer margin. The lower teeth have narrow, erect, triangular cusps with more finely serrated edges. Teeth number U 13 to 15–1 or 2–13 to 15, L 12 to 15–0 to 2–12 to 15. Color is bluish gray or gray above and paler below, occasionally with the sides and pelvic fins having a reddish tinge. Average size is about 90 cm (35 in); it reaches 134 cm (52 in).

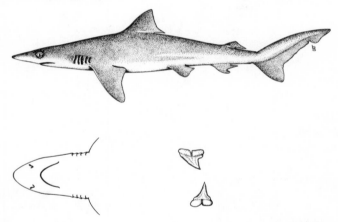

SIMILAR SPECIES: The sharpnose sharks have well-marked labial furrows and smooth-edged upper teeth. The other requiem sharks have the origin of the second dorsal fin anterior to the midpoint of the base of the anal fin.

RANGE: The smalltail shark inhabits the western Atlantic from the northern Gulf of Mexico to southern Brazil (no records from the Antilles) and the eastern Pacific from the Gulf of California to Peru. A similar form has been reported from off Vietnam and Thailand, suggesting a wider distribution.

BIOLOGY: This is a poorly known tropical and subtropical species, which inhabits shallow coastal waters and estuaries. It feeds on crabs and other small invertebrates and fishes.

REPRODUCTION: Development is viviparous. Embryos up to 22 cm (9 in) and litters of sixteen embryos have been reported.

RELATION TO MAN: It is occasionally marketed throughout its range.

FISHING: It is caught mainly on longlines.

REFERENCES: Bigelow and Schroeder 1948; Compagno 1978; de Menezes 1966; Garrick 1982.

## Night shark
*Carcharhinus signatus* (Poey) 1868

DESCRIPTION: The night shark is characterized by a snout *longer* than the width of the mouth, *large green eyes*, a relatively small first dorsal fin originating behind the free rear tips of the pectoral fins, and a low interdorsal ridge. The teeth are smooth-edged or finely serrated; *the upper teeth have increasingly oblique cusps with a pronounced notch on their outer margins and two to five coarse serrations from notch to base*; the lower teeth are symmetrical, narrow, and erect. Teeth number U 15–1 or 2–15, L 15–1–15. Color is grayish blue with scattered black spots above, grayish white below. Embryos are blue or silvery gray above and grayish white below. It grows to about 280 cm (110 in).

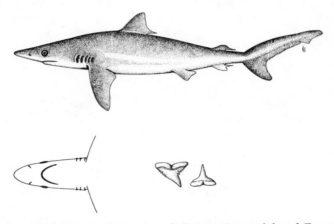

SIMILAR SPECIES: *Paragaleus pectoralis* has similar teeth but differs in having pronounced labial folds, a noticeable spiracle, and a much larger second dorsal fin. The combination of green eyes, the interdorsal ridge, and the characteristic teeth distinguishes the night shark from other requiem sharks in the area.

RANGE: This shark has been reported in waters from Delaware south to Brazil, including in the Gulf of Mexico. It has also been reported from West Africa. It is very abundant in deep waters off the northern coast of Cuba and the Straits of Florida.

BIOLOGY: This is a tropical species that seldom strays northward. The green eyes indicate that it is a deep-water species, usually found in depths greater than 150–200 fathoms during the day and at about 100 fathoms at night. It feeds on fishes and shrimp.

REPRODUCTION: Development is viviparous. Litters usually consist of about twelve to eighteen pups, which measure 68–70 cm (27–28 in) at birth. Little else is known about its reproductive processes.

RELATION TO MAN: It is of no economic importance in North America. In Cuba it is widely used for fish meal and oil.

FISHING: It is caught mainly on longlines in about 100 fathoms, usually at night.

REFERENCES: Bigelow and Schroeder 1948; Compagno 1978; Springer and Thompson 1957.

## Pico blanco
### *Carcharhinus velox* Gilbert 1896

DESCRIPTION: This shark is characterized by a very long and narrow snout (much longer than the width of the mouth) with *very large, transverse, closely set nostrils*, a first dorsal fin originating over the pectoral fin axil, and a second dorsal fin originating over the origin of the anal fin. The upper teeth have strongly oblique cusps with slightly serrated edges and a strong notch on their outer margins and wide bases. The lower teeth have very narrow erect cusps with very fine serrations. Teeth number about U 15–15, L 14–14. Color is bluish gray to brown above, whitish or grayish below. The *tip of the snout has a small black spot surrounded by white,* and the second dorsal fin tip is dusky. The species is known to reach 136 cm (54 in).

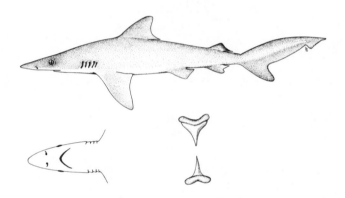

SIMILAR SPECIES: The Pacific sharpnose shark has pronounced labial furrows, more widely separated nostrils, and a second dorsal that originates well behind the origin of the anal fin. The blue shark has a more posterior dorsal fin originating well behind the free rear tips of the pectoral fins.

RANGE: The pico blanco has been reported from the Gulf of California, Panama, and Ecuador. Its range probably extends southward to Peru. In our area it is found only in the Gulf of California, where it is a rare catch.

BIOLOGY: This is apparently a species that inhabits shallow coastal waters. It is known to feed on small fishes and crabs. Nothing else is known of its habits.

REPRODUCTION: No data available.

RELATION TO MAN: None.

FISHING: It is caught on hook and line or in gill nets in shallow coastal waters.

REFERENCES: Beebe and Tee-Van 1941; Jordan and Evermann 1896; Kato, Springer, and Wagner 1967; Roedel 1950.

# Lemon shark
*Negaprion brevirostris* (Poey) 1868

DESCRIPTION: The lemon shark is characterized by a snout shorter than the width of the mouth and a *second dorsal fin that is nearly as large as the first*. The upper teeth have *narrow, triangular, smooth-edged cusps* and broad, finely serrated bases; the anterior teeth are erect, becoming progressively oblique toward the corners of the mouth. The lower teeth have narrow, triangular, erect, smooth-edged cusps. Teeth number U 15–1 to 3–15, L 13 or 14–3–13 or 14. Color is yellowish brown or olive gray above, occasionally dark brown; the undersides are yellowish. Its often characteristic *yellowish tinge* gives rise to the name lemon shark. Specimens 240–300 cm (94–117 in) are common. A specimen 290 cm (114 in) was reported to weigh 120 kg (265 lb). Maximum length is about 320 cm (10.5 ft).

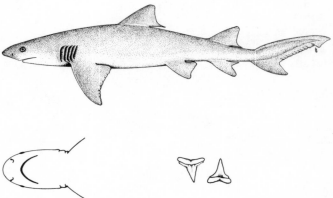

SIMILAR SPECIES: The bull shark has a similar snout, but its second dorsal fin is much smaller than the first, and its upper teeth are broadly triangular with serrated edges.

RANGE: It inhabits the western Atlantic from New Jersey to Brazil and the eastern Pacific from the Gulf of California to Ecuador. Its distribution is not well known because of confusion with other very similar species of "lemon sharks," which may prove to be synonymous. It is a summer visitor off North Carolina and only a stray to the north. It is common from South Carolina to Florida and most abundant in the Caribbean Sea.

BIOLOGY: This is a common shore species. It is active at night around docks, saltwater creeks, inlets, estuaries, bays, and sounds, retreating to deeper water during the day. It feeds mainly on bony fishes and rays, but it is also known to eat shrimp, crabs, small sharks, and sea birds. It appears to be capable of remaining motionless on the bottom.

REPRODUCTION: Development is viviparous. Maturity is reached at a length of 243 cm (96 in). Mating takes place in the spring; gestation lasts about twelve months. The pups measure about 60 cm (24 in) at birth. Litters range from five to nineteen pups, with eleven the average. Birth takes place from April to June in shallow nursery areas. Florida Bay is one of the nursery areas of the lemon shark, and large numbers of pregnant females are found in very shallow water during May and June.

RELATION TO MAN: This is an economically important shark pursued for its hide, flesh, and fins. In the past it was also pursued for its liver oil. It is also a hardy species, which often feeds in captivity, where it survives up to three or four years. Consequently, both small and large specimens are popular for experimental work. It has been suspected of a few attacks on bathers. Like any large shark that inhabits or enters shallow water, it must be considered potentially dangerous.

FISHING: This is a voracious fish that will take almost any bait day or night. Best fishing occurs at night in less than 20 fathoms.

REFERENCES: Banner 1972; Bigelow and Schroeder 1948; Compagno 1978; S. Springer 1950*a*, 1963.

## Blue shark
*Prionace glauca* (Linnaeus) 1758

DESCRIPTION: The blue shark has a snout longer than the width of the mouth, *very long pectoral fins* about as long as from the tip of the snout to the last gill slit, the midpoint of the first dorsal fin base closer to the pelvic fin origin than to the pectoral axil, and *weak keels* on the caudal peduncle. The upper teeth have triangular, curved cusps with serrated edges and overlapping bases. The lower teeth have triangular, erect cusps with smooth or finely serrated edges. Teeth number U 14–0 or 1–14, L 13 to 15–1–13 to 15. Color is *dark indigo blue on top*, shading to *bright blue on the sides*. The undersides are white. The blue color changes to slaty gray soon after death. Average size is 180–240 cm (71–94 in) and 30–52 kg (65–114 lb). The largest on record measured 383 cm (12.6 ft), but the species is said to reach 610 cm (20 ft).

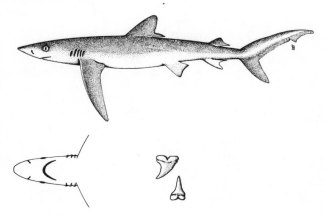

SIMILAR SPECIES: The shortfin mako has a similar blue color but differs in having a conical snout, long, smooth-edged teeth, pronounced caudal keels, and a lunate tail.

RANGE: The blue shark is cosmopolitan in tropical, subtropical, and temperate waters. Off North America it ranges from Newfoundland to Florida and from the Gulf of Alaska to California. There are no records of its presence in the Gulf of Mexico. It is common in deep waters throughout its range.

BIOLOGY: This is one of the most common and the widest-ranging of sharks. It is a pelagic species, which inhabits clear, deep, blue waters, usually in temperatures of 10–20°C (60–68°F), where the depth is greater than 100 fathoms, seldom venturing near land except in clear deep water around islands. Its diet consists primarily of small schooling fishes (anchovies, sardines, herring, etc.) and squid; however, it is an opportunistic feeder that will take any locally abundant fishes and will attack gill-netted salmon and wounded marine mammals. It is a sluggish shark usually seen cruising slowly on the surface, although when excited or feeding it is capable of rapid movements. Its migratory patterns are complex and encompass great distances but are poorly understood. Segregation by sex is known to occur in several areas. A population from New England waters is known to migrate to northeastern South America and also across the Atlantic.

REPRODUCTION: Development is viviparous. The blue shark reaches maturity at about 220 cm (87 in). This is probably the most prolific of the larger sharks; litters usually consist of 25 to 50 pups, and up to 135 pups have been reported. Gestation lasts nine to twelve months, and the pups measure 40–51 cm (16–20 in) at birth.

RELATION TO MAN: The blue shark is classed as a gamefish. It affects the mackerel, pilchard, and salmon fisheries by feeding on trapped or gill-netted fish and by becoming entangled in nets. It has often been implicated in attacks on victims of air or sea disasters. A commercial fishery is now developing on the west coast.

FISHING: It will take surface baits readily; large specimens may offer a challenge on light tackle.

REFERENCES: Bigelow and Schroeder 1948; Clarke and Stevens 1974; Gubanov 1978; Le Brasseur 1964; Pratt 1979; Sciarrotta and Nelson 1977; Stevens 1974, 1975, 1976; Strasburg 1958; Tricas 1979.

## Pacific sharpnose shark
*Rhizoprionodon longurio* (Jordan and Gilbert) 1882

DESCRIPTION: The Pacific sharpnose shark is identified by its pointed, long snout (longer than the width of the mouth), by the presence of well-marked *labial furrows around the corners of the mouth*, and by the position of its second dorsal fin origin, which lies well *behind* the origin of the anal fin. Teeth have oblique,

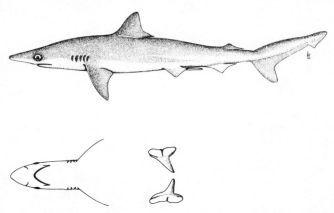

smooth-edged *cusps* (with very slightly serrated edges in large specimens) and a deep notch on their outer margins and are similar in both jaws. They number

U 13 to 15–1–13 to 15, L 13 or 14–13 or 14. Color is grayish brown above, shading to white below. Average size is 75–90 cm (30–35 in). Maximum reported size is 110 cm (43 in), but the species is said to grow to 152 cm (60 in).

SIMILAR SPECIES: The well-marked labial furrows and the position of the second dorsal fin distinguish it from other requiem sharks in the area.

RANGE: It inhabits the tropical eastern Pacific from southern California to Peru. It is common in the Gulf of California.

BIOLOGY: This little shark inhabits warm coastal waters, usually over soft bottoms in less than 15 fathoms. It feeds on small crustaceans and fishes. Very little is known about its habits.

REPRODUCTION: Development is viviparous. Males mature at over 60 cm (23 in), females at a slightly larger size. The pups measure 30–33 cm (12–13 in) at birth. Litters are usually small, three to five embryos having been reported.

REFERENCES: Beebe and Tee-Van 1941; Fowler 1941; Garman 1913; Hubbs and McHugh 1950; Kato, Springer, and Wagner 1967; Roedel and Ripley 1950; V. G. Springer 1964; Thomson, Findley, and Kerstitch 1979.

## Caribbean sharpnose shark
*Rhizoprionodon porosus* (Poey) 1861

DESCRIPTION: The Caribbean sharpnose shark is recognized by its long snout (longer than the width of the mouth) and by the presence of *long labial furrows around the corners of the mouth*. The teeth have *triangular, oblique, smooth-edged cusps* (very weakly serrated in large specimens), *strongly notched on their outer margins*, and are similar in both jaws. Teeth number U 12–1–12, L 12–12. Color is brown or grayish brown with metallic hues above, shading to white below, with the dorsal and caudal fins having darker edges. Average size is about 80 cm (31 in); the species reaches 110 cm (43 in).

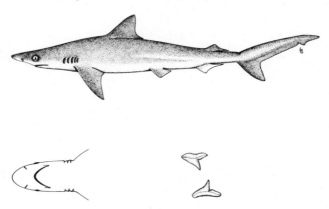

SIMILAR SPECIES: The smalltail shark lacks long labial furrows and has serrated teeth. The combination of long snout, labial furrows, and notched teeth distinguishes the Caribbean sharpnose shark from other requiem sharks in the area. The Caribbean sharpnose shark is replaced along the Gulf Coast and from Florida northward by a very similar, closely related species, the Atlantic sharpnose shark. These two species can be separated only on the basis of vertebral counts; the Caribbean form has sixty-five to seventy-five precaudal vertebrae, while the Atlantic form has fifty-eight to sixty-five precaudal vertebrae.

RANGE: It inhabits the Caribbean region from the Bahamas and the Antilles to the Central American coast, extending southward to Uruguay. It is common throughout the Antilles.

BIOLOGY: This is a tropical species that usually inhabits shallow coastal waters and estuaries, often entering rivers. It has also been reported from offshore waters at depths of 275 fathoms. It feeds on shrimp, mollusks, and small fishes.

REPRODUCTION: Development is viviparous. The pups measure about 25 cm (10 in) at birth. Litters usually consist of two to six pups.

RELATION TO MAN: It is used for fish meal or marketed fresh throughout the West Indies.

FISHING: It is easily caught with hook and line or in longlines throughout its range. It is often found in shrimp trawl catches. It is considered a nuisance by fishermen.

REFERENCES: Böhlke and Chaplin 1970; Compagno 1978; V. G. Springer 1964.

## Atlantic sharpnose shark
### *Rhizoprionodon terraenovae* (Richardson) 1836

DESCRIPTION: The Atlantic sharpnose shark is recognized by its long snout (longer than the width of the mouth) and by the presence of long *labial furrows around the corners of the mouth.* The teeth are *triangular, oblique, strongly notched on their outer margins,* smooth-edged (very weakly serrated in large specimens), and similar in both jaws. Teeth number U 11 to 13–1–11 to 13, L 12 or 13–12 or 13. Color is brownish, olive gray, or bluish gray, with metallic hues and a few scattered white spots above (adults only), shading to white below. Small specimens have black-edged dorsal and caudal fins. Average size is 95 cm (37 in) and 3.6 kg (8 lb). It grows to about 120 cm (47 in).

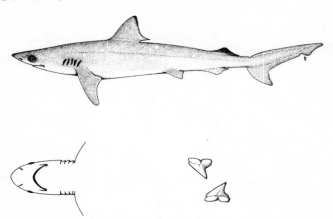

SIMILAR SPECIES: The combination of long snout, long labial furrows, and notched teeth distinguishes it from other carcharhinids in the area. The Atlantic sharpnose shark is replaced in the Caribbean by a very similar, closely related species, the Caribbean sharpnose shark. These two species can be separated only on the basis of vertebral counts; the Atlantic form has fifty-eight to sixty-five precaudal vertebrae, while the Caribbean form has sixty-five to seventy-five precaudal vertebrae.

RANGE: The Atlantic sharpnose shark inhabits the northeastern coast of North America from the Bay of Fundy (only as a rare stray) south to Yucatan. It is a year-round resident off South Carolina, Florida, the Keys, and the Gulf of Mexico.

BIOLOGY: This little shark is extremely common in coastal waters in summertime. It forms large schools composed of individuals of uniform size and sex. Off South Carolina it is found at depths of 7 fathoms or less in the summer, moving to waters deeper than 15 fathoms in winter. It feeds on shrimp, mollusks, and small fishes.

REPRODUCTION: Development is viviparous. Sexual maturity is reached at about 83 cm (33 in). The pups, usually four to seven, are born during early June in estuarine or shallow coastal waters and measure 22–35 cm (9–14 in).

RELATION TO MAN: This shark is often a nuisance to fishermen because it takes bait intended for more desirable, larger game. It is often marketed fresh; its meat is of excellent quality.

FISHING: It will take small hooks baited with shrimp or cut bait. It is usually too small to offer any challenge to the sportsman, except on very light tackle.

REFERENCES: Bigelow and Schroeder 1948; Clark and von Schmidt 1965; Compagno 1978; V. G. Springer 1964.

## Family Sphyrnidae—Hammerhead Sharks

The flat, wide, hammer- or shovel-shaped heads of these sharks is so characteristic that they cannot be confused with any other sharks. These medium to large sharks of the coastal areas of tropical and warm-temperate seas are considered to be the most advanced sharks, along with the closely related requiem sharks. They are characterized by flat and wide head, eyes with a well-developed nictitating membrane, and bladelike teeth with a single cusp, usually curved toward the corners of the mouth. Their development is viviparous. These are voracious fishes, which feed on rays, sharks, and many other fishes. Many species are migratory, often moving in large schools. They are economically important as food and gamefishes, and some are considered dangerous to man. The family comprises at least nine species, seven of which are found in our area.

The taxonomy of the hammerhead sharks has fluctuated considerably in recent times. The scientific names used here follow the latest revision of this family (C. R. Gilbert 1967); these names differ from those used in older literature.

| Current Names | Older Names |
|---|---|
| Sphyrna corona | Sphyrna corona |
| Sphyrna lewini | Sphyrna diplana |
| Sphyrna mokarran | Sphyrna tudes |
| Sphyrna media | Sphyrna media |
| Sphyrna tudes | Sphyrna bigelowi |
| Sphyrna zygaena | Sphyrna zygaena |

NOTE: Juveniles cannot be easily identified to species. In doubtful cases the excellent monograph by C. R. Gilbert (1967) should be consulted.

1.  Head shovel-shaped, anterior margin of head evenly rounded . . . .
    *Sphyrna tiburo* (p. 156)
    Head hammer-shaped, anterior margin of head undulated or nearly
    straight . . . . . . . . . . . . . . . . . . . . . . . . . . . . . . . . . . . . . . . . . . . . . . . .  2
2.  First dorsal fin free rear tip reaching the level of the pelvic fins . . . . . .  3
    First dorsal fin free rear tip not reaching the level of the pelvic fins . .  5
3.  Inner narial groove present, anterior margin of head with a deep
    central indentation . . . . *Sphyrna tudes* (p. 157)
    Inner narial groove absent, anterior margin of head with a shallow or
    no central indentation . . . . . . . . . . . . . . . . . . . . . . . . . . . . . . . . . . . . . .  4
4.  Length of snout (from anterior margin of head to front of mouth)
    greater than 40 percent of greatest head width, anterior margin of
    head with a shallow central indentation . . . . *Sphyrna corona* (p.
    152)
    Length of snout less than 40 percent of greatest head width, anterior
    margin of head without a deep central indentation . . . . *Sphyrna
    media* (p. 154)
5.  Anterior margin of head with a central indentation . . . . . . . . . . . . . . . . .  6
    Anterior margin of head lacking a central indentation . . . . *Sphyrna
    zygaena* (p. 158)
6.  Anterior margin of head nearly straight, pelvic fins with strongly
    curved rear margins . . . . *Sphyrna mokarran* (p. 155)
    Anterior margin of head strongly undulating, pelvic fins with nearly
    straight rear margins . . . . *Sphyrna lewini* (p. 153)

## *Sphyrna corona* Springer 1940

DESCRIPTION: This small hammerhead is characterized by a broadly rounded anterior margin of the head, occasionally with a shallow central indentation; a snout length (from the anterior margin of the head to the front of the mouth) *greater* than 40 percent of the greatest head width; *no inner narial groove*; and a free rear tip of the first dorsal fin that reaches the level of the pelvic fins. The upper teeth have oblique, smooth-edged cusps with a notch on their outer margins; the lower teeth are erect and smooth-edged. Teeth number U 14–14, L 14–1–14. Color is gray or grayish brown above and paler below, without fin markings. This is the smallest of the hammerheads, perhaps reaching 90 cm (35 in).

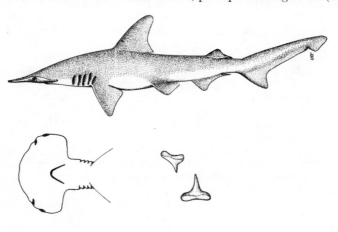

SIMILAR SPECIES: The scoophead has a shorter snout and an anal fin with a more curved rear margin and a more pointed apex.

RANGE: *S. corona* inhabits the eastern Pacific from southern Mexico to Colombia. It may be present in the Gulf of California.

BIOLOGY: This is a very poorly known small hammerhead that inhabits tropical coastal waters. Nothing else is known of its habits.

REPRODUCTION: No data available.

RELATION TO MAN: None.

FISHING: No data available.

REFERENCES: C. R. Gilbert 1967; Kato, Springer, and Wagner 1967.


## Scalloped hammerhead
*Sphyrna lewini* (Griffith and Smith) 1834

DESCRIPTION: The scalloped hammerhead is characterized by *a marked central indentation on the anterior margin of the head*, which gives it a "scalloped" look; a first dorsal fin rear tip that does not reach the level of the pelvic fins; and a *low and long second dorsal fin* (its length is about twice the height of the fin), which reaches almost to the precaudal pit. The teeth are triangular, smooth-edged (often weakly serrated in large individuals), and similar in both jaws; the central teeth are erect, while subsequent ones have oblique cusps. Teeth number U 15 or 16–0 to 2–15 or 16, L 15 or 16–1 or 2–15 or 16. Color is deep olive to brownish gray above, shading to white below. The *ventral tips of the pectoral fins are gray-black or black* in life; their color darkens with age, becoming black in large individuals. An albino specimen has been reported. A 208-cm (82-in) specimen weighed 43 kg (95 lb). The species grows to about 365 cm (12 ft).

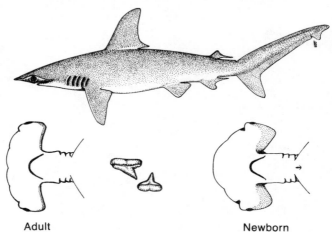

Adult　　　　　　　　　　　　　　Newborn

SIMILAR SPECIES: The great hammerhead has teeth with serrated edges and pelvic fins with curved rear margins. The smooth hammerhead lacks the central indentation on the anterior margin of the head. The rear tip of the first dorsal fin of the smalleye hammerhead, *S. media*, and *S. corona* reaches the level of the pelvic fins. The bonnethead has a shovel-shaped head.

RANGE: The scalloped hammerhead is circumtropical. In North American waters it ranges from New Jersey to Florida and the Gulf of Mexico and from southern California southward. It is one of the most common summer sharks in estuarine waters of the Carolinas and the Gulf of Mexico.

BIOLOGY: This is a warm-water species seldom found in water cooler than 22°C (72°F). It feeds on stingrays, sharks, shrimp, and crabs. It is believed to be a migratory species, but little is known about its movements. It is found both inshore and in oceanic waters.

REPRODUCTION: Development is viviparous. Adults probably mature at about 180 cm (71 in). Young are born at 38–45 cm (15–18 in) in late summer.

RELATION TO MAN: The scalloped hammerhead has been fished for oil, fish meal, and leather off Florida and the West Indies. It is classed as a gamefish. It is considered dangerous to divers and swimmers, like all large hammerheads.

FISHING: This is a voracious shark that will take bait easily. In the estuarine waters of the Carolinas the young will often take large hooks and baits intended for much bigger sharks.

REFERENCES: Clarke 1971; Fusaro and Anderson 1980; C. R. Gilbert 1967; McKenzie 1970.

## Scoophead
### *Sphyrna media* Springer 1940

DESCRIPTION: This hammerhead is characterized by a slightly rounded anterior margin of the head without a deep central indentation, a snout length (from the anterior margin of the head to the front of the mouth) *shorter* than 40 percent of the greatest head width; *no inner narial groove*, and a free rear tip of the first dorsal fin that reaches to the level of the pelvic fins. The upper teeth have oblique, smooth-edged cusps with a notch on their outer margins; the lower teeth are erect and smooth-edged. Teeth number U 12 to 14–0 to 2–12 to 14, L 13 or 14–1–13 or 14. Color is gray or grayish brown above, paler below, without fin markings. It reaches to at least 152 cm (60 in).

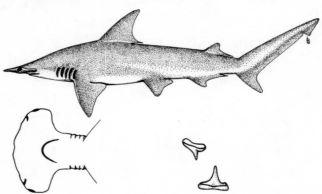

SIMILAR SPECIES: The smalleye hammerhead has a more pronounced notch on the anterior margin of the head. *S. corona* has a longer snout and an anal fin with a straighter rear margin and more rounded tip.

RANGE: This shark has been reported from the eastern Pacific from the Gulf of California to Ecuador, the southern Caribbean, and the southwestern Atlantic. The limits of its distribution are not well defined due to confusion with other hammerheads.

BIOLOGY: This is a poorly known species that inhabits tropical coastal waters. Nothing else is known of its habits.

REPRODUCTION: No data available.

RELATION TO MAN: None.

FISHING: No data available.

REFERENCES: C. R. Gilbert 1967; Kato, Springer, and Wagner 1967.


## Great hammerhead
*Sphyrna mokarran* (Rüppell) 1835

DESCRIPTION: The great hammerhead is characterized by a *nearly straight anterior margin of the head* (slightly rounded in young specimens) *with a deep central indentation*, a high second dorsal fin, and *pelvic fins with curved rear margins*. The teeth are triangular with *strongly serrated edges*, with cusps that become increasingly oblique toward the corners of the mouth. Teeth number U 17–2 or 3–17, L 16 or 17–1 to 3–16 or 17, and are similar in both jaws. Color varies from dark olive green to brownish gray above, shading to white below. Specimens up to 425 cm (14 ft) and 455 kg (1,000 lb) are common. A specimen 560 cm (18.3 ft) has been recorded. This species is the largest of the hammerheads, and it is reputed to reach 610 cm (20 ft).

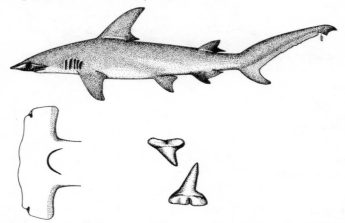

SIMILAR SPECIES: All the other hammerheads lack the strongly serrated teeth and the pelvic fins with curved rear margins.

RANGE: The great hammerhead is circumtropical. In North American waters it ranges from North Carolina southward to Florida and the Gulf of Mexico and from the Gulf of California southward to the tropics. It is common off the Carolinas during the summer months and off Florida during most of the year.

BIOLOGY: This large shark is found both in the open ocean and in shallow coastal waters. It feeds on rays, smaller sharks, and numerous bony fishes. It is a tropical species that wanders north in the summer.

REPRODUCTION: Development is viviparous. Maturity is reached at about 300 cm (118 in). Litters are usually large, twenty to forty pups. Young are born at about 70 cm (28 in), during the summer. The shape of the head of the young is more rounded than that of the adult, but it changes with growth.

RELATION TO MAN: In the past the great hammerhead was fished for its vitamin-rich liver. Its skin is often used for leather. This is a voracious and dangerous shark, and many attacks on man have been attributed to it.

FISHING: The great hammerhead is classed as a gamefish along with the other large hammerheads. It will take surface baits readily and offers exciting sport because of its large size.

REFERENCES: Bigelow and Schroeder 1948; Clark and von Schmidt 1965; C. R. Gilbert 1967; Gudger 1947.


## Bonnethead
### *Sphyrna tiburo* (Linnaeus) 1758

DESCRIPTION: The characteristic shovel- or bonnet-shaped head makes this hammerhead the easiest to identify. The *anterior margin of the head is evenly rounded between the eyes*. The frontal teeth have erect, smooth-edged cusps, while subsequent teeth have oblique cusps; the outermost teeth of the lower jaw are modified into flat crushers. Teeth number U 12 to 14–0 or 1–12 to 14, L 12 to 14–1–12 to 14. Color is gray or greenish gray above and paler below. Average size is 70–100 cm (28–39 in). Maximum size is about 110 cm (43 in).

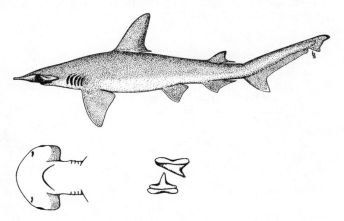

SIMILAR SPECIES: All the other hammerheads have hammer-shaped (not shovel-shaped) heads, and lack the evenly rounded anterior margin of the head. West coast specimens of the bonnethead have a more pointed head and are considered a different subspecies, *S. tiburo vespertina*.

RANGE: The bonnethead is confined to the warm waters of the western hemisphere. It ranges from New England, where it is rare, to the Gulf of Mexico and Brazil and from southern California to Ecuador. It is common in inshore waters of the Carolinas and Georgia in summer and off Florida and in the Gulf of Mexico in spring, summer, and fall.

BIOLOGY: The bonnethead inhabits shallow coastal waters, where it frequents sandy and muddy bottoms. It feeds on shrimp, crabs, mollusks, and small fishes. It is believed to migrate southward in winter or to deeper offshore waters in Florida and the Gulf of Mexico, but little is known about its movements. It often travels in schools of five to fifteen individuals. Migrating schools of hundreds and even thousands of these sharks have been reported. Juveniles are common in estuarine waters.

REPRODUCTION: Development is viviparous. Maturity is reached at about 75 cm (30 in). The pups are born in late summer and early fall and measure 30–32 cm (12–13 in) at birth. Usually eight to twelve pups are produced in each litter.

RELATION TO MAN: Although it is occasionally marketed, it is of little economic importance. One attack by this species has been recorded, but it is generally considered to be harmless. It is often exhibited in marine aquaria, where it usually survives for a few months.

FISHING: It is often caught in shrimp trawls. It takes shrimp or cut bait easily and offers lively sport on light tackle.

REFERENCES: Baldridge 1974; Bigelow and Schroeder 1948; Clark and von Schmidt 1965; C. R. Gilbert 1967; Hoese and Moore 1958; Myrberg and Gruber 1974; Schlernitzauer and Gilbert 1966; S. Springer 1940a, 1940b.

## Smalleye hammerhead
*Sphyrna tudes* (Valenciennes) 1822

DESCRIPTION: This hammerhead is characterized by the anterior margin of the head with a deep central indentation, a *well-developed inner narial groove*, and a free rear tip of the first dorsal fin that reaches the level of the pelvic fins. The upper teeth have oblique, smooth-edged cusps; the lower teeth have erect, smooth-edged cusps. Teeth number U 15 or 16–15 or 16, L 15 or 16–1–15 or 16. Color is gray or grayish brown above and much paler below, without fin markings. It grows to at least 152 cm (60 in).

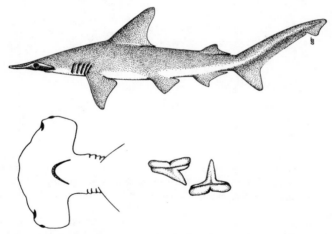

SIMILAR SPECIES: The great hammerhead, the scalloped hammerhead, and the smooth hammerhead have the free rear tip of the first dorsal fin well ahead of the origin of the pelvic fins. The scoophead has a more rounded anterior margin of the head and lacks the deep central indentation.

RANGE: The smalleye hammerhead has been reported only from the western Atlantic Ocean and the western Mediterranean Sea. In the western Atlantic it ranges from the Gulf of Mexico to Uruguay.

BIOLOGY: Because recognition of this species as distinct from other hammerheads is relatively recent, almost nothing is known about its habits. It is known to enter fresh water.

REPRODUCTION: No data available.
RELATION TO MAN: No data available.
FISHING: No data available.
REFERENCES: C. R. Gilbert 1967; S. Springer 1944.

## Smooth hammerhead
*Sphyrna zygaena* (Linnaeus) 1758

DESCRIPTION: The smooth hammerhead is characterized by the *anterior margin of the head that lacks a central indentation* (hence the name "smooth") and by a first dorsal fin free rear tip that does not reach the level of the pelvic fins. The teeth have oblique, smooth-edged cusps (occasionally with weakly serrated edges in large individuals) with a notch on their outer edges; they are similar in both jaws and number U 13 to 15−0 or 1−13 to 15, L 12 to 14−1−12 to14. Color is a deep olive to brownish gray above, shading to white below, occasionally with dusky or black-tipped pectoral fins. Adults up to 365 cm (12 ft) and 400 kg (881 lb) are not unusual. Maximum size is 370−396 cm (12−13 ft).

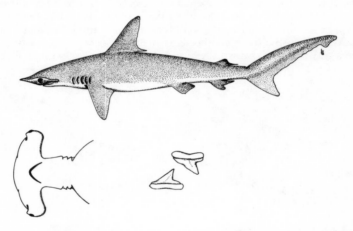

SIMILAR SPECIES: The combination of an anterior margin of the head without a central indentation and the relative position of its first dorsal fin distinguishes it from the other hammerhead sharks, except for the bonnethead, which has a shovel-shaped head.

RANGE: The smooth hammerhead inhabits warm-temperate waters throughout the world and is rare or absent in tropical waters. Off North America it ranges from Nova Scotia (summer only) to Florida and from central California to the Gulf of California. It has not been reported from the Gulf of Mexico.

BIOLOGY: This is a species often seen on the surface with the upper fins exposed. It feeds on stingrays (in southern areas), skates (in northern areas), sharks, including its own species, numerous bony fishes, crabs, and shrimp. It migrates along the east coast, northward in summer and southward in winter, often traveling in large schools.

REPRODUCTION: Development is viviparous. Maturity is reached at about 220 cm (87 in). The pups measure about 50 cm (20 in) at birth. Litters are large, usually twenty to forty pups.

RELATION TO MAN: The smooth hammerhead has been utilized for oil, fish meal, and leather. It is classed as a gamefish, grouped together with the other large hammerheads. It is considered dangerous to divers and swimmers.

FISHING: Like other hammerheads, it will take surface baits readily and offers lively sport to the angler.

REFERENCES: Bigelow and Schroeder 1948; C. R. Gilbert 1967; Leim and Scott 1966.

# APPENDIX

THIS appendix includes monotypic families (consisting of one species) of wide or unknown distribution. The sharks included here have never been reported from our area, but this may be because of their rarity or the difficulties involved in capturing them.

## Family Scapanorhynchidae—Goblin Shark

This is a family consisting of one species, the goblin shark, a very primitive, deep-water shark. Its distinguishing characteristics are a snout prolonged into a long flat blade and greatly protrusible jaws. The soft bodies of deep-water sharks are subject to deformation upon preservation; this fact and individual variation resulted in the description of several species early in this century. Presently they are all considered to be one widely distributed species. This species was described and named in 1898 as *Mitsukurina*, while an earlier described fossil form was known as *Scapanorhynchus*. They are both considered now to be one species, *Scapanorhynchus owstoni*, extant since the Cretaceous and widely distributed at present.

### Goblin shark
*Scapanorhynchus owstoni* (Jordan) 1898

DESCRIPTION: This is an unmistakable shark, it has a *snout prolonged into a long flat blade*, greatly protrusible jaws, a noticeable spiracle, the last gill slit over the pectoral fin. Its body is soft, and its skeleton is very flexible, like those of

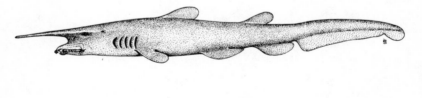

fishes inhabiting very deep waters. The teeth are long and narrowly cusped; the side teeth have lateral denticles. Teeth number about U 13–13, L 12–12, not counting the minute teeth in the back of the jaws. Color is light reddish gray above and lighter below, with the fins being darker brown (preserved specimens are gray). It has been reported to reach 335 cm (11 ft) and 160 kg (352 lb).

SIMILAR SPECIES: The prolonged, bladelike snout distinguishes it from all other sharks.

RANGE: The goblin shark has been reported in the eastern Atlantic off France, Portugal, and Guiana, the western Pacific off Japan, and the Indian Ocean off South Africa and southern Australia. It is obviously widely distributed in deep waters. It has never been reported from our area; however, this may be because of the lack of deep-water fisheries. It is one of the rarest sharks; few specimens have ever been caught.

BIOLOGY: Virtually nothing is known of its habits, which must be inferred from morphological characteristics. Depth-of-capture records indicate that this is one of the deepest-dwelling sharks; it is usually reported from 300 to 500 fathoms. Its flexible body is also typical of fishes inhabiting very deep waters. The long, slender, pointed teeth are designed for grasping, indicating it feeds on small prey, perhaps squid or small fishes. The function of the flat, flexible snout is unknown; one can speculate that it may serve as an enlarged area for sensory perception or detection of prey buried in the bottom ooze.

REPRODUCTION: Its mode of reproduction has not been described. The smallest known specimen measured 107 cm (42 in).

RELATION TO MAN: None.

FISHING: It is usually caught in deep-water trawls. This is one of the rarest sharks, and catches should be preserved and reported.

REFERENCES: Bass, D'Aubrey, and Kistnasamy 1975c; Hussakof 1909; Jordan 1898; Quero 1972.

# Megamouth Shark

Megamouth is the name given to a large deep-water shark that was collected in 1976. This shark represents not only a new species but also a hitherto unknown family. The formal description and scientific name have not yet appeared as this

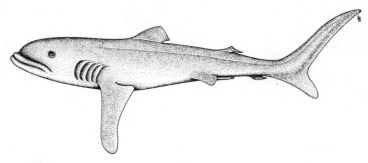

book goes to press (1982), but they should be available shortly. Megamouth is included here to round out the list of shark families and to call it to the reader's attention.

Megamouth was accidentally entangled in a sea-anchor deployed at a depth of 500 feet by a Navy vessel off Oahu, Hawaii. The shark apparently attempted to swallow the orange and white parachute anchor and died in the attempt. This shark is characterized by a *huge terminal mouth*, two relatively small dorsal fins, and a *uniformly colored back*. The only other sharks with similar terminal mouths are the whale shark and the frill shark. The whale shark is strikingly marked with white spots and bars; the frill shark has a single dorsal fin.

The only known specimen is a mature male that measured about 450 cm (15 ft) and weighed about 730 kg (1,600 lb). Presumably, this is a deep-water plankton-eater, whose habitat and indifference to baited hooks have kept it from fishermen and scientists. The formal description and more specimens are eagerly awaited.

# BIBLIOGRAPHY

Aasen, O. 1963. Length and growth of the porbeagle (*Lamna nasus* Bonnaterre) in the Northwest Atlantic. *Rep. Norw. Fishery Invest.* 13(6):20–37.

———. 1964. The exploitation of the spiny dogfish (*Squalus acanthias* L.) in European waters. *Rep. Norw. Fishery Invest.* 13(7):5–16.

Abe, T., S. Isokawa, T. Misu, T. Kishimoto, S. Shima, and H. Shima. 1968. Notes on some members of Osteodonti (Class Chondrichthyes). *I. Bull. Tokai Reg. Fish. Res. Lab* 56:1–6.

Alverson, D. L., and M. E. Stansby. 1963. The spiny dogfish (*Squalus acanthias*) in the northeastern Pacific. *U.S. Fish. Wildl. Serv. Spec. Sci. Rep. Fish.* 447. 25 pp.

Applegate, S. P. 1972. A revision of the higher taxa of Orectolobids. *J. Mar. Biol. Assoc. India* 14:743–51.

Backus, R. H., S. Springer, and E. L. Arnold, Jr. 1956. A contribution to the natural history of the white-tip shark, *Pterolamiops longimanus* (Poey). *Deep-Sea Res.* 3:178–88.

Baldridge, H. D. 1974. *Shark attack.* Anderson, S. Car.: Droke House/Hallux Inc. 297 pp.

Bane, G. W. 1966. Observations on the silky shark, *Carcharhinus falciformis*, in the Gulf of Guinea. *Copeia*, pp. 354–57.

———, and A. W. Bane. 1971. *Bay fishes of northern California* (with emphasis on the Bodega–Tomales Bay area). New York: Mariscos Publications. 143 pp.

Banner, A. 1972. Use of sound in predation by young lemon sharks, *Negaprion brevirostris* (Poey). *Bull. Mar. Sci.* 22:251–83.

Bass, A. J., and A. Ballard. 1972. Buoyancy control in the shark *Odontaspis taurus* (Rafinesque). *Copeia*, pp. 594–95.

———, J. D. D'Aubrey, and N. Kistnasamy. 1973. Sharks of the east coast of southern Africa. I. The genus *Carcharhinus* (Carcharhinidae). *Invest. Rep. Oceanogr. Res. Inst.* 33:1–168.

———, ———, and ———. 1975a. Sharks of the east coast of southern Africa. II. The families Scyliorhinidae and Pseudotriakidae. *Invest. Rep. Oceanogr. Res. Inst.* 37:1–63.

———, ———, and ———. 1975b. Sharks of the east coast of southern Africa. III. The families Carcharhinidae (excluding *Mustelus* and *Carcharhinus*) and Sphyrnidae. *Invest. Rep. Oceanogr. Res. Inst.* 38:1–100.

———, ———, and ———. 1975c. Sharks of the east coast of southern Africa. IV. The families Odontaspididae, Scapanorhynchidae, Isuridae, Cetorhinidae, Alopiidae, Orectolobidae, and Rhiniodontidae. *Invest. Rep. Oceanogr. Res. Inst.* 39:1–102.

———, ———, and ———. 1975d. Sharks of the east coast of southern Africa. V. The families Hexanchidae, Chlamydoselachidae, Heterodontidae, Pristiophoridae and Squatinidae. *Invest. Rep. Oceanogr. Res. Inst.* 43:1–50.

———, ———, and ———. 1976. Sharks of the east coast of southern Africa. VI.

The families Oxynotidae, Squalidae, Dalatiidae and Echinorhinidae. *Invest. Rep. Oceanogr. Res. Inst.* 45:1–103.

Bearden, C. M. 1965*a*. Occurrence of spiny dogfish, *Squalus acanthias*, and other elasmobranchs in South Carolina coastal waters. *Copeia*, p. 378.

———. 1965*b*. Elasmobranch fishes of South Carolina. *Contrib. Bears Bluff Lab.* 42:3–22.

Beck, B., and A. W. Mansfield. 1969. Observations on the greenland shark, *Somniosus microcephalus*, in northern Baffin Island. *J. Fish. Res. Board Can.* 26:143–45.

Beebe, W. 1941. External characters of six embryo nurse sharks, *Ginglymostoma cirratum* (Gmelin). *Zoologica* (N.Y.) 26:9–12.

———, and J. Tee-Van. 1941. Fishes from the tropical eastern Pacific (from Cedros Island, lower California, south to the Galapagos Islands and northern Peru). Pt. 2. Sharks. *Zoologica* (N.Y.) 26:93–122.

Berland, B. 1961. Copepod *Ommatokoita elongata* (Grant) in the eyes of the greenland shark—a possible cause of mutual dependence. *Nature* (London) 4790:829.

Bigelow, H. B., and W. C. Schroeder. 1940. Sharks of the genus *Mustelus* in the western Atlantic. *Proc. Boston Soc. Nat. Hist.* 41:417–38.

———, and ———. 1941. *Cephalurus*, a new genus of Scyliorhinid shark with redescription of the genotype, *Catulus cephalus* Gilbert. *Copeia*, pp. 73–76.

———, and ———. 1944. New sharks from the western North Atlantic. *Proc. New Engl. Zool. Club* 23:21–36.

———, and ———. 1948. *Fishes of the western North Atlantic. Pt. I. Lancelets, cyclostomes, and sharks*. New Haven: Mem. Sears Fdn. Mar. Res. 576 pp.

———, and ———. 1953. Fishes of the Gulf of Maine. *U.S. Fish Wildl. Serv. Fish. Bull.* 74. 577 pp.

———, and ———. 1954. Deep water elasmobranchs and chimaeroids from the northwestern Atlantic slope. *Bull. Mus. Comp. Zool. Harv.* 112:38–87.

———, and ———. 1957. A study of the sharks of the suborder Squaloidea. *Bull. Mus. Comp. Zool. Harv.* 117:1–150.

———, and ———. 1961. *Carcharhinus nicaraguensis*, a synonym of the bull shark, *C. leucas. Copeia*, p. 359.

———, ———, and S. Springer. 1953. New and little known sharks from the Atlantic and from the Gulf of Mexico. *Bull. Mus. Comp. Zool. Harv.* 109:213–76.

———, ———, and ———. 1955. Three new shark records from the Gulf of Mexico. *Breviora* 49:1–12.

Bjerkan, P., and E. Koefoed. 1957. Notes on the greenland shark *Acanthorhinus carcharias* (Gunn). *Fiskeridir. Skr. Ser. Havunders.* 11(10):1–12.

Böhlke, J. E., and C. G. Chaplin. 1970. *Fishes of the Bahamas and adjacent tropical waters*. Wynnewood, Pa.: Livingston Pub. Co.

Branstetter, S. 1981. Biological notes on the sharks of the north central Gulf of Mexico. *Contrib. Mar. Sci.* 24:13–34.

———, and R. L. Shipp. 1980. Occurrence of the finetooth shark, *Carcharhinus isodon*, off Dauphin Island, Alabama. *U.S. Fish Wildl. Serv. Fish. Bull.* 78:177–79.

Bright, D. B. 1959. The occurrence and food of the sleeper shark, *Somniosus pacificus*, in a central Alaska Bay. *Copeia*, pp. 76–77.

Bullis, H. R., Jr. 1961. Observations on the feeding behavior of white-tip sharks on schooling fishes. *Ecology* 42:194–95.

———. 1967. Depth segregations and distribution of sex-maturity groups in the marbled catshark, *Galeus arae*. In *Sharks, skates and rays*, ed. P. W. Gilbert, R. F. Mathewson, and D. P. Rall, pp. 141–48. Baltimore: Johns Hopkins Press.

Burgess, G. H., G. W. Link, and S. W. Ross. 1979. Additional marine fishes new or rare to Carolina waters. *Northeast Gulf Sci.* 3:74–87.

Cadenat, J. 1960. Notes d'Ichtyologie ouest-africaine. XXVIII—*Deania cremouxi*, sp. nov. des cotes du Senegal. *Bull. Inst. Fr. Afr. Noire* Ser. A 22(2):312–24.

Casterlin, M. E., and W. W. Reynolds. 1979. Diel activity patterns of the smooth dogfish shark, *Mustelus canis*. *Bull. Mar. Sci.* 29:440–42.

Castro-Aguirre, J. L., and F. de Lachica-Bonilla. 1973. Nuevos registros de peces marinos en la costa del Pacifico Mexicano. *Rev. Soc. Mex. Hist. Nat.* 34:147–81.

Chen, C., T. Taniuchi, and Y. Nose. 1979. Blainville's dogfish, *Squalus blainville*, from Japan, with notes on *S. mitsukurii* and *S. japonicus*. *Jpn. J. Ichthyol.* 26:26–42.

Clark, E. 1963. The maintenance of sharks in captivity, with a report on their instrumental conditioning. In *Sharks and survival*, ed. P. Gilbert, pp. 115–49. Lexington, Mass.: D. C. Heath and Co.

———, and K. von Schmidt. 1965. Sharks of the central gulf coast of Florida. *Bull. Mar. Sci.* 15:13–83.

Clarke, M. R., and J. D. Stevens. 1974. Cephalopods, blue sharks and migration. *J. Mar. Biol. Assoc. U.K.* 54:949–57.

Clarke, T. A. 1971. The ecology of the scalloped hammerhead shark, *Sphyrna lewini*, in Hawaii. *Pac. Sci.* 25:133–44.

Cohen, J. L. 1973. An albino grey smoothhound *Mustelus californicus* Gill. *Calif. Fish. Game* 59:210–11.

Collyer, R. D. 1953. The bramble shark (*Echinorhinus brucus*) at Guadalupe Island, Mexico. *Calif. Fish. Game* 39:266.

Compagno, L. J. V. 1970. Systematics of the genus *Hemitriakis* (Selachii: Carcharhinidae), and related genera. *Proc. Calif. Acad. Sci.* 38:63–98.

———. 1978. Sharks. In *FAO species identification sheets for fishery purposes. West Central Atlantic (Fishing Area 31)*, ed. W. Fischer. Rome: Food and Agriculture Organization of the United Nations. Unpaginated loose-leaf pub.

Cox, K. W. 1963. Egg-cases of some elasmobranchs and a cyclostome from Californian waters. *Calif. Fish. Game* 49:271–89.

Daugherty, E. 1964. The sand shark, *Carcharias ferox* (Risso), in California. *Calif. Fish. Game* 50:4–10.

DeGroot, S. J., and H. Nijssen. 1976. The shark *Dalatias licha* (Bonnaterre, 1788) caught alive in the coastal waters of the Netherlands (Pisces, Selacii, Dalatiidae). *Bull. Zool. Mus. Univ. Amsterdam* 5:73–76.

DeLacy, A. C., and W. M. Chapman. 1935. Notes on some elasmobranchs of Puget Sound, with descriptions of their egg cases. *Copeia*, pp. 63–67.

de Menezes, R. S. 1966. Some morphometric data on shark embryos. *Arg. Estac. Biol. Mar. Univ. Fed. Ceara* 6:143–46.

Dempster, R. P., and E. S. Herald. 1961. Notes on the hornshark, *Heterodontus francisci*, with observations on mating activities. *Occas. Pap. Calif. Acad. Sci.* 33:1–7.

Dodrill, J. W., and R. G. Gilmore. 1978. Land birds in the stomachs of tiger sharks *Galeocerdo cuvieri* (Peron & LeSueur). *Auk* 95:585–86.

———, and ———. 1979. First North American continental record of the longfin mako (*Isurus paucus* Guitart Manday). *Fla. Sci.* 42:52–58.

Dunbar, M. J., and H. H. Hildebrand. 1952. Contribution to the study of fishes of Ungava Bay. *J. Fish. Res. Board Can.* 9:83–128.

Edwards, H. M. 1920. The growth of the swell shark within the egg case. *Calif. Fish. Game* 6:153–57.

Eisert, C. F. 1969. Reproduction in the ovoviviparous sharks, *Etmopterus virens* and *Squalus acanthias*. Masters thesis, Cornell University. 90 pp.

Feder, H. M., C. H. Turner, and C. Limbaugh. 1974. *Observations on fishes associated with kelp beds in southern California*. Calif. Dept. Fish. Game Fish. Bull. 160. 144 pp.

Fitch, J. E. 1948. Use of DUKW's in the fishery for basking sharks *Cetorhinus maximus*. *Calif. Fish. Game* 34:219–20.

————. 1949. The great white shark, *Carcharodon carcharias* (Linneus) in California waters during 1948. *Calif. Fish. Game* 35:135–38.

————, and W. L. Craig. 1964. First records for the bigeye thresher (*Alopias superciliosus*) and slender tuna (*Allothunnus fallai*) from California with notes on eastern Pacific scombrid otoliths. *Calif. Fish. Game* 50:195–206.

Follett, W. I. 1976. First record of albinism in the leopard shark (*Triakis semifasciata* Girard). *Calif. Fish. Game* 62:163–64.

Ford, E. 1921. A contribution to our knowledge of the life histories of the dogfishes landed at Plymouth. *J. Mar. Biol. Assoc. U.K.* 12:468–505.

Forster, G. R., J. R. Badcock, M. R. Longbottom, N. R. Merrett, and K. S. Thomson. 1970. Results of the Royal Society Indian Ocean deep slope fishing expedition, 1969. *Proc. R. Soc. Lond.* B 175:367–404.

Fowler, H. W. 1941. Contributions to the biology of the Philippine Archipelago and adjacent regions. *Bull. U.S. Nat. Mus.* 100. Vol. 13. 879 pp.

Frøiland, O. 1975. Albinisme hos hai. *Fauna* (Oslo) 28:170–73.

Fusaro, C., and S. Anderson. 1980. First California record of the scalloped hammerhead shark, *Sphyrna lewini*, in coastal Santa Barbara waters. *Calif. Fish. Game* 66:121–23.

Garman, S. 1889. Reports on an exploration off the west coasts of Mexico, Central and South America, and off the Galapagos Islands, in charge of Alexander Agassiz, by the U.S. Fish Commission steamer "Albatross", during 1891. Lieut. Commander Z. L. Tanner, U.S.N., commanding. XXVI. The fishes. *Mem. Mus. Comp. Zool. Harv.* 24. 431 pp.

————. 1913. The plagiostoma (sharks, skates and rays). *Mem. Mus. Comp. Zool. Harv.* 36. 528 pp.

Garrick, J. A. F. 1960a. Studies on New Zealand elasmobranchii. Pt. X. The genus *Echinorhinus*, with an account of a second species. *Trans. R. Soc. N.Z.* 88:105–17.

————. 1960b. Studies on New Zealand elasmobranchii. Pt. XI. Squaloids of the genera *Deania*, *Etmopterus*, *Oxynotus* and *Dalatias* in New Zealand waters. *Trans. R. Soc. N.Z.* 88:489–517.

————. 1960c. Studies on New Zealand elasmobranchii. Pt. XII. Species of *Squalus* from New Zealand and Australia, and a general account and key to the New Zealand Squaloidea. *Trans. R. Soc. N.Z.* 88:519–77.

————. 1961. A note on the spelling of the scientific name of the immaculate spiny dogfish, *Squalus blainvillei* (Risso, 1826). *Trans. R. Soc. N.Z.* 88:843.

————. 1964. Additional information on the morphology of an embryo whale shark. *Proc. U.S. Nat. Mus.* 115 (3476):1–6.

————. 1967. Revision of sharks of genus *Isurus* with description of a new species (Galeoidea, Lamnidae). *Proc. U.S. Nat. Mus.* 118 (3537):663–90.

————. 1974. First record of an odontaspidid shark in New Zealand waters. *N.Z. J. Mar. Freshwater Res.* 8:621–30.

————. 1982. Sharks of the genus *Carcharhinus*. NOAA Tech. Rep. NMFS Circ. 445. Dep. of Commerce, Washington, D.C. 194 pp.

————, and J. M. Moreland. 1968. Notes on a bramble shark, *Echinorhinus cookei*, from Cook Strait, New Zealand. *Rec. Dom. Mus.* (Wellington) 6: 133–39.

————, and L. J. Paul. 1971. *Heptranchias dakini* Whitley, 1931, a synonym of *H. perlo* (Bonnaterre, 1788), the sharpsnouted sevengill or perlon shark, with notes on sexual dimorphism in this species. *Zool. Publ. Victoria Univ. Wellington* 54:1–14.

————, and S. Springer. 1964. *Isistius plutodus*, a new squaloid shark from the Gulf of Mexico. *Copeia*, pp. 678–82.

————, R. H. Backus, and R. H. Gibbs, Jr. 1964. *Carcharhinus floridanus*, the silky shark, a synonym of *C. falciformis*. *Copeia*, pp. 369–75.

Gilbert, C. H. 1905. II. The deep-sea fishes of the Hawaiian islands. *Bull. U.S. Fish. Comm.* 23 (Sect. II):575–713.

Gilbert, C. R. 1967. A revision of the hammerhead sharks (family Sphyrnidae). *Proc. U.S. Nat. Mus.* 119 (3539):1–77.

Gilbert, P., and D. A. Schlernitzauer. 1966. The placenta and gravid uterus of *Carcharhinus falciformis*. *Copeia*, pp. 451–57.

Goode, G. B., and T. H. Bean. 1896. *Oceanic ichthyology*. Smithson. Inst. Spec. Bull. 533 pp.

Gordon, B. L. 1956. The amazing angel shark. *Bull. Intl. Oceanogr. Fdn.* 2: 108–11.

Gotshall, D. W., and T. Jow. 1965. Sleeper sharks (*Somniosus pacificus*) off Trinidad, California, with life history notes. *Calif. Fish. Game* 51:294–98.

Grover, C. A. 1972a. Population differences in the swell shark *Cephaloscyllium ventriosum*. *Calif. Fish. Game* 58:191–97.

————. 1972b. Predation on egg-cases of the swell shark, *Cephaloscyllium ventriosum*. *Copeia*, pp. 871–72.

————. 1974. Juvenile denticles of the swell shark *Cephaloscyllium ventriosum*: function in hatching. *Can. J. Zool.* 52:359–63.

Gruber, S. H., and L. J. V. Compagno. 1981. Taxonomic status and biology of the bigeye thresher, *Alopias superciliosus*. *U.S. Fish Wildl. Serv. Fish. Bull.* 79:617–40.

Gubanov, Y. P. 1972. On the biology of the thresher shark *Alopias vulpinus* (Bonnaterre) in the northwest Indian Ocean. *J. Ichthyol.* (Engl. transl. *Vopr. Ikhtiol.*) 12:591–600.

————. 1974. The capture of a giant specimen of the mako shark (*Isurus glaucus*) in the Indian Ocean. *J. Ichthyol.* (Engl. transl. *Vopr. Ikhtiol.*) 14:589–91.

————. 1978. The reproduction of some species of pelagic sharks from the equatorial zone of the Indian Ocean. *J. Ichthyol.* (Engl. transl. *Vopr. Ikhtiol.*) 18:781–92.

Gudger, E. W. 1940. The breeding habits, reproductive organs, and external embryonic development of *Chlamydoselachus*, based on notes and drawings by Bashford Dean. *Bashford Dean Memorial Volume, Archaic Fishes* 7: 521–646.

————. 1941. The food and feeding habits of the whale shark, *Rhineodon typus*. *J. Elisha Mitchell Sci. Soc.* 57:57–72.

————. 1947. Sizes attained by the large hammerhead sharks. *Copeia*, pp. 228–36.

————. 1948a. The basking shark, *Cetorhinus maximus*, on the North Carolina coast. *J. Elisha Mitchell Sci. Soc.* 64:41–44.

————. 1948b. The tiger shark, *Galeocerdo tigrinus*, on the North Carolina coast and its food and feeding habits there. *J. Elisha Mitchell Sci. Soc.* 64:221–33.

————. 1949. Natural history notes on tiger sharks, *Galeocerdo tigrinus*, caught at Key West, Florida, with emphasis on food and feeding habits. *Copeia*, pp. 39–47.

————, and B. G. Smith. 1933. The natural history of the frilled shark, *Chlamydoselachus anguineus*. *Bashford Dean Memorial Volume, Archaic Fishes* 5:243–330.

Guitart-Manday, D. 1966. Nuevo nombre para una especie de Tiburon del genero *Isurus* (Elasmobranchii: Isuridae) de aguas Cubanas. *Poeyana Inst. Biol.* (Havana) Ser A 15:1–9.

Halstead, B. W. 1970. *Poisonous and venomous marine animals of the world*. Vol. 3. Washington, D.C.: Government Printing Office. 1,006 pp.

Hansen, P. M. 1963. Tagging experiments with the Greenland shark (*Somniosus microcephalus* (Bloch and Schneider) in subarea 1. *Intl. Comm. Northwest Atl. Fish. Spec. Publ.* 4:172–75.

Hart, J. L. 1973. Pacific fishes of Canada. *Bull. Fish. Res. Board Can.* 180. 740 pp.

Heemstra, P. C. 1973. A revision of the shark genus *Mustelus* (Squaliformes: Carcharhinidae). Ph.D. Dissertation, University of Miami. 187 pp.

Herald, E. S. 1968. Size and aggressiveness of the sevengill shark (*Notorynchus maculatus*). *Copeia*, pp. 412–14.

Hess, W. N. 1964. Long journey of the dogfish. *Nat. Hist.* 73:32–35.

Hisaw, F. L., and A. Albert. 1947. Observations on the reproduction of the spiny dogfish, *Squalus acanthias*. *Biol. Bull.* (Woods Hole) 92:187–99.

Hixon, M. A. 1979. Term fetuses from a large common thresher shark, *Alopias vulpinus*. *Calif. Fish. Game* 65:191–92.

Hoese, H. D. 1962. Sharks and rays of Virginia's seaside bays. *Chesapeake Sci.* 3:166–72.

————, and R. B. Moore. 1958. Notes on the life history of the bonnetnose shark, *Sphyrna tiburo*. *Tex. J. Sci.* 10:69–72.

Holden, M. J., and P. S. Meadows. 1962. The structure of the spine of the spur dogfish (*Squalus acanthias* L.) and its use for age determination. *J. Mar. Biol. Assoc. U.K.* 42:179–97.

Holland, G. A. 1957. Migration and growth of the dogfish shark (*Squalus acanthias* L.) of the eastern North Pacific. *Fish. Res. Pap. St. Wash.* 2:43–59.

Hubbs, C. L. 1951. Record of the shark *Carcharhinus longimanus*, accompanied by *Naucrates* and *Remora*, from the east-central Pacific. *Pac. Sci.* 5:78–81.

————. 1976. Comment on the proposed suppression of *Rhiniodon* Smith, 1838, in favour of *Rhincodon* Smith, 1829. Z.N.(S.) 2090. *Bull. Zool. Nomencl.* 33:70–71.

————, and F. N. Clark. 1945. Occurrence of the bramble shark (*Echinorhinus brucus*) in California. *Calif. Fish. Game* 31:64–67.

————, and W. I. Follett. 1947. *Lamna ditropis*, new species, the salmon shark of the North Pacific. *Copeia*, p. 194.

————, and J. L. McHugh. 1950. Pacific sharpnose shark (*Scoliodon longurio*) in California and Baja California. *Calif. Fish. Game* 36:7–11.

————, and L. R. Taylor, Jr. 1969. Data on life history and characters of *Galeus piperatus*, a dwarf shark of Golfo de California. *Fiskeridir. Skr. Ser. Havunders.* 15:310–30.

————, W. I. Follett, and L. J. Dempster. 1979. *List of the fishes of California.* Occas. Pap. Calif. Acad. Sci. 133. 51 pp.

————, T. Iwai, and K. Matsubara. 1967. External and internal characters, horizontal and vertical distribution, luminescence, and food of the dwarf pelagic shark, *Euprotomicrus bispinatus*. *Bull. Scripps Inst. Oceanogr. Univ. Calif.* 10:1–81.

Huish, M. T., and C. Benedict. 1977. Sonic tracking of dusky sharks in the Cape Fear River, North Carolina. *J. Elisha Mitchell Sci. Soc.* 93:21–26.

Hureau, J. C., and T. Monod. 1973. Check-list of the fishes of the northeastern Atlantic and of the Mediterranean. Paris: UNESCO. 677 pp.

Hussakof, L. 1909. A new Goblin Shark, *Scapanorhynchus jordani*, from Japan. *Bull. Am. Mus. Nat. Hist.* 26:257–62.

Jensen, A. C. 1966. Life history of the spiny dogfish. *U.S. Fish Wildl. Serv. Fish. Bull.* 65:527–54.

————. 1969. Spiny dogfish tagging and migration in North America and Europe. *Intl. Comm. Northwest Atl. Fish. Res. Bull.* 6:72–78.

Jensen, A. S. 1914. The selachians of Greenland. *Mindeskrift for Japetus Steenstrup* (Copenhagen) 2(30):1–40.

Jensen, N. H. 1976. Reproduction of the bull shark, *Carcharhinus leucas*, in the Lake Nicaragua–Rio San Juan system. In *Investigations of the ichthyofauna of Nicaraguan Lakes*, ed. T. B. Thornson, pp. 539–59. Lincoln: School of Life Sciences, University of Nebraska. 663 pp.

Johnson, C. S. 1978. Sea creatures and the problem of equipment damage. *U.S. Nav. Inst. Proc.* 104-8-906:106–107.

Jones, E. C. 1971. *Isistius brasiliensis*, a squaloid shark, the probable cause of crater wounds on fishes in cetaceans. *U.S. Fish Wildl. Serv. Fish. Bull.* 69:791–98.

Jordan, D. S. 1898. Description of a species of fish (*Mitsukurina owstoni*) from Japan, the type of a distinct family of lamnoid sharks. *Proc. Calif. Acad. Sci.* (3) *Zool.* 1:199–204.

————, and B. W. Evermann. 1896. The fishes of North and Middle America. *Bull. U.S. Nat. Mus.* 47. 1,240 pp.

Joseph, D. C. 1954. A record-size thresher from southern California. *Calif. Fish. Game* 40:433–35.

Kato, S., S. Springer, and M. H. Wagner. 1967. *Field guide to eastern Pacific and Hawaiian sharks*. U.S. Fish Wildl. Serv. Circ. 271. 47 pp.

King, J. E., and I. I. Ikehara. 1956. Some unusual fishes from the central Pacific. *Pac. Sci.* 10:17–20.

Krefft, G. 1968a. Neue und erstmalig nachgewiesene Knorpelfische aus dem Archibenthal des Sudwesatlantiks, einschliesslich einer Diskussion einiger *Etmopterus*-Arten sudlicher Meere. *Arch. Fischereiwiss.* 19:1–42.

————. 1968b. Knorpelfische (Chondrichthyes) aus dem tropischen Ostatlantik. *Atl. Rep.* 10:33–76.

Kritzler, H., and L. Wood. 1960. Provisional audiogram for the shark, *Carcharhinus leucas*. *Science* (Wash., D.C.) 133:1480–82.

Le Brasseur, R. J. 1964. Stomach contents of blue shark (*Prionace glauca* L.) taken in the Gulf of Alaska. *J. Fish. Res. Board Can.* 21:861–62.

Lee, R. S. 1969. The filetail catshark, *Parmaturus xaniurus*, in midwater in the Santa Barbara Basin off California. *Calif. Fish. Game* 55:88–90.

Leim, A. H., and W. B. Scott. 1966. Fishes of the Atlantic coast of Canada. *Bull. Fish. Res. Board Can.* 155. 485 pp.

Limbaugh, C. 1963. Field notes on sharks. In *Sharks and survival*, ed. P. Gilbert, pp. 64–94. Lexington, Mass.: D. C. Heath and Co.

Lineaweaver, T. H., III, and R. H. Backus. 1970. *The natural history of sharks*. New York: J. B. Lippincott Co. 256 pp.

McAllister, D. E. 1968. Poisonous and venomous fishes of Canada. *Nat. Mus. Can. Nat. Hist. Pap.* 42:2–3.

McKenzie, M. D. 1970. First record of albinism in the hammerhead shark, *Sphyrna lewini* (Pisces:Sphyrnidae). *J. Elisha Mitchell Sci. Soc.* 86:35–37.

Mathews, C. P. 1975. Some observations on the ecology of *Galeus piperatus* Springer and Wagner, a little known shark endemic to the northern Gulf of California. *J. Fish. Biol.* 7:77–82.

————, and M. F. Ruiz D. 1974. *Cephalurus cephalus*, a small shark, taken in the northern Gulf of California, with a description. *Copeia*, pp. 556–60.

————, and V. Guardado France. 1975. Potencial pesquero y estudios ecologicos de Bahia Magdalena. II. Las existencias de gatas. Heterodontidae. *Ciencias Marinas* 2:60–66.

Matthews, L. H. 1950. Reproduction in the basking shark, *Cetorhinus maximus* (Gunner). *Philos. Trans. R. Soc. Lond. B Biol. Sci.* 234:247–316.

————. 1962. The shark that hibernates. *New Sci.* 280:415–21.

————, and H. W. Parker. 1950. Notes on the anatomy and biology of the basking shark. *Proc. Zool. Soc. Lond.* 120:535–76.

Maul, G. E. 1955. Five species of rare sharks new for Madeira including two new to science. *Notulae Naturae* 279:1–13.

Merrett, N. R. 1973. A new shark of the genus *Squalus* (Squalidae: Squaloidea) from the equatorial western Indian Ocean; with notes on *Squalus blainvillei*. *J. Zool.* (London) 171:93–110.

Miller, B., and D. W. Greenfield. 1965. A juvenile six-gilled shark (*Hexanchus corinus*) from the San Juan Islands, Washington. *J. Fish Res. Board Can.* 22:857–59.

Miller, D. J., and R. N. Lea. 1972. *Guide to the coastal marine fishes of California*. Calif. Dept. Fish. Game Fish Bull. 157. 235 pp.

Morrow, J. E. 1955. A thresher shark from Long Island Sound. *Postilla* 24. 3 pp.

Moss, A. 1972. Nurse shark pectoral fins: An unusual use. *Am. Midl. Nat.* 88:496–97.

Musick, J. A., and J. D. McEachran. 1969. The squaloid shark *Echinorhinus brucus* off Virginia. *Copeia*, pp. 205–206.

Myers, B. W. 1977. Shark in miniature, keeping a horn shark in a home aquarium. *Oceans* 10:39–41.

Myrberg, A. A., Jr., and S. H. Gruber. 1974. The behavior of the bonnethead shark, *Sphyrna tiburo*. *Copeia*, pp. 358–74.

Nakamura, H. 1935. On the two species of the thresher shark from Formosan waters. *Mem. Fac. Sci. Agric. Taihoku Imp. Univ.* 14:1–6.

Nakaya, K. 1971. Descriptive notes on a porbeagle, *Lamna nasus*, from Argentine waters, compared with the north Pacific salmon shark, *Lamna ditropis*. *Bull. Fac. Fish. Hokkaido Univ.* 21:269–79.

Neave, F., and M. G. Hanavan. 1960. Seasonal distribution of some epipelagic fishes in the Gulf of Alaska region. *J. Fish. Res. Board Can.* 17:221–33.

Nelson, J. S. 1976. *Fishes of the world*. New York: John Wiley and Sons. 416 pp.

Nichols, J. T. 1917. Ichthyological notes from a cruise off southwest Florida, with description of *Gobiesox yuma* sp. nov. *Bull. Am. Mus. Nat. Hist.* 37:873–77.

————. 1927. A new shark from the continental slope off Florida. *Am. Mus. Novit.* 256:1–2.

Noble, E. R. 1948. On the recent frilled shark catch. *Science* (Wash., D.C.) 108:380.

Norris, H. W. 1923. The occurrence of *Mustelus lunulatus* on the California coast. *Copeia*, pp. 1–2.

Otake, T., and K. Mizue. 1981. Direct evidence for oophagy in thresher shark *Alopias pelagicus*. *Jpn. J. Ichthyol*. 28:171–72.

Parin, N. V. 1964. Data on the biology and distribution of the pelagic sharks *Euprotomicrus bispinatus* and *Isistius brasiliensis* (Squalidae, Pisces). *Transactions of the Institute of Oceanology Academy of Sciences, U.S.S.R.*, pp. 163–84. Translated by E. Roden in *Fishes of the Pacific and Indian Oceans: biology and distribution*, ed. T. S. Rass, pp. 173–95. Israel Program for Scientific Translations, 73.

Penrith, M. J. 1972. Earliest description and name for the whale shark. *Copeia*, p. 362.

Pequeño, G. 1979. El genero *Notorhynchus* en Chile (Elasmobranchii: Hexanchidae). *Rev. Biol. Mar.* 16:247–54.

Phillips, J. B. 1948. Basking shark fishery revived in California. *Calif. Fish. Game* 34:11–23.

———. 1953. Sleeper shark, *Somniosus pacificus*, caught off Fort Bragg, California. *Calif. Fish. Game* 39:147–49.

Pratt, H. L. 1979. Reproduction in the blue shark, *Prionace glauca*. *U.S. Fish Wildl. Serv. Fish. Bull.* 77:445–70.

———, J. C. Casey, and R. B. Conklin. 1982. White sharks, *Carcharodon carcharias*, off Long Island, New York. *U.S. Fish Wildl. Serv. Fish. Bull.* 80:153–56.

Quero, J. C. 1972. Capture de deux *Scapanorhynchus owstoni* (Jordan, 1898) (Selachii, Scapanorhynchidae) par des chalutiers de la Rochelle. *Ann. Soc. Sci. Nat. Charente-Maritime* 5:168–70.

Randall, J. E. 1968. Caribbean reef fishes. Neptune City, N.J.: T.F.H. Publ. 318 pp.

———. 1973. Size of the great white shark (*Carcharodon*). *Science* (Wash., D.C.) 181:169–70.

———, and M. F. Levy. 1976. A near-fatal shark attack by a mako in the northern Red Sea. *Isr. J. Zool.* 25:61–70.

Ripley, W. E. 1946. The soupfin shark and the fishery. *Calif. Dep. Fish. Game Fish. Bull.* 64:7–37.

Robins, C. R., et al. 1980. *A list of common and scientific names of fishes from the United States and Canada.* American Fisheries Society Special Publication No. 12. Fourth edition. Bethesda, Md.

Roedel, P. M. 1950. Notes on two species of sharks from Baja California. *Calif. Fish. Game* 36:330–32.

———. 1951. The brown shark, *Apristurus brunneus*, in California. *Calif. Fish. Game* 37:61–63.

———, and W. E. Ripley, 1950. California sharks and rays. *Calif. Dep. Fish. Game Fish. Bull.* 75:1–88.

Rogers, A. 1922. Process of treating shark skins and the like. U.S. Pat. 1,412,968. U.S. Patent Office.

Rosenblatt, R. H., and W. J. Baldwin. 1958. A review of the eastern Pacific sharks of the genus *Carcharhinus*, with a redescription of *C. malpeloensis* (Fowler) and California records of *C. remotus* (Dumeril). *Calif. Fish. Game* 44:137–59.

Russo, R. A. 1975. Observations on the food habits of leopard sharks (*Triakis semi-*

*fasciata*) and brown smoothhounds (*Mustelus henlei*). *Calif. Fish. Game* 61: 95–103.

Scattergood, L. W. 1962. First record of mako, *Isurus oxyrinchus*, in Maine waters. *Copeia*, p. 462.

Schlernitzauer, D. A., and P. W. Gilbert. 1966. Placentation and associated aspects of gestation in the bonnethead shark, *Sphyrna tiburo*. *J. Morphol.* 120:219–32.

Schuck, H. A., and J. R. Clark. 1951. Record of a white-tipped shark, *Carcharhinus longimanus*, from the northwestern Atlantic. *Copeia*, p. 172.

Schwartz, F. J. 1959. Two eight-foot cub sharks, *Carcharhinus leucas* (Müller and Henle), captured in Chesapeake Bay, Maryland. *Copeia*, pp. 251–52.

———. 1960. Additional comments on adult bull sharks *Carcharhinus leucas* (Müller and Henle), from Chesapeake Bay, Maryland. *Chesapeake Sci.* 1: 68–71.

———, and G. H. Burgess. 1975. *Sharks of North Carolina and adjacent waters*. Morehead City: North Carolina Department of Natural and Economic Resources, Division of Marine Fisheries. 57 pp.

Sciarrotta, T. C., and D. R. Nelson. 1977. Diel behavior of the blue shark, *Prionace glauca*, near Santa Catalina Island, California. *U.S. Fish Wildl. Serv. Fish. Bull.* 75:519–28.

Seigel, J. A. 1978. Revision of the dalatiid shark genus *Squaliolus*: anatomy, systematics, ecology. *Copeia*, pp. 602–14.

———, T. W. Pietsch, B. H. Robison, and T. Abe. 1977. *Squaliolus sarmenti* and *S. alii*, synonyms of the dwarf deepsea shark, *Squaliolus laticaudus*. *Copeia*, pp. 788–91.

Silas, E. G., and G. S. D. Selvaraj. 1972. Descriptions of the adult and embryo of the bramble shark *Echinorhinus brucus* (Bonnaterre) obtained from the continental slope of India. *J. Mar. Biol. Assoc. India* 14:395–401.

Slaughter, B. H., and S. Springer. 1968. Replacement of rostral teeth in sawfishes and sawsharks. *Copeia*, pp. 499–506.

Smith, B. G. 1937. The anatomy of the frilled shark, *Chlamydoselachus anguineus* Garman. *Bashford Dean Memorial Volume, Archaic Fishes* 6:331–520.

———. 1942. The heterodontid sharks: their natural history, and the external development of *Heterodontus japonicus* based on notes and drawings by Bashford Dean. *Bashford Dean Memorial Volume, Archaic Fishes* 8:649–770.

Smith, H. M., and L. Radcliffe. 1912. The squaloid sharks of the Philippine Archipelago, with descriptions of new genera and species. *Proc. U.S. Nat. Mus.* 41 (1877):677–85.

Smith, J. L. B. 1967. The lizard shark *Chlamydoselachus anguineus* Garman in South Africa. *Occ. Pap. Dep. Ichthyol. Rhodes Univ.* 10:105–14.

Snodgrass, R. E., and E. Heller. 1905. Papers from the Hopkins-Stanford Galapagos expedition XVII. Shore fishes of the Revillagigedo, Clipperton, Cocos and Galapagos Islands. *Proc. Wash. Acad. Sci.* 6:333–427.

Springer, S. 1939a. Two new Atlantic species of dog sharks, with a key to the species of *Mustelus*. *Proc. U.S. Nat. Mus.* 86 (3058):461–68.

———. 1939b. The great white shark, *Carcharodon carcharias* (Linnaeus) in Florida waters. *Copeia*, pp. 114–15.

———. 1940a. Three new sharks of the genus *Sphyrna* from the Pacific coast of tropical America. *Stanford Ichthyol. Bull.* 1:161–69.

———. 1940b. A new species of hammerhead shark of the genus *Sphyrna*. *Proc. Fla. Acad. Sci.* 5:46–52.

————. 1943. A second species of thresher shark from Florida. *Copeia*, pp. 54–55.

————. 1944. *Sphyrna bigelowi*, a new hammerhead shark from off the Atlantic coast of South America with notes on *Sphyrna mokarran* from New South Wales. *J. Wash. Acad. Sci.* 34:274–76.

————. 1946. A collection of fishes from the stomachs of sharks taken off Salerno, Florida. *Copeia*, pp. 174–75.

————. 1948. Oviphagous embryos of the sand shark, *Carcharias taurus*. *Copeia*, pp. 153–57.

————. 1949. *An outline for a Trinidad shark fishery*. Proc. Gulf Caribb. Fish. Inst. 2nd ann. sess. Miami Beach. 10 pp.

————. 1950*a*. Natural history notes on the lemon shark, *Negaprion brevirostris*. *Tex. J. Sci.* 3:349–59.

————. 1950*b*. A revision of North American sharks allied to the genus *Carcharhinus*. *Am. Mus. Novit.* 1451:1–13.

————. 1957. Some observations on the behavior of schools of fishes in the Gulf of Mexico and adjacent waters. *Ecology* 38:166–71.

————. 1959. A new shark of the family Squalidae from the Carolina continental slope. *Copeia*, pp. 30–33.

————. 1960. Natural history of the sandbar shark *Eulamia milberti*. *U.S. Fish Wildl. Serv. Fish. Bull.* 61 (178):1–38.

————. 1963. Field observations on large sharks of the Florida-Caribbean region. In *Sharks and survival*, ed. P. W. Gilbert, pp. 95–133. Lexington, Mass.: D. C. Heath and Co.

————. 1966. A review of western Atlantic cat sharks, Scyliorhinidae, with descriptions of a new genus and five new species. *U.S. Fish Wildl. Serv. Fish. Bull.* 65:581–624.

————. 1967. Social organization of shark populations. In *Sharks, skates and rays*, ed. P. W. Gilbert, R. F. Mathewson, and D. P. Rall. Baltimore, Md.: Johns Hopkins Press.

————. 1979. *A revision of the catsharks, family Scyliorhinidae*. NOAA Tech. Rep. NMFS Circ. 422. Dep. of Commerce, Washington, D.C. 152 pp.

————, and H. R. Bullis. 1960. A new species of sawshark, *Pristiophorus schroederi*, from the Bahamas. *Bull. Mar. Sci. Gulf Caribb.* 10:241–54.

————, and P. W. Gilbert. 1974. The basking shark, *Cetorhinus maximus* from Florida and California, with comments on its biology and systematics. *Copeia*, pp. 47–54.

————, and V. Sadowsky. 1970. Subspecies of the western Atlantic cat shark, *Scyliorhinus retifer. Proc. Biol. Soc. Wash.* 83:83–98.

————, and J. R. Thompson. 1957. Night sharks, *Hypoprion*, from the Gulf of Mexico and the Straits of Florida. *Copeia*, p. 160.

————, and M. H. Wagner. 1966. *Galeus piperatus*, a new shark of the family Scyliorhinidae from the Gulf of California. *Los Angeles Cty. Mus. Contrib. Sci.* 110:1–9.

————, and R. A. Waller. 1969. *Hexanchus vitulus*, a new sixgill shark from the Bahamas. *Bull. Mar. Sci.* 19:159–74.

Springer, V. G. 1964. A revision of the carcharhinid shark genera *Scoliodon, Loxodon*, and *Rhizoprionodon. Proc. U.S. Nat. Mus.* 15 (3493):559–632.

Standora, E. A., and D. R. Nelson. 1977. A telemetric study of the behavior of free-swimming Pacific angel sharks, *Squatina californica. Bull. South. Calif. Acad. Sci.* 76:193–201.

Stevens, J. D. 1974. The occurrence and significance of tooth cuts on the blue shark (*Prionace glauca* L.) from British waters. *J. Mar. Biol. Assoc. U.K.* 54:373–78.

————. 1975. Vertebral rings as a means of age determination in the blue shark (*Prionace glauca* L.). *J. Mar. Biol. Assoc. U.K.* 55:657–65.

————. 1976. First results of shark tagging in the northeast Atlantic, 1972–1975. *J. Mar. Biol. Assoc. U.K.* 56:929–37.

Stillwell, C. E., and J. G. Casey. 1976. Observations on the bigeye thresher shark, *Alopias superciliosus*, in the western North Atlantic. *U.S. Fish Wildl. Serv. Fish. Bull.* 74:221–25.

Strasburg, D. W. 1958. Distribution, abundance, and habits of pelagic sharks in the central Pacific Ocean. *U.S. Fish Wildl. Serv. Fish. Bull.* 58:335–61.

————. 1963. The diet and dentition of *Isistius brasiliensis*, with remarks on tooth replacement in other sharks. *Copeia*, pp. 33–40.

Svetlov, M. F. 1978. The porbeagle, *Lamna nasus*, in Antarctic waters. *J. Ichthyol.* (Engl. transl. *Vopr. Ikhtiol.*) 18:850–51.

Talent, L. G. 1973. Albinism in embryo gray smoothhound sharks, *Mustelus californicus*, from Elkhorn Slough, Monterey Bay, California. *Copeia*, pp. 595–97.

————. 1976. Food habits of the leopard shark, *Triakis semifasciata*, in Elkhorn Slough, Monterey Bay, California. *Calif. Fish. Game* 62:286–98.

Taylor, L. R., Jr. 1972*a. Apristurus kampae*, a new species of Scyliorhinid shark from the eastern Pacific Ocean. *Copeia*, pp. 71–78.

————. 1972*b*. A revision of the shark family Heterodontidae (Heterodontiformes, Selachii). Ph.D. diss. Univ. Calif. San Diego. 176 pp.

————, and J. L. Castro-Aguirre. 1972. *Heterodontus mexicanus*, a new horn shark from the Golfo de California. *An. Esc. Nac. Cienc. Biol. Mex.* 19:123–43.

Templeman, W. 1963. Distribution of sharks in the Canadian Atlantic (with special reference to Newfoundland waters). *Bull. Fish. Res. Board Can.* 140:1–77.

————. 1968. Grand Bank tagged dogfish moves to Iceland. *Fish. Res. Board Can. Atl. Prog. Rep.* 70:28–30.

Tester, A. 1969. *Co-operative Shark Research and Control Program. Final Report 1967–1969.* Univ. Hawaii. 47 pp.

Thomson, D. A., L. T. Findley, and A. N. Kerstitch. 1979. *Reef fishes of the Sea of Cortez*. New York: John Wiley and Sons. 302 pp.

Thornson, T. B. 1976. The status of the Lake Nicaragua shark: an updated appraisal. In *Investigations of the ichthyofauna of Nicaraguan Lakes*, ed. T. B. Thornson, pp. 561–74. Lincoln: University of Nebraska, School of Life Sciences. 663 pp.

————, D. E. Watson, and C. M. Cowan. 1966. The status of the freshwater shark of Lake Nicaragua. *Copeia*, pp. 385–402.

Tibbo, S. N., and R. A. McKenzie. 1963. An occurrence of dusky sharks, *Carcharhinus obscurus* (Lesueur) 1818, in the northwest Atlantic. *J. Fish. Res. Board Can.* 20:1101–1102.

Tortonese, E. 1956. *Fauna D'Italia*. Vol. II: *Leptocardia ciclostomata, selachii*. Bologna: Edizioni Calderini. 334 pp.

Tressler, D. K., and J. McW. Lemon. 1951. In *Marine products of commerce*, pp. 538–49. New York: Reinhold Publ.

Tricas, T. C. 1979. Relationships of the blue shark, *Prionace glauca*, and its prey species near Santa Catalina Island, California. *U.S. Fish Wildl. Serv. Fish. Bull.* 77:175–82.

Vorenberg, M. M. 1962. Cannibalistic tendencies of lemon and bull sharks. *Copeia*, pp. 455–56.

Walford, L. A. 1935. The sharks and rays of California. *Calif. Dept. Fish. Game Fish. Bull.* 45:1–66.

Wass, R. C. 1973. Size, growth, and reproduction of the sandbar shark, *Carcharhinus milberti*, in Hawaii. *Pac. Sci.* 27:305–18.

Wheeler, A. 1962. New records for distribution of the frilled shark. *Nature* (London) 196:689–90.

Whitley, G. P. 1940. *The Fishes of Australia. Pt. 1. The sharks, rays, devil-fish, and other primitive fishes of Australia and New Zealand.* Sidney: R. Zool. Soc. N.S.W., Aust. Zool. Handb. 280 pp.

# INDEX